Quebec and its Historians

The Twentieth Century

Books by Serge Gagnon

Quebec and its Historians: 1840 to 1920
Montreal, Harvest House, 1982

Man and His Past: the Nature and Role of Historiography
Montreal, Harvest House, 1982

Serge Gagnon, et al.
L'Eglise et le village au Québec, 1850 à 1930
Montreal, Leméac, 1979

Quebec and its Historians
The Twentieth Century

Serge Gagnon

Translated by
Jane Brierley

Harvest House
Montreal, 1985

Deposited in the Bibliothèque Nationale of Quebec, 3rd Quarter 1985.
Typography and Cover: Original design by Book Design and Production Associates, Bynum, N.C., adapted by Naoto Kondo.

Printed in Canada

First Harvest House Edition

For information address Harvest House Ltd., 2335 Sherbrooke St. West, Montreal, Canada H3H 1G6

Canadian Cataloguing in Publication Data

Gagnon, Serge, 1939-
Quebec and Its Historians: The Twentieth Century

Includes index.
Bibliography: p.
ISBN 0-88772-026-9

1. Quebec (Province)—Historiography. 2. Quebec (Province)—20th century.
3. Historians—Quebec (Province). I. Title.

FC2909.G34 1985 971.4'007'2 C85-090131-6
F1052.95.G34 1985

To Marie-Reine Regina Gaudreault, my mother,
who taught me the pleasure of reading
and the love of intellectual work.

Translator's Note

I would like to express my thanks and appreciation to the author, Serge Gagnon, for his unfailing interest and patience throughout the months in which this translation was being prepared. Despite his enormously busy teaching and research schedule, he always found time to give his undivided attention to the various questions that arose. Working with him has been an enjoyable privilege. My thanks are also due to the editor, Maynard Gertler, for the vision and guidance that helped bring this book to the English-speaking public.

The first three chapters of this work originally appeared as articles: "Pour une conscience historique de la révolution québécoise," *Cité libre* (Jan. 1966): 4-19; "Le XVIe Siècle canadien de Narcisse-Eutrope Dionne à Marcel Trudel (1891-1963)," Pierre Savard, ed., *Mélanges d'histoire du Canada français offerts au Professeur Marcel Trudel*, (Ottawa: Editions de l'Université d'Ottawa, 1978), 65-83; and "The Historiography of New France, 1960-1974: Jean Hamelin to Louise Dechêne," *Journal of Canadian Studies*, 13, no. 1 (Spring 1978): 80-99. The author has taken the opportunity of making various slight revisions. Any changes in editorial style have been made in the interests of consistency, in consultation with the author and the editor.

Contents

Foreword

Over the past twenty years I have often remarked that history is the child of its time, as the French historian Lucien Febvre pointed out. I have taken as my creed Croce's dictum that all history is contemporary. Some of my colleagues, however, have had misgivings about my opinions concerning the inevitable subjectivity of the historian's thinking, be he layman or scholar. "Is not history a science like sociology or economics?" they ask. My fellow historians deserve a few words of explanation.

I should point out that I have never denied the scientific nature of the study of history. I have merely emphasized its social and ideological dimensions. In many cases my remarks could have applied equally well to other disciplines. Certain parallels obviously exist between the development of the oldest of human sciences and the progress in method of younger, synchronological sciences. We have borrowed many techniques from the latter, notably the structuralist approach. It is therefore unfortunate that historians should have developed a sort of inferiority complex vis-à-vis scholars in other fields. Modern-day historical dissertations are no more subjective than those of the sociologist or psychoanalyst. A competent historian produces work that is as well-informed as that of any good political analyst. Errors in calculating the outcome of elections, for example, put the reliability of the expert's calculations into question. Such errors, however, can always be attributed to some unforeseen but decisive event within the forty-eight hours preceding election day. In a more general way, the predictions of opinion polls are the product of an "inexorable" array of figures, combined with wishful thinking and convictions of a prophetic or mythical nature that closely resemble the outpourings of soothsayers and astrologers, past and present. Even economists are continually consulting curves and graphs in order to predict the future, a process that reminds one uncannily of the seer and his crystal ball. Who is to say that the results are any more reliable?

It is time we read more critical studies of man the sociologist. The urge to know and to question is not characterized by indifference, either in the social sciences or the humanities. This is as true of historians as of other scholars. Results in the human sciences tend to be unreliable, as the failures of various advertising campaigns based on opinion polls make all too evident. In medicine, to take another example, the swing between progress and setback proves that even the less "human" sciences are merely groping their way forward. Unlike the botanist who classifies varieties of leaves from clover to maple, the student of human relations is dealing with a being who is free to choose.

History, along with philosophy, is one of the oldest forms of critical discussion of the human race. Long after Herodotus and Livy, Renaissance humanists conceived the idea of studying the past scientifically. The Age of Enlightenment and the positivist era saw the first revolution in knowledge of our discipline: the use of historical criticism to establish facts. French-speaking Quebec historians assimilated the positivist revolution some fifty to a hundred years after their colleagues in France, Germany, Great Britain, the United States, and English Canada. During the 1930s, the theology of history still dominated Quebec historiography. Before then, the few renegades who suggested a secular approach to the past, only marginally related to the Christian, Roman Catholic credo, had their knuckles rapped. The application of methodical doubt in Quebec history was pioneered by scholars like Marcel Trudel and Guy Frégault who, between 1940 and 1950, inaugurated a fully scientific history. And yet, despite its underlying positivism, we now realize that modern critical history contains a perceptible strain of subjectivity. I remember a discussion with Trudel, my professor at Laval University, following one of his brilliant lectures on the seigneurial regime. Before the lecture I had read a piece by Frégault praising the merits of this form of land tenure. Trudel, however, took the view that in the final analysis the system was a major handicap to economic development in the St. Lawrence Valley. The idea for the first article reprinted in this collection was born of this contradiction. A philosopher friend had just initiated me into the mysteries of Hegelian logic, and—as I have frequently been told—I have probably overstated the differences between the nationalist standpoint of the Montreal School and the liberal or "modernist" antithesis propounded by the Quebec School. I trust my readers will pardon a youthful enthusiasm.

Over the past few decades there has been a gradual second revolution in Western historiography. This is the New History, which explores the lot of the silent majority and the slow changes in systems and outlook that affect its destiny. While retaining the contributions of classical historical criticism, the new form also relies on statistical calculations, rather excessively on occasion. In its belated use of quantitative methods, history has come to resemble the other scientific disciplines, as we can now recognize. But the philosophical critique of history as a science of the past has somewhat discredited it by an overinsistence on the subjectivity of historical knowledge.[1] Historians who believe that their research can bring to light underlying causes of social change feel that this sort of friendly "attack" is responsible for the illusion that they are less "scientific" than anthropologists, geographers, demographers, or those pet oracles of Western culture, sociologists.

Historians such as Fernand Ouellet, Louise Dechêne, and the Jean Hamelin of *Economie et société en Nouvelle-France* (Quebec: PUL, 1960), were in the vanguard of this new scientific approach in French Canada. In analyzing their works I have not limited myself exclusively to their value judgments, but have also tried to show the scientific merit of their work. This emphasis on the scientific aspect reflects a change in my concerns as a historian. My aim is to give the scientific discipline to which I belong its fair share of credibility. History is now one of the human sciences concerned with revealing the true, or at least exact, state of things, just like any other specialty in the large family of related disciplines. It is to be hoped that historians will soon move beyond immediate political considerations and that the field of history will regain its former respectability. I would like the reader to close this book thinking that scientific history is a branch of human knowledge that is as serious, and surely as wise, as its younger brethren.

Trois-Rivières   S.G.

Acknowledgments

I wish to thank the university community of Trois-Rivières: its administrators, who have shown their concern for maintaining scholarly activity in these years of uncertainty by giving me their full support in the preparation of this book; and my fellow professors, with whom I share my daily task of teaching and research.

This translation has been published with the help of a grant from the Social Science Federation of Canada, using funds provided by the Social Sciences and Humanities Research Council of Canada. We also gratefully acknowledge a translation grant from the Canada Council.

Introduction

These collected essays show recent developments in Quebec's historiography without necessarily attempting to be exhaustive. Whatever the field, encyclopedic inventories of intellectual works inevitably result in lists of authors and titles—information that can be found in the many and varied reference sources available. Some other procedure is needed to recognize underlying currents of thought and to take note of tendencies that presage far-reaching change. The books under consideration deal with the pre-1850 period, and some readers may be surprised to find such authors as Claude Galarneau or Jacques Monet omitted, although they have written major works in this area.[1] Despite their importance, however, these and many other historians have had less impact than those featured in the present study. I sincerely hope that the considerable number who are not included will forgive the necessity for their exclusion. The interested reader can learn more by consulting the forty-odd bio-bibliographies in the *Dictionnaire pratique des auteurs québécois* (Montreal: Fides, 1976) by Reginald Hamel, John Hare, and Paul Wyczynski.

The scholarly production that has come to the fore in French Canada was not spontaneously generated. Here as elsewhere, the use of modern methods in historical research had its precursors. The debt owed by such historians as Jean Hamelin and Fernand Ouellet to their predecessors is difficult to estimate. We do know, however, that they were influenced by the works of archivist Ivanhoe Caron (1875-1941) and journalist Aegidius Fauteux (1888-1957), as well as Herald Innis and Donald Creighton; moreover they were profoundly affected by European thinking, which marks every aspect of their work.[2]

It is a significant but perhaps little known fact that between the wars four French Canadians received doctorates in history from a French university and published their theses.[3] Nevertheless, until the 1940s, scholars came to the field of history in a variety of ways. Léon Gérin entered the field of scholarly

1

historical research equipped as a sociologist, but this was an exception. The more usual route to history was through the neighboring discipline of literary studies. Marcel Trudel, for example, one of the founders of the Institute of History at Laval University, received his doctorate in literature during the 1940s.

What distinguished postwar historiography in Quebec from earlier periods was the emergence of a handful of professional historians who no longer earned their living as journalists, curators, archivists, teachers in classical colleges, or civil servants of some kind; nor were they notaries, lawyers, doctors, or priests merely indulging in a retirement hobby. The universities' initiative in setting up history programs gave professors and researchers the means and the time to write scholarly books on a professional basis. Furthermore, this phenomenon was not limited to historians, but was indicative of the developing importance of the humanities and the social sciences in Quebec French-language universities.

The methods initially adopted by these scholars reflected the ideological ferment of what one might call the "Quiet Modernization." In the mid-1960s even works concerning the French colonial period were somehow linked to modernizing Quebec. The Quiet Revolution cannot be understood without emphasizing the historians' contribution, and indeed the first chapter of this book demonstrates the politicization of historical discourse in the 1960s. This was the period when historians were invited to round table radio and television discussions in which they thrashed out Quebec's future. Even Marcel Trudel, the most positivist historian of his generation and a highly disciplined scholar, succumbed to a present-minded interpretation of the discovery of America, and we find Trudel's Jacques Cartier abandoning the evangelical mission attributed to him by earlier historians.

Mid-twentieth-century, secular Quebec turned its back on the theological view of history in order to construct a collective, materialist view of the past, in keeping with the prevailing economism. Sixteenth-century explorers were portrayed as eager for knowledge and anxious to discover new resources. Jean Hamelin moved historiography away from classical historical analysis to the New History—the term used in France then and since for a reconstruction of the past that rejects the importance once accorded great men and events. His *Economie et société en Nouvelle-France* actually initiated the use of serial, quantitative methods in Quebec historiography. Subsequent historical debate has tended to be methodological rather than ideological. With Louise Dechêne's *Habitants et marchands de Montréal au XVII siècle* (Paris: Plon, 1974), French historical methods became firmly embedded in French-Canadian historiography.

The central figure of those years of methodological renewal between 1960 and 1970 was Fernand Ouellet, a historian of great vitality and flair who chose the 1760-1850 period in Quebec as his field. His work has aroused considerable controversy, which is perhaps an indication that despite sophisticated historical methods, ideology is still a factor in historical scholarship. I have attempted to deal with this possibility in the final two chapters of this book.

I

Historians and
the Quiet Revolution

A Look at the Debates of
the Mid-Sixties

This radically different approach in the two regions
[Quebec and Montreal] is a constant factor in the history
of French Canada. There is a distinct feeling that
Montrealers are kept in a state of almost continual tension
by their Anglo-Saxon surroundings...[whereas those in]
the old capital [are] more accustomed to American or
English-Canadian tourists than capitalists.... This difference accounts in large part for the divergent views of the
two schools of history, Montreal and Laval.

—*Denis Vaugeois*[1]

The two schools of thought that characterize mid-twentieth-
century Quebec historiography took their impetus from two
archetypal figures: Canon Lionel Groulx of Montreal, and
Abbé Arthur Maheux of Laval University in Quebec City. Each
typified certain regional attitudes that crystalized during the
1940s to form a distinct approach. If, as we shall discover, our
historical development is seen from two perspectives, it is partly
because these two historians aroused considerable controversy
at the same period. Both men had their followers and headed
the two history institutes founded by Laval University and the
University of Montreal after the Second World War.

Working in the tradition of our first national historian, François-Xavier Garneau, Canon Groulx was the moving spirit behind the nationalist movement of the period between the wars, aimed at creating a French-speaking Catholic state in North America. The ideological basis for this "Laurentian dream," as it has been called, came from Maurice Barrès and the founder of *L'Action française*, Charles Maurras. The back-to-the-land nationalism of Barrès supported the cause of a rural Quebec, riveted to its traditions and fettered by a rigid opposition to change that one can scarcely imagine today. The monarchism of Charles Maurras contributed to prolonging an ultramontane mentality fiercely opposed to democratic ideals. This eminently conservative nationalism soon became linked to a form of racism, inherited from the disciples of Gobineau whom Groulx encountered while studying at the University of Freiburg. Such, very briefly, is the background to the interpretation of history put forward by Groulx, who was adulated by nationalist youth for his advocacy of French minorities and his rejection, implicit or explicit, of the pan-Canadian nationalism of Sir Wilfrid Laurier, Mackenzie King, and Henri Bourassa.

French-Canadian nationalist thinking, which had affinities with the racial struggles of the two world wars, received a serious setback at the end of World War II. It began with a motion by Senator Athanase David recommending the adoption of a single history textbook for Canada. The senator's proposal was quickly seconded by his colleague, Senator Damien Bouchard, who on June 21, 1944, made a stinging attack on the absurdity of "racial" battles in Canada. Among the causes he evoked was the partisan teaching of national history, which had contributed to keeping anti-English hatred alive in the younger generation. Instead of seeing written history as a story of persecution, Bouchard proposed a version that would stimulate goodwill and acknowledge the characteristic weaknesses of French Canadians as a national group.

The forces of reaction pounced on Bouchard as a traitor to his "race." The man who had often been described as an apostate was now literally jeered at by the public, especially after Cardinal Villeneuve had officially condemned him at the

St. Hyacinthe eucharistic congress that opened on the very day of his senate speech.

Hope was not lost, however. For some years past a Quebec City university professor had been working on a history promoting national unity. Well-known to the English-speaking community as a lecturer, Abbé Arthur Maheux, mentioned by Bouchard in his speech, had published a little book in 1941 that aroused a storm of protest in nationalist circles.[2] In it he showed that French Canadians had no cause to complain about their fate since 1760. Recalling the conciliatory spirit of Governor Murray, he concluded that the Conquest did not lead to oppression and had in no way diminished the church's freedom. Two years later, the CBC published a series of talks by Maheux on the French network, on the general theme of "Why Are We Divided?"[3] According to him, hatred of the English went against evangelical principles. Absence from the business world, an evil deplored by everyone, was due to the exclusive interest in agriculture, an interest that had been promoted, in the name of a false mystique, as the national vocation of French Canadians. However, if one really read the history of New France, one found that the French in North America were mostly artisans and soldiers without peasant traditions. The charter of the Company of One Hundred Associates clearly demonstrated that France had intended to make its colony an industrial power. Furthermore, colonial nobles did not look down on business as an occupation. In fact, the intention was to prevent the French clergy and nobility from bringing with them their disdain for commerce and industry. The examples given by Intendant Talon and Bishop Laval, who had built a vocational school at St. Joachim, contradicted the myth of the peasant origins of the French Canadians. Maheux concluded:

We still have among us a certain number of "nobles" who look down on the bustle of business, the smoke of industry, and the wheelings and dealings of commerce. They should heed the words of Cardinal Richelieu and rid themselves of this disdain. Let them not lead our people astray.[4]

In reading these lines one is inevitably reminded of Canon Groulx's remark:

There are riches and riches; we know that there are races that can do without gold and silver more easily than others, and that the spire of a church or monastery, despite appearances to the contrary, reaches higher toward heaven than a smokestack.[5]

In his radio talks Abbé Maheux continually preached moderation, collaboration, and discussion with English-speaking countrymen. When he spoke of democracy he praised British liberties in contrast to the despotism of the French regime. Admittedly, the Act of Union aimed at assimilation; but, he pointed out, the achievement of responsible government had come about through open collaboration among all moderate Canadians. In line with Harold Innis's thinking, Maheux noted that the country's geography tended to unite rather than divide Canadians. He then spoke out against ridiculous English-Canadian fears of possible "French domination" resulting from their high birth rate. Reminding his listeners that their English-Canadian partners also had a survival problem in the face of American pressures, he urged them to strive for conquest, not domination.[6] And what did conquest mean for French Canada? In the first place, it meant setting up a system of education based on a healthy pragmatism. In his celebrated report, Lord Durham had deplored the deficiencies of the Quebec education system. Despite his observations, however, the role of science in a modern school was not recognized for over a century. Conquest, therefore, meant exchanging theoretical teaching for an education that dealt with concrete problems; it meant creating technical, agricultural, mining, and forestry schools. Abbé Maheux concluded with this fairly acute observation:

Political economy is beyond our grasp because we do not study it. All our schools, even the most elementary, should teach children about the demands of practical, everyday life, and the laws of supply and demand.[7]

In a talk on mother countries, he criticized English Canadians for their colonial mentality, which stood in the way of

Canadian unity.[8] He ended his talks by reminding listeners of his concern for reducing the dissension that divided the two Canadian "races."[9]

The distribution of Abbé Maheux's book—especially in the province's classical colleges—produced a flood of protest, as might be expected. *Le Devoir* likened Maheux's ideas to those of Bouchard and the other proscribed liberal thinker of the period, Jean-Charles Harvey. The intellectuals of English Canada, on the other hand, greeted the book with the utmost satisfaction. In *Macleans's* of August 15, 1944, Blair Fraser praised the author for dealing the "Groulx myth" a shattering blow. Such an attack could not go unanswered. The response came from one of Canon Groulx's young disciples, who refuted Fraser's allegations about the supposed racism of his mentor. He insisted that Groulx's historical works were a contribution to scientific scholarship, and treated Abbé Maheux's remarks with withering sarcasm. This disciple was Guy Frégault.[10]

The Montreal School

There is now a new interpretation of French Canada's history.... The historians who have brought it forward...no longer accept the interpretation of the "winning team".... In their approach to French-Canadian history they have also been influenced by the English-Canadian Laurentian School of historians who, under the leadership of H.A. Innis, Donald G. Creighton, and John B. Brebner, have emphasized the functioning of metropolitanism in Canadian history. The most striking fact about this new school of French-Canadian historians is that because of their clear-sighted knowledge of English-Canadian history, they are in a better position to rewrite French Canada's history.
—*Michel Brunet*[11]

Guy Frégault[12]

Guy Frégault was the first of the six historians discussed here to publish monographs based on modern historical methods. *Iberville le conquérant* and *La Civilisation de la Nouvelle-France* appeared in quick succession in 1944, initiating a new phase in French-Canadian historiography. His disciplined technique, quality of style, and abundantly documented material presaged a successful career. The author of *The War of the Conquest* (originally published in 1955 and brought out in English by Oxford University Press in 1969) proved to be an excellent biographer as well.

Ideologically speaking, the Montreal professor's work was clearly linked to Lionel Groulx's thinking, despite the fact that in his major works he dissociated himself from this key figure. For example, *Iberville le Conquérant* was characterized by Frégault's emotional tone when speaking of his hero. As for *The War of the Conquest*, while not peopled by supermen it was nevertheless based on the nationalist conception of the French regime.[13]

What did New France represent for Frégault? His pamphlet *Canadian Society in the French Regime* provided a good summary of his interpretation.[14] He pointed out that the underpopulated French colony drew the bulk of its revenue from the fur trade. According to accounts by both the voyageurs and the colony's leaders, the inhabitants enjoyed a relatively high standard of living and education. The colony possessed "keen men of business" and experienced remarkable prosperity. After the Cession of 1763, however, this business class no longer existed. Its disappearance coincided with the colony's "collapse," causing the political and economic framework of New France to disintegrate. "The control of the all-important fur trade passed into the hands of the British merchants in Montreal," noted the pamphlet. Those historians who did not consider the Conquest a disaster judged the inhabitants of New France on the basis of the atrophied society that succeeded it. Cut off from metropolitan France and therefore unable to develop normally, French-Canadian society was doomed to mere survival.

Frégault consistently maintained this vision of a tragic destiny. In the last chapter of *La Civilisation de la Nouvelle France* he noted the existence of nationalist sentiment among Canadians during the French regime. Despite limited numbers, under French guidance they had built up distinctly Canadian institutions. The French colony was in fact "a complete social entity, a new nation whose links with a powerful past were shaping its future."[15]

Frégault adopted a similar perspective in the final pages of *La Guerre de la Conquête*, his last important work, subsequently published as *The War of the Conquest*. The year 1760 was "cataclysmic" for the French colony. Although French monopoly-holders, Bigot chief among them, contributed to the catastrophe, the operative factor was the capitulation to British rule that altered the course of French-Canadian history for the next two centuries. This time, however, he was categorical: "It [the French-Canadians' position after 1760] is the direct consequence of the Conquest; it dislocated society, doing away with the existing framework and weakening its internal dynamics."[16]

The real significance of the French defeat was overlooked, Frégault felt, mainly because the history of New France was seen as an epic of saints and heroes, and examination of its material basis neglected. Traditional historiography portrayed French-Canadian society under British rule as continuing to produce supermen for the reader's edification. This heroic approach effectively suppressed the tragic aspect of the Conquest for French-Canadian society.

Two years after the original publication of *The War of the Conquest*, Frégault definitively stated his historical position in an article.[17] He may have been accused on occasion of representing the French regime as the golden age of French-Canadian history. In any event, he defended his thesis very ably. He again emphasized the "normal development" of New France, pointing out that the colony's political structure did not stifle individual initiative. New France had its prominent businessmen, he urged, insisting that there was no foundation to allegations about the dynamism of the bourgeois elite having been "undermined by economic *dirigisme*, by the monopolies, or by the officials' stranglehold on economic activity." In fact, he intimated, those who now put forward a view of Quebec history similar to his, based on the views of Sombart, Weber, Tawney, and the *Annales* School, were right. The mistaken idea that New France was arbitrarily run was initiated by Francis Parkman in the late nineteenth century; English-Canadian historians such as Creighton, Lower, and Mason Wade in his *French Canadians*, had merely parroted Parkman's hypotheses.[18]

The thrust of Frégault's thinking was that in the eighteenth century "Canada was already a distinct community endowed with economic, political, social, religious, and cultural institutions." He cited numerous facts in support of the idea that, despite major difficulties, the two generations preceding the Conquest contained prominent business figures. They backed numerous ventures such as shipbuilding and industrial metallurgy. The closing of three hat-manufacturing businesses in Montreal in 1735 did not prove that metropolitan France had ceased to encourage its transatlantic colony, in his view. This normal source of support was to disappear at the Conquest, however, with a concomitant drop in dynamism. The country's development passed into the hands of its new masters. With the backing of their own metropolitan power, English settlers in turn built a second colonial empire. The last lines of Frégault's article could have applied equally well to the unrest in Quebec during the Quiet Revolution:

> One understands the present situation in French Canada better when one realizes what historical forces have influenced its development in the past two hundred years.

What in fact was the history of the British regime in relation to French Canadians as a national group? It fell to Maurice Séguin to take up the story.

Maurice Séguin[19]
Maurice Séguin's scholarly publications are few. In fact, his Ph.D. thesis, defended in the 1940s, was only published in 1970 under the title *La "Nation canadienne" et l'agriculture (1760-1850)* by Les Editions du Boréal Express. But his career as a teacher and researcher have placed him among French Canada's recognized historians. He provided an interesting version of the British regime along the lines of Frégault's analysis of the earlier period.

Briefly, for both Séguin and Frégault, French Canadians did not inherit their economic inferiority from the French colonial regime. Séguin wrote:

Then came the catastrophe of 1760-63. The Conquest was ratified by the Cession; this meant that a tiny people, which had barely begun to develop in the various economic sectors, was brought into a new empire with different political and economic relationships from those that had shaped its previous existence. The question arose of what forces would now influence the French Canadian's economic life, and how that life would be altered. In other words, what would be the effects of the Conquest and of keeping the French-Canadian people of 1760 in the British Empire by force? This was a problem worth looking at closely. If we ignore the facts of history we run the risk of making superficial judgments about the contemporary economic situation. To go back to the origins, particularly to the first hundred years after the Conquest, is no idle pastime. By studying the French Canadians' way of life at a period of great upheaval, we might find the explanation of the current economic crisis.

This "great upheaval" began with the French-Canadian nation turning toward agriculture as the only economic activity permitted the conquered people. But farming as a sole activity could not enable the national group to develop normally. Crop surpluses were unable to move profitably to British Empire markets, to which the fortunes of war had linked the former French colony. Quite apart from the natural obstacles of distance and climate, American wheat offered exceptionally stiff competition that was soon increased by wheat from Upper Canada. Such market conditions provided no incentive for the French-Canadian farmer to improve growing methods, particularly since the British were not interested in promoting agricultural education.

The absence of markets and technical knowledge was further aggravated by a scheme of land distribution detrimental to the French Canadians. They had quickly occupied all the available territory in the established seigneuries, and demanded new grants under the system of seigneurial tenure. This mode of ownership with its annual rent was perfectly suited to their modest means. Their request was refused, however, at the very moment that the authorities were selling land in the Eastern Townships almost exclusively to British newcomers.

The conjunction of these three factors triggered a crisis that reached serious proportions in 1850 and has continued ever since. The first sign of it was a rural exodus. This would not be surprising in a progressive economy where people normally leave the land for big business, industry, and finance. But the French Canadians, although forced from the land, were unable to enter these sectors of economic activity as they might have done ordinarily. Foreign occupation had obliged them to trade within an imperial network where they could not compete with the newcomers. The latter easily eliminated them from the fur trade, and took over the wheat as well as the lumber trade, which had burgeoned during the first half of the nineteenth century. As a result they found it impossible to amass the capital to industrialize French Canada. By the time the industrial revolution got under way here, French Canadians were historically predisposed to becoming a proletariat exploited by "foreign" businessmen.

The French Canadians may have tried to escape their fate, but were incapable of doing so, Séguin felt. In the first place, the Conquest had reduced them to the point of believing that they had a collective vocation for agriculture. Economically speaking, they needed to reestablish their links with the tradition of the French regime, and gain independence at any cost. Only thus "could they have eradicated the political source of their economic troubles." This was what the revolutionaries of 1837 tried to do without success. Then came the Act of Union, an assimilative force that accentuated French Canada's alienation, followed by Confederation, which effectively lulled its consciousness of being an individual "nation." This blinding of French Canadians to their individuality induced them to collaborate with the occupying power. It was a permanent collaboration, in the tradition set by Sir Louis-Hippolyte Lafontaine and Etienne Parent.[20] Just for good measure, French-Canadian political leaders took up the notion of a rural Quebec, smugly exalting life on the farm. We must not be too hard on them, Séguin cautioned. Nineteenth-century Quebec was not ready for the separatist adventure:

However, the necessary solution to the French Canadians' economic problem was merely deferred.... In time they, as a nation, would have an opportunity to revert to their pre-1837 traditions without fearing the consequences, and to rid their economy of the paralyzing constraints of the Occupation.[21]

In essence, Séguin asserted that the economic inferiority of French Canada was due to the presence of the British. After 1760 a minority that subsequently became a majority gained political power over the whole of Canada, thereby assuring its domination of the national economy. The terms "minority" and "majority" were to assume new dimensions in Michel Brunet's version of British rule.

Michel Brunet

It was Michel Brunet who brought Maurice Séguin's interpretation of history to a wider public. This does not mean that Brunet's work was unoriginal, however. His particular field was the first generation following the defeat of 1760. Incidentally, Brunet was trained as a specialist in American history. Moreover, he was a political scientist and therefore concentrated on the political phenomenon—whatever his claims to the contrary. His work was polemical in nature, although this had nothing to do with his academic training. His temperament seemed suited to sweeping denunciations of the sort that have made him French Canada's best known and most controversial historian of the sixties and early seventies.[22]

Michel Brunet's French regime was identical to that of his colleague, Guy Frégault. The tragedy of the Conquest was that "it forced the fledgling colony to live unassisted. New France was too young to lose its parent country."[23]

After 1760 the British installed themselves in the now-defunct New France, and a second Canadian realm took shape in the St. Lawrence Valley. Brunet felt that if one analysed the immediate reactions of the conquered people vis-à-vis their new masters, one could observe a submissive desire induced by the "nightmare" of fear and the benevolence of the conquerors. Even so, hope remained that the Conquest was not final; their early diffidence gave way to an optimism that blinded them to the seriousness of their defeat and to their newly-assigned role of "pariahs." They were not to be blamed, however, as they were living in an era of absolute monarchy and had no idea of the "liberal and democratic nationalism" that was to shake the foundations of the Old Regime in Europe. For them, the Conquest simply meant a change in monarchs.[24]

One of the first effects of the Conquest on French-Canadian society was the disappearance of its bourgeois class.[25] Brunet maintained that an entrepreneurial class had existed in New France since the formation of the Company of Habitants in 1645. Throughout the French regime this class was involved in various enterprises, and by the eighteenth century had amassed enough wealth to acquire political influence. During the final fifteen years of New France especially, fabulous fortunes for the period were made by Bigot, Cadet, Péan, and similar figures. They most probably would have put their wealth to work for their country, but for the catastrophe of the Conquest. Admittedly they were dishonest, but it should be remembered that dishonesty was often the price of great wealth.

This commercial elite went back to France after the defeat. Those who stayed "were among the least rich or the most needy. They were not the entrepreneurs of big business, monopoly holders, or war profiteers." This qualitative weakness was compounded by difficulties that eventually completed their downfall. First the card money was devalued, then relations with suppliers in metropolitan France were broken off, and finally it proved impossible to establish profitable relations with British suppliers. As a result both the import and fur trades passed into the hands of British merchants who settled in the country. The few French traders who wished to continue in business were assigned the least profitable posts at the very time that their line of credit was seriously diminished.

Generally speaking, Brunet said, the history of the first thirty years of British rule was that of a bourgeoisie being gradually eliminated from the commercial sector. This bourgeoisie was rarely associated with major transactions, although it occasionally played a middleman role. Not surprisingly, therefore, it lost that inclination for taking risks which had been an accustomed feature of life in New France. The French Canadians fared no better politically, since the new order relegated them to lesser positions.

All was not lost, however. Toward the end of the eighteenth century a new elite rose up "that dissociated itself from the seigneurial and military class"—a class generally on good terms with the foreigners. Made up of small village shopkeepers, notaries, lawyers, doctors, surveyors, and clerks, this new elite supported the measures that subsequently gave birth to representative institutions. It was convinced that it could promote the interests of the French-Canadian community in a house of assembly, where it would by definition be in the majority.[26] There were other interested parties, however, and the parliamentary institutions demanded by the new elite operated to its distinct disadvantage, as events proved. The British merchants already dominated the Canadian economy; now, strengthened by Loyalist support, they could be sure of carrying the day within the new political structure. True, the division of the colony into Upper and Lower Canada frustrated their hopes of creating a British stronghold; but the history of Lower Canada was one of constant struggle between a triumphant British minority and the new spokesmen for French Canada, who called for responsible government in the legislative assembly without success.

Canadians of British origin, backed by London, which had granted them Union, resumed their attempts to assimilate the French, begun with the establishment of the Royal Institution for the Advancement of Learning in 1801. Boatloads of immigrants arrived regularly from England, soon reversing the population ratio of the two peoples. Between 1840 and 1850 French Canadians became a minority in their own country, suffering demographic as well as economic defeat. The granting of responsible government, now no longer a threat to British North America's continued existence, was the conqueror's crowning achievement in the struggle for domination.

Did Confederation improve the situation of the defeated people? Brunet maintained that it did not, since their minority status in a strong, centralized state placed them in a position of permanent inferiority. The provincial arena was still open to them, but French Canadians did nothing to transform it into a national state. Lulled by the comforting illusion of traditional nationalism, they limited themselves to defending their laws, language, and schools, as well as their farm and parish-oriented culture. This was not surprising; the Conquest, by removing their control of public and private business, had left them with a diminished concept of economic life. As citizens of a state governed by foreigners, they came to believe that it was a bad thing to use public power to promote economic activity. Their attitude was further confirmed by the belief that French Canadians had some sort of Catholic and French mission in America.[27]

In Brunet's view, certain politicians, as well as a great many intellectuals, had adopted the mistaken idea that equality was possible between the two Canadian "nations." This hoary myth seriously affected the chances of liberation. A minority could not govern a majority, and those who supported the two-nation concept should realize that they were playing into the hands of the pan-Canadian majority by giving the myth credence. But such people, although still technically French Canadians, had long been assimilated by the majority in any case.[28]

Among the apostles of Canadian unity were eminent statesmen like Sir Wilfrid Laurier, Ernest Lapointe, and Louis St. Laurent.[29] It was St. Laurent who encountered one of the first defenders of provincial autonomy, Maurice Duplessis. The Quebec premier obstructed the assimilating aims of the Massey Report, particularly by his refusal to accept federal government university grants.[30]

However indulgent Brunet might be toward politicans, he gave no quarter to French-Canadian intellectuals who deliberately undermined the interests of their own community. By approving federal aid to universities they were supporting the central government's offensive tactics.[31] But the crucial aspect of their national betrayal was to be found in their writings. In trying to discover why Quebec was economically backward, these writers described past generations of French Canadians as being addicted to political combat and inspired by a mistaken devotion to the spiritual life; French Quebec lacked an education system geared to the demands of the Industrial Revolution and suffered from a stifling, family-oriented approach to business. Such writers made no mention of the one really significant event that had been eating away at the foundation of the French-Canadian "nation" for two centuries. Their explanations were merely symptoms of the malady.[32]

These scholars refused to serve the French-Canadian community, Brunet averred, and consequently condemned nationalism as the cause of all ills.[33] They were in fact the blind tools of federal Canadian nationalism, having failed to understand that a renewed French-Canadian nationalist philosophy would guarantee Quebec the necessary arguments for its emancipation.

What was this "neo-nationalist" philosophy? Its prime trademark was the rejection of the traditional nationalist arsenal.[34] No more struggles to safeguard customs, language, and faith: future combats must be centered on a nationalist platform of economic development—one that would be feasible if Quebec had maximum provincial autonomy. This meant reducing to a minimum the "number of institutions in which the minority was obliged to associate with the majority."[35]

As Toronto historian Ramsay Cook has so aptly put it, Michel Brunet became the national historian of French Canada.[36] Heir and successor to Garneau and Groulx, he shared their conviction that scholarship was useful in so far as it served the interests of the national group. Such scholarship had a mission to raise French-Canadian consciousness and stimulate action, and had no room for those not imbued with this sense of duty toward society.

The Quebec School:
The "New" Liberals from Laval University

God knows...we love to talk about the Conquest and its responsibility for the entire subsequent development of French Canada. Some of our historians have even taken it as the sole explanation for the history of a whole people.
—*Claude Galarneau*[37]

Marcel Trudel
Marcel Trudel, like Frégault, turned his attention to the French regime. He too was interested in political and religious history, and wanted to rid French-Canadian historiography of its mythical element. In this respect his *Champlain* and "L'Affaire Jumonville" were comparable to Frégault's *Frontenac*.[38] Problems of method brought them together. As Trudel himself

remarked in his foreword to *Louis XVI, le Congrès américain et le Canada*: "In adopting the scientific approach to history I am merely following the method so brilliantly employed by that erudite historian, Guy Frégault."

Trudel's work provided few clues to his interpretive criteria—one might almost say none, since its analytical nature in one sense confined it to descriptive narrative.[39] On the other hand, this very limitation guaranteed a sort of authenticity that was probably without equal in French Canada. My business, however, is to find out whether Trudel had a comprehensive concept of Quebec's historical evolution, and a 1957 article entitled *La Nouvelle France* gives us a good idea of his perspective.[40]

Trudel considered the colony's economic structure just before the Conquest to be weak. There was "no established, large-scale industry; shipbuilding had been tried, but it soon became clear that it cost more to build a ship in Quebec than in France. Shipbuilding would only have become profitable if the government had been prepared to allow major secondary industries in New France; but France jealously guarded its right to process raw material." Industry in the Trois-Rivières region was confined to canoe-building and iron production. Montreal was little more than a meeting ground for Indians and traders.

Generally speaking, the only important economic activity in New France was the fur trade, and even this was very much threatened by British competition. The new string of western trading posts had never compensated for the loss of the fur-rich Hudson Bay in the Treaty of Utrecht. One means of remedying this economic drawback would have been to make New France an industrial power, but the schemes of Champlain and Talon for major development in this sector came to nothing.[41] In fact, since the beginning of the eighteenth century France had expressly forbidden the setting up of any industry that might compete with production in France.

This negative policy was compounded by the lack of settlers. What were 65,000 inhabitants compared to the colony's immense territory? What had the residents of Louisiana or Acadia in common with those of the St. Lawrence Valley?

Apart from language and family, they had no ties capable of cementing the fragile unity of this overly vast country. "For all these reasons, New France rapidly disintegrated under the impact of the Seven Years' War." This was hardly an encouraging picture of New France, showing as it did that the colony foundered because of internal weakness. The Conquest merely gave the *coup de grâce* to an already moribund country.

French Canada was still burdened with this legacy of weakness after 1760. During a conference on the current separatist crisis, Trudel summed up the major stages of French-Canadian history in these terms:

Our weakness goes back for three centuries. As a French colony we lagged desperately behind the fantastic development of the American colonies. It was a colony to which only 10,000 French immigrants came over a period of 150 years; where development of natural resources was expressly forbidden by France after 1704; a colony that, according to the firsthand account of one intendant, could not provide a living for a single printer. Conquered by the British and ceded by France, the people of this colony remained illiterate for many years. Frozen in time, antagonistic to anything in the nature of progress, it opposed the introduction of a parliamentary system in 1791.... The Durham Report gave us the most brutally realistic insight into our condition.... As an ethnic group, we were in a very bad way in 1839. It is because Durham appreciated the good qualities of French Canadians, as enumerated in his report, that he wished to save them from what he considered a doomed situation by assimilating them into English society. Union as an instrument of assimilation did not augur well, and yet it was under this repressive regime that French Canada made astonishing progress in every field, perhaps for the very reason that we are always at our best when threatened with destruction....

Then we entered Confederation.... We allowed English Canada to reap the benefit of the advantages that Confederation brought us—for Confederation did bring advantages. In the first place, from the economic point of view, we were now in a country that stretched from the Atlantic to the Pacific and offered the business world unprecedented opportunities for expansion. Despite its backwardness in this sector, French Canada should have participated in this expansion. What did it do? It made a point of training people for the liberal professions. Bishop Pâquet even gave official religious sanction to these social roles, with a corresponding disapproval of commerce and industry. French Canada, said the theologian, had a more noble mission—a spiritual one; business belonged to the materialists. Consequently the business world slipped through our fingers, and English Canada found itself virtually without competition.[42]

These last lines put forward the idea that a misguided emphasis on things spiritual had governed past generations.[43]

Jean Hamelin

The task of taking stock of Marcel Trudel's New France fell to another member of the Quebec School, Jean Hamelin. Unlike his predecessor, however, he analyzed the French colony's development in terms of social and economic history.

Hamelin's monograph, *Economie et société en Nouvelle-France*, began with a brief survey of the French regime.[44] He then discussed the schemes of Champlain and Talon for turning the colony into a major economic power. Champlain's scheme was unfortunately dropped. Talon's development policy was equally short-lived because of his limited sojourn in New France and the absence of a successor of his calibre at a time when British pirates and the Iroquois posed a serious threat. The War of the Spanish Succession (1701-1714) produced a crisis that crippled production and overseas trade during the first twenty years of the century, one of the major factors being the overproduction of oak masts. On the other hand, the decline in trade with metropolitan France stimulated local economic effort and the establishment of several industries. The two subsequent decades marked an upswing. Agriculture made significant progress, particularly in the Trois-Rivières region, due to diversified production and the opening of the Quebec-Montreal road. The leading industries were the Quebec shipyards and the St. Maurice ironworks. Nevertheless the colony lagged behind in manufacturing, still importing such commodities as soap, brick, tile, and cloth. Although the fishing industry showed relative progress, this did not close the unhealthy gap between industry and agriculture. It was obvious that New France suffered from economic weakness that could not be explained in terms of short-lived circumstances. Hamelin tended toward the view that the colony's economic development was hampered by permanent conditions.

In his analysis of New France's socio-economic structures, Hamelin concluded that the colony's main drawbacks were lack of capital, skilled labor, and consequently a big business bourgeoisie. Briefly, this was because the lion's share of fur trade profits went to metropolitan merchants. France, on the other hand, had no need to buy wheat from its colony, since it produced enough of its own. Furthermore, it did not send out the skilled labor needed in industry. With little capital and an insufficient labor force, there were predictably few industrial enterprises in New France.

If the colony were so unprosperous, how could we account for the forty millionaires at the end of the French regime? Peculation and profiteering enabled them to get rich in a wartime economy, said Hamelin. Moreover, those who claimed that this group would have invested in colonial enterprise, but for the Conquest, forgot that its capital was not in the form of hard cash. Paper money had already been devalued, and it was highly probable that the French king would only have redeemed it at part of its face value. If France had won, those who had misappropriated public funds might well have had to answer to the law. Such considerations proved, thought Hamelin, that the existence of a big business bourgeoisie at the end of the regime was merely a convenient fiction.

In general, Hamelin attributed the colony's inability to foster a big business class to the "absence of wealthy immigrants" and the rapid turnover of itinerant traders who only came to make their fortune, as well as to the ill-judged actions and the "megalomania" that encouraged the local bourgeoisie to spend extravagantly instead of saving and reinvesting its money. Predictably, under such conditions the colony was plunged into total economic stagnation. The very fact that part of its bourgeois class emigrated at the time of the Conquest proved that it was not engaged in long-term activity.[45]

Whether or not the Conquest changed the pattern of economic development, those left behind were faced with the problem of how to deal with the switch in allegiance.[46] The economic stagnation of the final years of the French regime

continued unabated, even though the very presence of the
conqueror was an invitation to progress. Incoming British
merchants, "formed in the Calvinist school where riches were
a sign of God's blessing," demanded a house of assembly. They
tried to involve the French Canadians in this project, but realized that their efforts were wasted. French Canadians were
accustomed to absolute monarchy and followed the advice of
their traditional leaders, the seigneurs, who were supported
by a clergy opposed to popular sovereignty. In other words,
parliamentary rule was an achievement of the British, and the
French Canadians refused to take part.

Fernand Ouellet

Fernand Ouellet's numerous articles have earned him the
reputation of an expert on the first hundred years after the
Conquest.[47] As with Hamelin, his research centered on social
and economic history. It is worth noting, however, that his
view of the British regime had a great deal in common with
Creighton's.[48]

Ouellet thought of the post-Conquest development of
French Canada as a continuation of the French regime.[49] It
was a mistake to suppose that the change to British rule had
deprived the colony of a big business class, the existence of
which was more likely "a projection of neo-nationalist historiography." Such an elite could never have been formed in
New France, primarily because of a despotic monarchy and
officialdom's stranglehold on the fur trade, as well as the
absence of a capitalist mentality.

Ouellet did not consider the Conquest to be the direct cause
of the French Canadians' weakness; on the contrary, it brought
benefits because it opened up the wheat markets of the British
Empire to the colony. At last the breadstuffs of the St. Lawrence
Valley could find the outlets that France had been unable to
provide. Furthermore, the French Canadians continued to
play an important role in the fur trade until the American
Revolution, when they were gradually replaced by Scottish
traders. This reversal was not due to the presence of new
competitors, but rather to the inability of the "native" business
class to meet the challenge of emerging capitalism. French

Canadians hesitated to become involved in large companies and diversify their investments. Moreover, the French legacy of extravagant consumer habits prevented them from reinvesting profits, which was partly why the early nineteenth century was a period of decline for the French-Canadian business bourgeoisie in favor of the English-speaking commercial class.

The English became increasingly identified with commercial capitalism as the fur trade waned. Lumber exports during the Napoleonic wars became the almost exclusive preserve of English-Canadian capitalists. The underlying reasons for this were all linked to the French Canadians' refusal to adapt to new economic structures. To begin with, traditional education continued to shut out bourgeois values. The economic necessities of the period called for a system of education that would supply the much-needed, dynamic businessmen, skilled laborers, and farmers familiar with modern techniques. Primary school education, however, did not develop in this direction during the first half of the nineteenth century. University education did not exist, although a university was actually proposed in 1789 by the English-speaking bourgeoisie. It was to have been mixed and non-sectarian, and consequently the Roman Catholic authorities of the province rejected it.[50]

Secondary education for French Canadians was the exclusive preserve of the church, which founded a considerable number of classical colleges during the period. The teaching in these establishments leaned far too much toward the traditional humanities, Ouellet felt, to produce an elite alive to the realities of capitalist society. It had the opposite effect of training large numbers of professional men, thus perpetuating the trend of French-Canadian society to develop counter to the prevailing current.[51] As a result, this professional elite became too large a group for the needs of the community, obliging it to turn toward political power as a source of prestige and security. The rural background and classical training of this group prevented it from making common cause with the English commercial bourgeoisie. Consequently, as the rebellion drew nearer, it sought to extend its power within the legislative assembly, defending its group interests under the guise of progressive ideas and making itself the spokesman for a restive rural class.

According to Ouellet, early nineteenth-century farmers were affected by a crisis caused by their negligence and ignorance of modern farming methods.[52] Demographic tensions produced by the scarcity of arable land added to their discontent. (The statistical measurement of such agricultural and demographic problems will be dealt with in detail in chapter 5.) Normally, since it was unaware of its own deficiencies, the rural population would have resigned itself with traditional fatalism.

The "professional" bourgeoisie, however, sought a scapegoat for popular misfortunes in order to rouse the people, and seized upon its rival for political power—the colony's commercial class with its connections in the legislative and executive councils. This is why the French-Canadian professional class obstructed executive projects in the assembly. Opposition to a St. Lawrence canal system was a classic example. It also explained the stubborn defense of institutions like the seigneurial system that actually accentuated the economic inferiority of the nation that it was claiming to save.[53]

This version of French Canada's history threw a new light on the events of 1837-1838. The Troubles, as they were called, no longer appeared as the revolt of an oppressed nation, but as the normal outcome of a society unable to adjust to the demands of progress. Armed insurrection became a plot fomented by a social class that hid its desire for domination behind imported European principles of liberal nationalism.

The Lower-Canadian clergy had watched this stormy development with misgiving. The church did not oppose conservative nationalism; but it condemned the political agitation of Papineau and his lieutenants because of its liberal and democratic aspect. The first bishop of Montreal, Monseigneur Lartigue, cleansed the nationalist ideology of its liberal overtones. Bishops Laflèche and Bourget soon followed suit, thus insuring the triumph of right-wing nationalism, which subsequently dominated the evolution of French Canada. The petite bourgeoisie gradually dissociated itself from the principles of liberalism emanating from France. The few dissident voices in the Institut canadien talked in vain of badly needed reforms: they were powerless to stop the rising ultramontane, anti-materialist tide. This tide was the logical outcome of the new direction taken by French-Canadian nationalism. However, nationalism in the latter half of the nineteenth century did not lead to separatism, Ouellet noted, since the national enemy tended to be identified with a few left-wing activists who had survived the rebellion.

As the twentieth century dawned, events took a different turn. The close association of Britain's colonies with imperial policy was to revive French Canadians' hatred of the British, never far from the surface. The subject of Canada's contribution to Great Britain's war effort aroused the old "racial" conflict, which this time deflected the attention of the leading groups from the problems of adapting to industrial society. Ethnic conflicts born during the conscription debate were aggravated by the Great Depression of the thirties, and it was then that the separatist ideology reappeared. The Second World War brought about a fresh national crisis and a final period of intransigent nationalism.

Shortly after the war ended, Quebec turned toward the more productive goal of gaining autonomy. Ouellet saw this change in attitude as the work of the Duplessis regime. However, despite the warning indicated by the growing opposition of a new elite trained in the social sciences, this regime made the mistake of not reorganizing Quebec's social structure. The overthrow of the Duplessis regime led to the much needed and continuing reform of traditional institutions. This reform did not have universal support, he noted, and separatist ideology was once more on the rise. Perhaps nationalist agitation was merely the result of "the inevitable growing pains that go with modernizing our institutions." In any case, Ouellet thought that the main concern should be the achievement of internal reform. Once this was achieved, it would be time to ask "whether Confederation was a fool's bargain."

The Implications of the Quiet Revolution
I can see no end to English Canadian domination of the machinery of production in Quebec except the abandon-

ment by the French of their attitude to life and their acceptance of ours [in conformity with the Protestant ethic]—either that, which they will not deliberately make— or the invocation of the power of the state to take over English enterprise and thus a slipping back into a more or less efficient paternalistic socialism, in which the intellectuals at last have all the *postes* they want as public factory managers.

—A.R.M. Lower[54]

In *L'Option politique du Canada français*, sociologist Philippe Garigue remarked that almost all Quebec studies have centered on the causes of the province's economic inferiority. With the exception of Trudel, French Quebec historiography has followed a similar path. Understandably, historians have reflected the major choices facing contemporary Quebec society. One might say that developments which took place in the 1960s were more or less connected with the new historical consciousness. This does not mean that such studies have actually given rise to political action,[55] but that they are related to the "Quiet Revolution," as it has come to be called. The following discussion attempts to look at this phenomenon.

Autonomy or Independence

The Montreal School of history introduced a more realistic attitude toward the "national" question, and this was probably its major contribution. It recognized the imperatives of a pluralist society and avoided all religious discussion. There was still some evident confusion on this score in certain sectors,[56] but nonetheless there was a marked tendency to strive for secular objectives. The old slogan about "language defender of the faith" was no longer meaningful. It had been replaced by *maîtres chez-nous*, "the right to self-determination," and "special status." The general idea was that one could not save culture without mastering economy. This was what Claude Ryan meant when he wrote:

It is no longer our language demands for Quebec that disturb our English-speaking countrymen, but rather the extent of economic sovereignty that Quebec means to gain in order to realize its ambitions.[57]

This anxiety was one of the first consequences of renewed Quebec nationalism. A few English Canadians understood the gravity of the situation,[58] but for the most part these were intellectuals without the support of political leaders or the electorate. The current question, "What does Quebec want?" was proof of this. During a visit to the province of Quebec, Premier Duff Roblin of Manitoba talked of the French Canadians as a young people, thereby showing the ludicrous ignorance in western Canada concerning Quebec's "national" problem. It seemed that the general public still believed that French Canada responded to symbolic concessions such as those involving the flag or the national anthem.

Religion, Modernity, and Education

The Quebec School did not blame the Conquest and subsequent British occupation for French Canada's inferior position. Instead, it challenged the refusal to question the whole set of values and institutions that prevented Quebec society from modernizing itself. Actually, the sociologists of French Canada had traditionally held this view. The tradition stemmed from such writers as Léon Gérin, Horace Miner, Everett Hughes, Robert Redfield, and the many French-Canadian sociologists whom they had inspired. All these researchers studied the structures and development of French-Canadian society without any mention of the cataclysm supposedly unleashed by the Conquest.[59] They emphasized the conservative nature of Quebec Catholicism, which they saw as the main cause of collective weaknesses. *Témoins*, a new magazine of the 1960s, summed up their position in these terms:

For many years the socio-cultural future of French Canada was mistakenly viewed as linked to some divine destiny: first, by the suggestion that the nation had a spiritual vocation that compensated for its social and economic powerlessness [sic]; and second, by transferring the community's awareness of genuine political concerns to supposedly religious ones (and therefore apparently more noble), while minimizing political realities as being too "profane."

Secular life was cluttered with pseudo-religion (philosophy, the arts, literature, and even economics had a distinctly religious flavor), and was influenced by a fairly open invitation to spurn the things of this world. Eventually the faithful adopted a mentality character- ized, not by Jansenism, as is too often stated, but by a willingness to forego a material future in favor of eternal life. Hence the frequent use in sermons of the New Testament parable of the rich young man.[60]

Such statements meant that the church in Quebec no longer disdained a dollar bill, or to put it another way, it had become reconciled to industrial society.[61] Meanwhile, a new, lay elite was already preparing the ground for restructuring and reorienting Quebec society toward secular goals. It wanted to fill in the gaps in the education system. The Parent Report, on which current reforms were based, seemed to be a clearcut response to the challenges of technological society.[62]

II

Changing Views of the Canadian Sixteenth Century

From Narcisse-Eutrope Dionne (1891)
to Marcel Trudel (1963)

A conservative ideology dominated the intellectual life of
French Quebec for many years after the abortive 1837-1838
attempt to do away with colonial rule. It was an ideology
defined by the clergy and a large sector of the petite bourgeoisie. These middle class groups supported a general view of
society that has been repeatedly described and analysed in
numerous studies on Quebec ideology, and it is therefore
unnecessary to summarize the main features of it here. Instead,
I wish to show the influence of what I call clerico-conservative
nationalism on the historical reconstruction of the "nation's"
distant past. Furthermore, the way in which Quebecers perceive
their past has changed since World War I, and I would like
to consider this in relation to the works of Marcel Trudel. We
will then be in a position to understand the influence of liberal
ideology on the collective self-questioning that occurred at the
time of the Quiet Revolution. In examining Trudel's work,
we will discover a retrospective vision of the French-Canadian
destiny—a vision that was shared by "activist" intellectuals
during the 1950s and 1960s, and generally by the recently-
emerged sector of the Quebec petite bourgeoisie described by
various authors as the new elite or new middle class.[1]

31

I have chosen two authors to demonstrate the areas of comparison and confrontation between the clerico-conservative concept of society and its liberal counterpart, which emerged in the middle of the twentieth century. Narcisse-Eutrope Dionne (1848-1917) and Marcel Trudel published two distinct reconstructions of the sixteenth century.[2] Although often using the same documents, they were working three-quarters of a century apart.

Narcisse-Eutrope Dionne

In several respects, Dionne is typical of Quebec's traditional elites. After four years of theology and philosophy at the Grand Séminaire in Quebec, he went on to study medicine. Following a few years of practice, he moved into clerico-conservative journalism, was subsequently named librarian of the Quebec legislature (1892), and in 1897 was promoted to provincial secretary-archivist, a post which he occupied until 1912. Like several nineteenth-century civil servants in Ottawa and Quebec, Dionne devoted his leisure time to history. A prolific and erudite amateur, he published several lengthy works, mainly on the early days of French Canada.[3]

In 1891 Dionne published *La Nouvelle-France de Cartier à Champlain, 1540-1603*,[4] a scholarly work by contemporary standards. It contained many clarifications of detail, including corrections of place names and dates that previous histories had left obscure, and dealt not only with discoveries but with map-making and economic conditions in the sixteenth century. There is no doubt that it represented a great advance in detailed knowledge. What concerns us, however, is to distinguish what sociological and ideological perspectives served as a basis for interpretation.

For nineteenth-century historians, founding a colony presupposed considerable devotion, generosity, and disinterestedness. Colonial enterprise was only legitimate if undertaken for the greater glory of God, the need for converting the Amerindians being taken for granted. The next most important assumption was that colonists should be chosen according to moral criteria rather than the needs of economic development. According to nineteenth-century standards, therefore, the founding of Montreal was an ideal form of colonization. The city of Quebec, on the other hand, only attained the primarily moral and religious standards of colonization after 1600. These standards were set by the same people who defined the clerico-conservative concept of society, and it was this historical concept that served Dionne as an invisible yardstick in chronicling the sixteenth century. Of the work of Champlain and de Maisonneuve, he wrote:

These two great Frenchmen laid the foundation of our nationhood and—astute builders that they were—rested it upon the immutable rock of the Catholic religion.... Could they have built a solid and unshakable structure otherwise? Never. I have no hesitation in saying so, because I am convinced that without religion as the mainstay, successful colonization is not possible. Even today, it is still true that the Christian ideal must preside over any undertaking of this nature. What is necessary today was no less so in past centuries [p. 17f.].

In stating the guiding principles of his work, Dionne was not merely justifying the role of colonizing missionaries who oversaw pioneer settlements in Quebec after 1840. He was confirming the theological argument whereby human enterprise conducted under the sign of the cross was destined to endure, whereas works not inspired by Catholicism would inevitably perish. Dionne saw sixteenth-century history in the St. Lawrence region as a story of greed and cupidity. He explained the temporary nature of French colonial ventures during the first century of the modern era as follows:

Crass materialism nearly resulted in all being lost, and it is always surprising to find that such was not the case. No one can deny that, had providence not directly intervened in the affairs of Canada, France's fate in North America would have been sealed forever; its disappearance would only have been a matter of years.[5]

Dionne placed special emphasis on the expeditions of Cartier and Roberval, and of the Marquis de La Roche to Sable Island, in order to demonstrate their value and significance.

Roberval[6] cut a rather sorry figure beside Jacques Cartier. Dionne perceived Cartier as having a missionary ambition comparable to that of "the saintly and herioc figure of Columbus" (p.12), a vocation also mentioned in his earlier biography of Cartier (1889). Roberval was not of the same calibre. When Cartier abandoned him to return to France in 1542 with what he thought was a cargo of gold, Dionne did not feel that the navigator was acting out of self-interest. His refusal

to return to Charlesbourg-Royal with the leader of the expedition [Roberval] when they met by chance in the port of St. John's...is easily explained.... Hakluyt's account says that Cartier decamped for fear of losing the credit for his discoveries. Mere common sense should make it clear that this is ridiculous. Cartier had no new discovery to report to his king.... He was returning to his country because he realized the futility of trying to colonize Canada with such inadequate resources, and possibly because he saw that Roberval could not handle the situation [p. 54].

The number of settlers accompanying Roberval was indeed inadequate. But a further reason for Dionne's approval of Cartier's flight was that the settlers recruited for the expedition were nothing but a "band of scoundrels." According to Dionne, fear of the pioneers' morals, not the Amerindians, dissuaded Cartier from founding a new settlement:

What could he really expect from these hardened criminals.... To colonize a country with scoundrels and sinners would have been a colossal error. Cartier's noble soul and religious sentiments prevented him from supporting an enterprise doomed from the start. He was therefore right, all things considered, in allowing Roberval to go on alone [p. 30f.].

Dionne spoke to Roberval across the years, as though calling on him to return to France as well. Canada had no need of felons, Dionne insisted.[7] Roberval's expedition failed, as we know. In Dionne's view, "the failure of this attempt at colonization was a stroke of luck for Canada" (p. 40). The only service rendered the Canadian nation by Roberval was to have "repatriated every single one of the felons that had accompanied him" (p. 50).

Dionne felt that Roberval had done little for posterity, but took a more lenient view of the Marquis de La Roche.[8] It was true that La Roche's recruits "were apparently ill-fitted to form the nucleus of a healthy settlement" (p. 173), but he launched the enterprise from the noblest of motives. His good intentions won him general absolution in the opinion of clerico-conservatives. Although he "abandoned [his settlers] to their sad fate," leaving it to "providence to come to their rescue" (p. 174), this was no reason to sully his memory as the expedition's leader. He was unable to carry out his work of settlement, most likely because of opposition from "Calvinist sectarians" who feared the spread of Catholicism (p. 177). Dionne refuted the marquis's detractors, whose views had been disseminated by a certain "liberal" historiographer, and invoked Champlain's testimony:

> According to the founder of Quebec, whom one cannot suspect of ignorance or even less of partiality in this matter, the aim of the marquis . . . was not so much to recoup a broken-down fortune, as to work for the glory of God by raising Christ's standard on our shores, peopled by infidels.
> Although he would have liked to carry on, his work was impeded by those of his compatriots whose religious views differed from his. Was he wrong? [P. 178f.]

Religious intolerance and hatred of capitalist "materialism" were the hallmarks of the clerico-conservative perspective. For example, Henri IV was seen as the major culprit of the sixteenth century. He granted "certain trading and mining privileges...to courtiers who were more eager to enrich themselves than to found colonies" (p. 10). Although described as "having given new life to our former mother country," Henri IV was nevertheless reproached for "his compliance toward his erstwhile co-religionists" (p. 152) after his conversion to Catholicism. At least under his predecessor, "the celebrated war known as the 'War of the League'" had as an "ostensible aim...saving the Catholic religion from the Calvinists" (p. 153). "Despite his recantation, which ought to have made him devoted to the Catholic cause, Henri IV could never bring himself to break with his former co-religionists completely.... He often favored them, on the ridiculous pretext of being just and impartial toward all his subjects without distinction" (p. 212). In short, clerico-conservatives did not accept the principle of religious tolerance. The rejection of this liberal premise was widespread among nineteenth-century clergy and the petite bourgeoisie. One can get a fairly clear sense of their attitude by reading a series of lectures on liberalism by the Abbé Benjamin Pâquet. He stated that although the church had not the right to force heathen to share the Catholic faith, the same was not true when dealing with Protestants:

> With regard to heretics and apostates, the church always has the right, and even the duty—when persuasion is not sufficient to bring them back to the truth—to use physical constraint and corporal punishment, either for correction or to keep the faithful from the contagion of error.[9]

Not only did the church have the right, it had the power. The church's history and certain propositions in the *Syllabus* provided legitimate precedent for such action, Pâquet went on to say.[10] What is more, the state should cooperate in the work of reconverting the Protestants. If it did not, it placed itself in peril:

> Heresy is not just an individual error of no consequence. It is a social crime. Wherever it penetrates it negates the divine authority of the church. The collapse of this authority leads to further ruin. The downfall of civil authority soon follows, bringing with it the denial of the most sacred family and individual rights. Then it is that ancient monarchies totter on their foundations and crumble with a roar; the nations rush headlong into barbarism, in comparison with which the most primitive tribe of savages would seem highly civilized.[11]

This may seem extreme, and yet Abbé Pâquet's adversaries considered him a "liberal."[12] In any event, this theologian's thinking sheds a singular light on Dionne's interpretation of the sixteenth century. Among those who believed in the subordination of state to church, what better ally than Benjamin Pâquet to condemn the principle of religious liberty? One can understand why, given this perspective, the Edict of Nantes might appear as a politico-religious heresy. Dionne commented:

> The Edict of Nantes,...by placing Huguenots on the same footing as Catholics, gave them access to all offices, both in the judiciary and in finance. As a result the Calvinists, Huguenots, and all those belonging to the so-called reformed religion, often occupied the most important posts at court, whereas Catholics could only gain some

favor by submitting to the yoke of those people whom the old religious quarrels had made extremely fanatic [p. 195f.].

It was because of the supreme error of the Edict of Nantes that the Protestants "were able to keep the upper hand," both in government and colonial enterprise (p. 196), a position that force of circumstances had given them before the proclamation of the Edict granted religious liberty. Henri IV preferred to give exclusive trading privileges to the Protestant Chauvin[13] rather than to La Roche or to Cartier's St. Malo successors (p. 200). It should be noted that Dionne felt that Chauvin symbolized the "cupidity" and "avarice" of Protestant merchants:

Canada owes very little to Pierre de Chauvin, who did nothing...for French colonization.... Chauvin wished to make money first and foremost.... In any case, what motives would have induced the Norman speculator to colonize New France? As a member of a Calvinist sect, he was not particularly concerned about establishing a faith other than his own on our soil.... For then as now, many Protestants bowed down before the golden calf rather than before God in heaven [p. 211].

At least Chauvin did not attempt to make converts, Dionne went on to say. For this reason he was "less to blame" than the "Huguenot merchants who later ruined the French colony through religious zeal pushed beyond the limits permitted by the court." However, "their habit of dumping settlers of every persuasion on the shores of the St. Lawrence seems to have begun under Chauvin" (p. 211).

Dionne clearly attributed the failure of several French colonial enterprises to the Protestant influence, particularly in Brazil, Florida, and Acadia.[14] For those with a clerico-conservative view of society, it was imperative that French America not become a dumping-ground for rebel elements from France. Traditional historians, with a few rare exceptions, did not feel that France could have profited from the British example.[15] They saw New France as the exclusive homeland of virtuous Catholics. Dionne contrasted the "baseness" of economic motives with the nobility of missionary intentions. Among European nations competing for American domination, Portugal acted solely from ambition (p. 13), and England only wanted to find a passage to the East Indies. Spain was in the grip of "a mad desire for monopoly" (p. l4). This "ambitious nation" asserted that France could not undertake exploration without its permission. "The French were the first to object to conditions that adversely affected the missionaries' evangelical conquests" (p. 79). The terms in which Dionne denounced the Spaniards' "materialism" was typical of the scale of values that he relied upon when writing history. The ultramontane historians felt that only the French cared about converting the Amerindians to Catholicism while at the same time respecting their cultural roots. France's competitors, on the other hand, had opted for "genocide" or for reducing the natives to servitude.

Hungry for gold, they [the Spaniards] threw themselves on America as though on a prey.... The Indian was soon nothing more than an enemy to be vanquished, if not destroyed. It is repugnant to see a civilized nation ignore the basic principles of justice in this manner...for love of a few ingots of gold. A nation does not gain power and prestige by such dishonorable means [p. l52f.].

The Spaniards, greedy for riches, were more barbarous than the savages,...contrary to what one might expect. In order to appropriate the treasure of these [Indian] nations, idolatrous and ignorant, perhaps, but attached to their homeland nonetheless,...the Spaniards believed that the most expeditious method was to reduce them to servitude or simply kill them off [p. 93f.].

The Portuguese were treated to a similar tirade (p. 94), while the French, in Dionne's words, "were immediately able to gain the respect of the savage nations with which they traded their products."[16] He emphasized Franco-Amerindian friendship in order to refute certain interpretations then current in the United States, which alleged that the French did not always deal fairly with native peoples. Dionne contended that "the French name has always sounded pleasant to Indian ears in both the Americas" (p. 92). Despite the wars against the Iroquois and abuses by certain coureurs de bois, "these individual cases, however deplorable, will never give the lie to the fine testimony of the Englishman Isaac Weld," who after visiting Canada at the end of the eighteenth century "noted that 'nature seems to have implanted in their hearts a reciprocal affection between Frenchman and Indians' and that 'an Indian, even at this day, will always go to the house of a poor French farmer in preference to that of a [rich] Englishman'" (p. 92). Even so, Dionne retained the spirit of Western racism: the white man was "the amiable and civilized man...the superior man" (p. 97).

Missionary work only began in the seventeenth century, as we know, and therefore Dionne did not disguise the self-serving motives underlying the friendliness of the French in an earlier age. He remarked that communication between the French and the Amerindians, who helped the colonizers discover the continent's resources, had already given birth to good relationships. This was heartening to note, as other nations seemed deliberately to have made themselves detested by their behavior, often unworthy of civilized peoples (p. 90).

All the same, French participation in the race for colonies would have had to increase considerably to make any real impact during the sixteenth century. To Dionne, the failure of settlement was the result of a basic flaw—and here we are dealing with the theology of history: God was not on their side.

The hour fixed by providence for opening up this land to our ancestors was merely delayed, and when it did strike, we would witness a far more encouraging sight. Each nation has its special destiny, but the various peoples do not grow strong unless they tread the path indicated by the great Master. The kings of France had dreamed of forming another France in America, but God decreed that it should not come to pass until his apostles and missionaries had arrived on the scene. The great sixteenth-century explorers brought only transitory colonizing elements with them. Except for Jacques Cartier, none of them thought of bringing priests; yet priests had always been regarded as the only men capable of injecting vigor into a new colony. It was they who could rekindle spirits and maintain respect for the authority of God and man. After seven years spent laying the foundations of his city, Champlain fully realized that he would never succeed in uniting his countrymen on the rock of Quebec unless he brought a few men of the cloth with him. Although his was as bold an undertaking in its way as Cartier's had been, it was the priests who supplied the solid base that had been lacking prior to 1615. They had scarcely set foot on our soil before they were at work, unmindful of their health in their eagerness to bring new vigor to Champlain's enterprise. One by one, they returned to France to place the settlers' needs and grievances before the king and to ask support for the settlers from generous souls, never flagging in carrying out so difficult a mission [p. 194f.].

In order to fulfil the designs of providence, however, it was first necessary to replace the king's minister, Sully, who had no gift for colonization (p. 15f.). His successor was Richelieu, hailed by Dionne as an ardent colonizer, and one who "could...distinguish between the man suited to command and direct, and the masses who are bound to obey" (p. 16f.)—in a word, the man seconded by Champlain, the man "taken by providence from the ranks of the people,...[the man] who realized that Canada offered a vast field for propagation of the faith...and for greater French renown" (p. 12). Note the order of priorities in what was presumed to be Champlain's social scheme: faith, then language. This accurately reflected the clerico-conservative concept of national destiny, according to which survival was subordinate to the maintenance of moral and religious integrity and the furtherance of missionary work. Modern-day Quebec has forgotten the epigraph attributed to Champlain that was quoted admiringly for many years by the traditional elite of French Canada, not to mention several generations of schoolchildren and college students. Dionne cited it twice:

The taking of fortresses, the winning of battles, and the conquest of countries are nothing compared to the salvation of souls...the conversion of one heathen is worth more than the conquest of a realm.[17]

Marcel Trudel's Early Career (1945-1963)

It should be stated at the outset that I am not attempting to assess Trudel in terms of his knowledge of Quebec's past. This distinguished historian has taught a generation of researchers the rudiments of historical science. He is recognized for his remarkable scholarly production, which adheres faithfully to the stringent demands of critical history and is inspired in varying degrees by positivist methodology.[18] We are indebted to the pioneers of the historian's craft in Quebec for the introduction of this scientific theory of history—a theory that devotees of clerico-conservativism regarded as an intellectual practice bordering on atheism.[19] In the view of the clergy and the conservative sector of the petite bourgeoisie, historians such as Marcel Trudel and others, whose work began to appear after World War II, were responsible for destroying the influence of Christian theological doctrines of history. The gradual disappearance of this influence followed the declining curve of French Canada's traditional elites.[20] If these historians were indeed responsible, there must have been an underlying polemical element in their work, despite protestations of neutrality or objectivity. In other words, this first change in historiographical perspective in Quebec was connected to a social conflict, the extent and significance of which we can now measure, given the passage of time. To relate Trudel's social environment to his historical scholarship, we will examine his account of the sixteenth century. In the process, we will also have a chance to look at the ideology of the new middle class in Quebec. This newly emerged sector of the petite bourgeoisie was the moving spirit behind the Quiet Revolution.

Of course, with a writer of Marcel Trudel's calibre, value judgments are far from obtrusive. Often they are expressed in terms of silent comment or the inclusion of revealing material from primary documentary sources. Nevertheless, value judgments do exist. Trudel threw down the gauntlet to clerico-conservative tradition early on with a controversial choice of subject: *L'Influence de Voltaire au Canada* (1945). He was the first to demonstrate and perhaps even exaggerate the importance of eighteenth-century philosophical thought among the post-Conquest Quebec intelligentsia. A strange subject, this, for a doctoral thesis written by a Quebec student in the early 1940s, even though he condemned the importation of rationalism, "which imperiled the church in Canada," diverted the press from the struggle for survival, and "distorted Garneau's history."[21] The revelation of the existence of a liberal, lay, and anticlerical current constituted the first breach in what had been a collective sense of the past fabricated by the Quebec clergy and the petite bourgeoisie during the century following the rebellion.

Much could be said on the subject of Marcel Trudel's revelations in connection with his works on the Seven Years' War. At various points the church in Quebec appeared tainted with "weaknesses" known only to historians, who until then had been careful not to put them in writing.[22] Some were shocked to see the "new" historians revealing "scandalous" behavior to the general public. The best that could be said, for example, of Trudel's biography of Chiniquy[23] was that "it took a lot of courage to deal with such a subject in a country where...it was often considered preferable to hide the existence of Judas rather than recount the story of his treachery."[24] For the liberal-minded, Trudel was in search of "objective truth" and dared to speak "the whole truth."[25] In company with Guy Frégault and Michel Brunet, with whom he had published *Histoire du Canada par les textes* (1952), he was highly praised by the liberal sector of the petite bourgeoisie. This sector attacked clericalism and favored secular, industrial modernism combined with government intervention, as exemplified by the Lesage regime of the 1960s. "We congratulate them on their firm stand against the fine-sounding lies and pious omissions" of their predecessors, wrote journalist Jean-Marc Poliquin in 1955.[26] Not all truth makes suitable telling, replied the clerics and the conservative petite bourgeoisie who had remained true to the traditional vision of national destiny. Lucien Lemieux, one of Dionne's successors at the Quebec legislative library, confided to a curé friend in 1957: "The history being written these days is a vast conspiracy against the truth."[27] In many respects, the debate took on the character of a duel between idolaters and iconoclasts. Monseigneur Albert Tessier criticized "certain university circles" that enjoyed "methodically belittling our great historical figures."[28] Tessier had chosen the publication of Trudel's *Champlain* in the Fides "Classics" series as an occasion for intervening. Trudel was doing more than sully the memory of a hero in this edition of texts; he was attacking the agrarianism of the clerico-conservative group. Champlain, in Marcel Trudel's view, wished to found a "commercial colony." "The word recurs like an obsession," deplored Monseigneur Tessier.[29] Group resistance to changes in the social structure since the beginning of the Industrial Revolution has been remarkably tenacious, as illustrated in Pierre-Georges Roy's preface to *Terres de la Grande-Anse des Aulnaies et du Port-Joly* (1951) by Léon Roy. "Monsieur Roy...has produced more than a work of research; he has been instrumental in encouraging young people to feel a greater sense of attachment to the family farm.... There is no question that rural areas are being deserted at a rate that is alarming to those who care for the future of our people. Country folk are attracted by the deceptive allure of city life, much as those who look too long are drawn into the abyss."[30] The writing of Firmin Létourneau (*Histoire de l'agriculture*, 1950) and others contained numerous nostalgic anxieties of this kind concerning the irreversible process of industrialization and urbanization. Behind Trudel's denial of an agrarianist Champlain, therefore, lay the implicit proposal of a whole new conception of the French-Canadian national vocation. At the beginning of the twentieth century, the traditional elites, disquieted by the increasing rate of industrialization, had erected a bronze statue of Louis Hébert, symbol of the Quebec people's rural calling. In Trudel's view, Hébert was nothing more than an "improvised farmer who settled on top of a cape to farm instead of working the good earth in the valley."[31] Albert Tessier fully grasped the significance of this criticism of an eminent figure of traditional national mythology:

> It is not enough to demolish individuals. The rural class is also attacked—the class that formed nearly 75 percent of the total population until the end of the last century, and that constituted our great reservoir of moral and national strength. All the evils that our people endure are imputed to the "myth of agrarianism," as it is labeled.[32]

To put it briefly, however much Trudel may have wanted to remain aloof from contemporary debate, his scholarly work involved him in the ideological confrontation of the mid-twentieth century, perhaps in spite of himself. In this confrontation, progressives of liberal tendencies opposed the clerico-conservative group whose influence was gradually being eroded. Trudel's works formed part of what was seen as a subversive literature that both reflected and fueled the questioning of that ideal Quebec envisaged by the clergy and the conservative members of the professions. It need hardly be said that Albert Tessier was not alone in considering that Quebec's founder had been insulted.[33]

Clerico-conservative chauvinism underwent a further trial with the publication of Trudel's history of slavery in 1960.[34] In the view of the Dominican Antonin Lamarche, this study was a slur on "the nobility of our origins."[35] Although Trudel's monograph was a scholarly work, it had far-reaching effects. With all the prestige attached to the then newly-employed statistical method, it portrayed the Quebec people as partisans of slavery. From the end of the seventeenth century until the beginning of the nineteenth, reported Trudel, 86.7 percent of all slave-owners were French-speaking, "which enables us to state," he concluded, "that slavery was practised much more frequently here by French Canadians than by the English."[36] A reader more familiar with statistical inference would be quick to point out that a Briton could hardly have owned slaves under the French regime. Trudel did distinguish between the period of New France and the first decades of the British regime. However, he neglected to mention for the latter period that French-speaking residents (of whom 477 owned 937 slaves) accounted for about 90 percent of the population, whereas English-speaking residents (of whom 217 owned 420 slaves) represented some 10 percent. Therefore it was the British, not the French Canadians, who owned proportionately more slaves during the first decades of British rule. The use of arbitrary statistics that did not take into account the "ethnic" proportions of the population showed Trudel's evident bias. An unbiased statistical reading would have made it clear that even after the arrival of the Loyalists the Lower-Canadian population was still 85 to 90 percent French-speaking.[37]

By the beginning of the 1960s, Marcel Trudel had acquired sufficient knowledge and mastery of his craft to devote himself to writing a monumental synthesis of the history of New France, employing the unassailable erudition that is the hallmark of all his work. True to positivist theories, although he had already recognized that the historian is himself part of history,[38] Trudel gave notice in the foreword to the first volume that this would be an "objective" work.[39] This first volume dealt with the sixteenth century, covering the period of *vaines tentatives* or "vain attempts" to found a settlers' colony in the St. Lawrence Valley. It is this work that I shall analyze in detail to illustrate the distance between this reconstruction of the past, written at the time of the Quiet Revolution, and the clerico-conservative reconstruction offered by Dionne.

Trudel's *Les Vaines Tentatives* was unavoidably a succession of travel accounts. Like a good tourist guide well-versed in the territory through which he was leading us, the author noted things not seen by the explorers whom he was accompanying. Attempts at dramatization, revealed by the occasional exclamation point, reminded us that we were dealing with perilous journeys into the unknown, exotic odysseys fraught with mystery. The picturesque was not lacking in this account reconstructed for twentieth-century readers. The explorers' chronicles appeared to be an invitation to travel. Even the kidnapped natives seemed "gratified...at the prospect of a trip abroad" (p. 83)—the first Canadian tourists in Europe. Trudel's Amerindians generally made little complaint about their fate. This was very much the classic liberal perspective, fairly insensitive to the phenomenon of domination. "The native was not despoiled" (p. 268), he stated rather summarily in connection with the colonizers' invasion of Amerindian territory.

The advent of Renaissance humanism meant that acquired knowledge was no longer considered subordinate to Christian revelation. The new men of the sixteenth century founded their knowledge on reasoning, criticism, and experience. Scientific empiricism, which became part of liberal rationalism after 1700, overrode the theocentric perception of the universe, and progress in knowledge of the physical world through exploration and cartography has accordingly been a feature of the modern era. Trudel therefore chronicled the discoveries of the sixteenth century from the standpoint of a Renaissance humanist, with astonishing emphasis on scientific progress. That is why someone like Verrazano, the first explorer employed by France and almost unknown in traditional historical writing, was a key figure in the sixteenth century of Marcel Trudel (pp. 47-49). Although the Venetian's expedition was "a commercial disappointment" (p. 66), it was nevertheless a "spectacular success" (p. 47) because it significantly increased knowledge about the world. All through his account, with an almost obsessive regularity, Trudel registered progress and failure in extending knowledge of the continent.[40] According to him, the explorers were more eager to gain knowledge (p. 90f.) than to spread the Gospel. Jacques Cartier himself possessed a taste for science. When wintering over in Quebec, he occupied his "leisure time by increasing his knowledge" (p. 104). Trudel saw him leave Hochelaga with regret, for he might have remained there "at least a few weeks" in order "to acquire valuable information" (p. 100). It comes as no surprise to the reader to find that Champlain was the hero *par excellence* whose advent was heralded at the end of the book. From the time of his first sojourn in America (1603), Champlain had taken an interest in the geography of the continent, studying the native population and the country's natural resources. A man of science, unconcerned with worldly goods and consequently superior to the merchants, Champlain had brought about "immense progress" (p. 264) in mapping the Laurentian region, according to Trudel. In short the historian, who claimed to be "fair" in recognizing "true worth" (p. 258), represented Champlain and Verrazano as cultivated men of the Renaissance—the new superstars in the national pantheon. Moreover, in the course of changes in outlook undergone by postwar Quebec historians, the father of New France and founder of the city of Quebec had lost his missionary vocation. No longer did he venture to assert that the salvation of a soul was worth more than the conquest of an empire.

And how did Cartier, the central figure in the story, fare at the hands of a historian who belonged to a generation of iconoclasts? As late as the mid-1930s, clerico-conservative historiography had made Cartier a great Christian hero, an explorer with the soul of an apostle, who noted that the Amerindians would be easy to convert and who set up crosses for their "edification," not just to take possession of the territory.

Cartier, that "man of faith" who made his men pray to heaven to cure their scurvy and who recited the Gospel according to St. John to the Amerindians, was not merely an explorer chosen by providence to prepare the way for colonization and evangelization. He possessed a plethora of human qualities, endowed by historiographic tradition. This "intrepid idealist" was not lacking in ingenuity either, and knew how to unmask the duplicity, envy, and cupidity of the Amerindians. Such was the superman presented by Canon Lionel Groulx in 1934.[41] During these Depression years, which, incidentally, were a vindication of ruralist ideology, Groulx attributed to Cartier the wish to establish an agrarian colony. "The admirable thing about these sailor's accounts," he wrote, "is the part devoted to the land, to the beauties and fruitfulness of the soil, to what one could call his foreordained rural calling."[42]

Groulx's edifying reconstruction of history vanished with the Quebec modernism of the Quiet Revolution. "Jacques Cartier, seeker after gold? Why not?" Trudel asked (p. 69). In order to make this fundamental "revelation," he resorted to a strategic alliance with a historian of the old school. Had not Canon Groulx put forward a similar thesis thirty years earlier? What more effective way to convince the astounded reader of the soundness of Trudel's own interpretation. Taken in context, however, Groulx's statement was not quite so categorical.[43] In his estimation it was the sovereigns who desired gold—a hypothesis that did not rob Cartier of credit for his missionary intentions.[44] Trudel, on the contrary, felt that Cartier was no better than his king when it came to missionary matters:

In certain circles, where precious metals and the riches of Asia are considered objects too base for the attention of great men, Cartier has been seen preferably as a sort of missionary, a man preoccupied mainly with spreading the Gospel.... Neither the royal decree of 1534, or any known official document, nor the account of the first voyage, authorizes us to give the pilot Cartier a halo: he was seeking what he had been asked to find—gold and the route to Asia! [P. 70].

Although clever, wily, even a liar on occasion (p. 144), was Cartier really enough of an opportunist to use religion to dupe the natives? To read Trudel, this was a plausible hypothesis.[45] As for the crosses set up by the navigator, they were signs of possession or navigational landmarks, nothing more (pp. 81f, 90). Trudel's passionate insistence on making Cartier some sort of agent for the Quiet Revolution by bringing his supposed missionary intentions into disrepute is symptomatic of a period that saw the break-up of clericalism, assisted by the sort of frontal attack revealed in these exclamatory lines:

The pretext advanced by Cartier [against baptism] was that one cannot baptize without holy oil, and natives who had seen solemn baptism celebrated in Brittany believed him! But why this false pretext? One may certainly baptize without holy oil! Where is the missionary zeal in this? The native language was known, or in any case interpreters were available; there was time to teach the rudiments of religion, and the Iroquois were themselves asking for baptism. Cartier refused! Furthermore, what missionary zeal is demonstrated by the fact that Domagaya and Taignoagny spent eight months in France and returned to America without being baptized! It is true that in the prologue to the 1535 account, when speaking of the material advantages of the discovery, he adds: "Which things give those who have seen them some hope of the future increase of our aforesaid holy faith." This hope gets short shrift amid all the material preoccupations mentioned, and does not offset the fact that Cartier refused Christianity to the natives who asked for it.[46]

André Vachon was quite justified in writing that Trudel's own missionary zeal had an ironic touch. "Trudel would have blamed Cartier greatly for being so precipitate, had he baptized these Indians after a hasty instruction through interpreters. He would have deplored Cartier's 'weakness' for missionary work as he did in his second volume[47] in the case of Abbé Fléché, whom he accuses . . . of having been 'prodigal with his sacraments.' "[48]

In addition to documenting the lack of missionary activity to the point of being redundant, Trudel included other revelations likely to diminish the traditional Cartier cult. The fallen hero was possibly a privateer (p. 124). He liked to drink (p. 165). Although subordinate to the Protestant Roberval on his third voyage, he was known to have deserted the St. Lawrence Valley without his commander's consent, believing himself to be in possession of a cargo of gold that he was anxious to transport to France. Trudel's version portrayed Roberval, who turned up with settlers taken from the jails of France, as superior to Cartier, at least at the time of the expedition. Trudel felt that Cartier made himself ridiculous by fleeing, and revealed a capacity for self-willed insubordination that compromised the work of settlement, since he was familiar with the terrain.[49] According to Groulx's 1934 version, Roberval was nothing but a debt-ridden megalomaniac, an adventurer with the instincts of a pirate, whom Cartier did well to abandon.[50]

Trudel wanted settlers for New France, whatever their antecedents or religious affiliation, not new converts to swell the celestial kingdom. This was very much in line with liberal views between 1950 and 1960. It accounted for his not being scandalized, as was Dionne, by Roberval and La Roche having recruited prisoners to form the nucleus of a settlement.[51] After listing the misdemeanors of which Roberval's pioneers were guilty, Trudel wrote that this "gives us some idea of the variety of offences committed by the conscripts, ranging from petty theft to homicide; but one must bear well in mind," he immediately added, "that under the Old Regime one could be classed as a criminal for offences that today are excused with greater tolerance!" (P. 141.) This tolerant attitude toward a certain level of common criminality is typical of recent liberal historical writing, as exemplified by the works of such writers as Raymond Boyer and André Lachance.

The principle of religious tolerance, or even tolerance of unbelief, is an important aspect of liberal thought. It is the basic premise behind the Mouvement laïque de langue française that came into being around 1960. It is more than coincidence that Trudel was a member of this French-language lay movement.

It must be remembered that the sixteenth century was one of schism for Western Christianity. Not surprisingly, the pluralist historian of the 1960s felt no animosity toward Protestants, unlike proponents of the clerico-conservative philosophy of history. Trudel was sympathetic to Protestants encountered in his travel accounts. When royal masters excluded Protestants from the colony, Trudel felt that reasons of state alone lay behind their decision (p. 224), and he criticized Champlain, who did not share his tolerance for the disciples of Calvin. Champlain, he wrote, "lacks . . . objectivity" with regard to the Protestant Chauvin (p. 239). Trudel also devoted a chapter to Protestant colonization in Brazil and Florida. In his estimation, if France had carried out its policy of settlement using Protestant elements it would have outstripped British colonization and "would have totally altered the history of Protestantism in America; French Protestantism would have had a dominant and long-lasting influence here" (p .212). Trudel was again emphasizing the need for settlers, even if they were non-Catholics. When Garneau advanced a similar hypothesis in the 1840s, he was obliged to retract such an unorthodox view.

Trudel's historical thinking clearly fell within the category of nationalist historiography. It was "our history" (p. 252) that he was recounting. In passing, he censured the nation's enemy, that is, France, for entrusting the work of colonization to private enterprise without any guarantee that a population of settlers would be provided. In his approach to the period, Trudel was therefore prepared to forego liberal principles of free-trade economics in the higher interests of the emerging nation. Such a reading of the Quebec sixteenth century was made in the light of post-Keynesian changes in liberal economies and, in particular, of the state intervention implemented by agents of the Quiet Revolution and advocated by its intellectual supporters. Trudel was anti-capitalist, but not for the same reasons as the clerico-conservative nationalists. He offered what was basically an implicit justification of the merchant companies' profit-seeking (pp. 84, 146), whereas the clerico-conservatives denounced their materialism. Nevertheless, Trudel regretted that the companies had "entirely mercantile preoccupations" (p. 244). They wanted to make New France a trading-post and nothing more: "either free trade for all and no colonization, or exclusive monopoly and colonization. In 1588 this dilemma arose for the first time, and free trade carried the day. This victory would be followed by many others, to the detriment of New France" (p. 266).

Trudel's nationalism was distinct from that of the neo-nationalists, however. For him, France was the national enemy, not English Canada. In fact, writers of the Quebec School brought no indictment against English Canadians. Trudel's interpretation of the sixteenth century partook of the pan-Canadian sense of goodwill characteristic of the Laval historians. His manner of dealing with the issue of who discovered Canada is an example. In the French-Canadian nationalist tradition, Cartier was credited with the discovery of Canada.[52] Nevertheless, with the rise of English-Canadian nationalist feeling at the beginning of the nineteenth century, the British in Lower Canada queried Cartier's title. One finds mention of "the English claim to the discovery of Canada" being refuted in the early 1800s by a member of the Quebec petite bourgeoisie.[53] The Cartier hypothesis was acceptable to the clergy and generally to the clerico-conservative camp that dominated historical writing from mid-nineteenth century on, and it was propounded in numerous published works in French Canada. Dionne subscribed to it without question in *La Nouvelle France de Cartier à Champlain* (330f.). Then, toward the end of the nineteenth century, a wave of imperialism swept English Canada. John Cabot became the symbol of the English Canadians' struggle for supremacy. For those who championed the Cabot-discoverer-of-Canada view, the fourth centenary of his expedition coincided very neatly with the sixtieth anniversary of Victoria's reign. Controversy raged, with Cabot and Cartier being somewhat battered in the process.[54] Trudel revived the debate in the early 1960s. "Was Cartier the discoverer of Canada?" asked a section heading in his book (p. 116). His reply conformed in all respects to the tolerant spirit of the Quebec School, submitting that, since Confederation and the extension of Canadian territory, the St. Malo navigator no longer had a claim to the title. In fact, he noted, the debate had been over since 1949, the year of Newfoundland's entry into Confederation, making Cabot the first modern explorer to have completed an official mission to the Atlantic seaboard of Canada as it exists today (p. 116ff.). Perhaps, as André Vachon remarked in a review of *Les Vaines Tentatives*, it might have occurred to Trudel to give Cartier the title of discoverer of Quebec.[55]

In the foregoing, I have sketched the social and ideological backgrounds that have conditioned our awareness of the Canadian sixteenth century. Instead of a concept of society buttressed by the pillars of church and the soil, Trudel proposed a colonial scheme founded on tolerance and the growth of all sectors of society. Like his predecessors, he developed his hypothesis within the framework of existing national life, and like them, he overestimated the influence of political and religious factors. For example, he referred to France— that is, the state—losing or regaining interest in the colonial venture, when in fact it was the merchant companies that were in question. So deep-rooted is this politico-religious perspective that French Quebec has not yet produced a writer capable of envisaging the early history of the territory as an extension of free-trade economics. The description of capitalist development in the sixteenth century as a vain attempt is surely not justified. In contrast, by 1901 English Canada—fairly insensitive to the problems of survival, and more interested in capitalists' exploits than their religious affiliations—had already produced a version of the sixteenth century in Canada that emphasized the bourgeois virtues of the early entrepreneurs of the St. Lawrence region.[56]

III

The Historiography of
New France, 1960-1974

Jean Hamelin to Louise Dechêne

In one of his essays, Professor J.R. Hexter[1] has questioned
the validity of applying the sociology of knowledge to the study
of historians and their craft. His basic premise is that historians can be judged only by their peers, that the society of
historians has an exclusive claim to pass judgment on the
strengths and weaknesses of its members. In so arguing, Hexter
suggests that the attempt to find relationships between historiography and society as a whole has no particular value or
relevance—or at least this appears to be implied by his criticism of the ideas of E.H. Carr. Since I, on the other hand,
take a great interest in the impact of society on knowledge
and vice versa,[2] my first reaction to Hexter's views was a negative one. Having overcome this initial response, however, I
recognized a possible basis for agreement.

History has now acquired the status of a "scientific" activity,
the validity of which is comparable to that of any other field
of knowledge. It is thus the responsibility of professional historians to determine whether their work represents an accurate
analysis and factual account of past societies. In general, such
judgments are passed in the book review sections of scholarly
journals, or in the evaluations of a jury during a thesis defence.
Does the candidate deserve to be a member of the historians'
guild? Did he successfully apply the methods and tools of his
science? The fact remains, however, that the historian's decision to study one subject as opposed to another reflects, to

some degree, a connection between his field of investigation and some aspect of current public thought or opinion.[3] Of course, some inquiries into the past bear little, if any, direct relation to the current ideologies of the historian's own society. The influence of climate on crops is a good example of such a study, but social historians usually put very little emphasis on the apparently neutral aspects of life.

The work of historians, then, is determined, at least to some degree, by their personality and social environment. Nor does this influence necessarily call into question the excellence of their work as a genuine contribution to knowledge. Would one, for example, condemn a sociologist because in studying the characteristics of underdevelopment he implicitly or explicitly compared the society under observation to the standards of the industrialized world? In so doing, however, the social scientist passes judgment on the values of Western civilization. To cite a further instance from the field of natural science, it has been revealed by psychoanalysis that Jean Rostand's interest in the study of monster frogs was in some way linked with the monsters created by his dramatist father, a possibility which Rostand himself admitted. Would biologists therefore conclude that Rostand is a poor scientist? In effect, then, the sociology of knowledge and the evaluation of research results are distinct but not necessarily opposite dimensions of science.

It is with these considerations in mind that I shall proceed with the first part of this review of recent historical literature on New France. It is not my intention to cover everything that has been published. Good bibliographies are available in the *Canadian Historical Review* and, since 1967, in the *Revue d'histoire de l'Amérique française*. I have chosen, instead, to draw the reader's attention to a number of the major debates or conflicting interpretations in the field. To begin with, I will attempt to demonstrate the close connection between debates among historians and the evolution of French Canada in recent years. Secondly, I will examine a new variety of historiography, characterized by the attempt to write a more "scientific" history.

Contemporary Quebec and its Historians

Since the beginning of the twentieth century, the province of Quebec has experienced cultural changes rooted in demography and economics. The migration of rural French Canadians to the industrial cities led ultimately to a decline in the birth rate, thus threatening their survival as a distinct "national" group. New values gradually replaced old ones. The process of secularization which followed urbanization undermined the once powerful role of the church. In the 1950s, a new group of leaders emerged in Quebec society. The newcomers, many of whom had been educated abroad in the social sciences, began to accept the idea that the future of Quebec was irrevocably bound to the new industrial age, while the traditional elite, composed of or trained by the clergy, never really acknowledged the social impact of industrialization. Because Quebec has been and continues to be economically dominated by outsiders of English cultural background, the new "lower middle class" attempted to explain why French Canadians had not assumed control over the development of the "national" territory. Why, in effect, was there not a significant group of powerful French-Canadian entrepreneurs among Quebec businessmen?[4] The two explanations that have been offered place the blame either on the clergy or on the minority position of French Canada.[5]

Professional historians in Quebec were deeply involved in the debate. Whereas the traditional elite group had seen the conquest of Canada by the British as part of a providential design to save the French Catholics from the evils of the French Revolution, some of the new secular minds began to argue that 1760 had, in the long run, deprived the French of their entrepreneurs in North America. As Richard Colebrook Harris wrote: "The conquest has always loomed over the literature on the French regime, and the most recent historiographic manifestation of the conquest psychosis is the debate over the role, if any, of a Canadian bourgeoisie. An earlier Quebec looked back to a golden agricultural age. An urbanized Quebec which has pulled up its rural roots...is inclined to see, if it looks back at all, an age when French Canadians controlled the commerce of the lower St. Lawrence."[6] And, in fact, during

the last two decades an increasing number of French Canadian intellectuals have come to view the Conquest as an irre-
parable disaster. During the same period, another school of
thought argued that the British conquerors were by no means
responsible for the fact that French Canadians had played
such a minor role in their own economic development, a fact
which they argued must be attributed to France, or to the
French Canadians themselves. New France had never had a
group of solid entrepreneurs who might have been capable
of maintaining control of the commerce of the colony after
the Conquest.[7]

The controversy over the bourgeoisie in New France arose
in the fifties, and continued to enliven historical debate
throughout the sixties. The conclusion of Jean Hamelin's
Economie et société en Nouvelle-France of 1960 can be considered
the springboard for those who did not believe in the existence
of a powerful bourgeoisie during the French regime. In 1965,
"La Bourgeoisie canadienne-française et ses fondements
historiques" was the theme of a symposium held at Laval
University in Quebec.[8] Like Guy Frégault and Michel Brunet,
Cameron Nish attempted to disprove Hamelin's thesis. His
Les Bourgeois-Gentilhommes de la Nouvelle-France (Montreal:
Fides, 1968) actually involved much more than the thesis of
the existence of a bourgeoisie: Nish pointed out that the notion
of the landed aristocracy as a rural community collecting rents
was false. The seigneurs in fact lived in towns and many of
them had acquired their fortunes in commercial ventures.
Nish's seigneurs were thus entrepreneurs rather than nobles
disdainful of business. Hence his title, *Les Bourgeois-Gentilhommes*. Nish's argument was supported by the many marriages
arranged between members of influential families from both
groups in order to acquire still more wealth or prestige and/
or the protection of the state in the fur trade. But above all,
Nish wanted to prove that Jean Hamelin and Fernand Ouellet[9]
had been wrong, and that there had, in fact, been a viable
entrepreneurship in the French colony.[10]

Since 1968, Nish's thesis has been challenged many times.
His critics contend that Nish has supported his argument for
the existence of great entrepreneurs by reference to a few

cases of individuals involved in big business. But had there been a social group capable of overthrowing the non-bourgeois values which were dominant in colonial politics? Was capitalism strong enough to overcome the social values of the Old Regime? Did the businessmen of the colony really reject the way of life of the Old Regime aristocracy? Here the support for Nish's thesis was weak. Since he was only interested in establishing the existence of individuals who made profits, he did not examine the values or the world view of his entrepreneurs. It must also be remembered that some of his great merchants ultimately lost their fortunes, hardly an indication of a healthy bourgeoisie. Y.F. Zoltvany's "Some Aspects of the Business Career of Charles Aubert de la Chesnaye (1632-1702)" contained a major attack on Nish's thesis. Zoltvany suggested that Hamelin was probably right in stating that there had been no powerful business community in New France:

The story could have been different had la Chesnaye succeeded in building a large fortune in Canada. For this might have encouraged other important businessmen to invest in the colony and a class of powerful Canadian *entrepreneurs* might then have emerged. La Chesnaye, however, had failed. His debt in 1702 amounted to 408,000 *livres* while his assets consisted of little more than his Quebec house, a few seigneuries, 43,000 *livres* of *rentes* and accounts receivable of which 200,000 *livres* had to be written off as bad debt. Such a discouraging precedent might explain the subsequent reluctance of private enterprise to risk capital in Canada, which, in turn, forced the state to expand its economic role. If this should be the case, la Chesnaye's failure would not merely be that of an individual but, more basically, that of a type of entrepreneurship.[11]

The controversy over the bourgeoisie did not end with Nish and Zoltvany in 1968. In the same year, Denis Vaugeois introduced new evidence on the Conquest period in *Les Juifs et la Nouvelle-France* (Trois-Rivières: Boréal Express, 1968), part of which was devoted to a narrative account of the role of the Jews in the war economy of the 1760s. In 1970, at the annual meeting of the Institut d'histoire de l'Amérique française, many historians were again engaged in the debate.[12] More recently, José Igartua has argued that "patronage relationships between British military officals and British traders...deprived the

Canadians of an equal chance in the competition for furs"
after 1760 in Montreal.[13] It may well be, as Louise Dechêne
has pointed out, that the question is nothing but a "superficial
argument about poorly-defined concepts."[14] In so far as the
contribution to knowledge is concerned, Professor Dechêne
is probably right. However, the prominence of the issue in
historical discussion reflects the importance of current ideologies in contemporary Quebec: why *is* it that the French province is underdeveloped, or developed by outsiders? The
nationalist argument assumes that the economic assets of New
France were sound and that the British conquest then deprived
the French Canadians of their businessmen.[15] The contemporary nationalist school of historians has thus argued against
the liberal tradition which, since Parkman, has contended that
New France was an authoritarian, hierarchical society. They
have attempted to establish the existence of what Rosario Bilodeau has referred to as the "economic and political freedom
of the Canadians under the French regime."[16] On the opposite side of the debate, liberal historians such as Fernand Ouellet argued (and in so doing perpetuated a long liberal tradition
in English-Canadian historiography) that the existence of
monopolies, state control over the economy, and the involvement of military and civil administrators in fur trading were
factors which stunted the growth of a national bourgeoisie.
Moreover, he contended that those engaged in business were
attracted by the noble way of life, and tended to squander
their profits on personal luxuries rather than invest their gains
in profitable enterprises.[17]

The election of Jean Lesage's Liberal government in 1960
opened a new era in Quebec history, popularly known as the
"Quiet Revolution," in which liberalism flourished throughout Quebec society. The intellectuals of the fifties, who had
been labelled anti-clericals, atheists, or communists,[18] could
now rely on the provincial government, within the limits of
its jurisdiction, to protect individual freedom against the power
of the Catholic church, which had hitherto controlled social
life in Quebec. In fact, the emergence of the welfare state
under the Lesage government signified a radically altered
status for the church in Quebec.[19] In the field of education,

a department of education was established, encroaching directly upon the empire of the church. Similarly, in the realm of health, social welfare, and public services in general, the state took effective control away from the Catholic clergy. The secularization of Quebec, a process that had begun long before the early 1960s, called for political initiatives to promote civil liberties. Laws providing for civil marriage and divorce were enacted. The rights of non-Catholic minorities to have their own schools were recognized, and the state began to acknowledge the pluralistic character of Quebec society. As one might expect, the church did not give up without a fight. But ultimately the supremacy of the state triumphed over the greatly diminished power of the clergy.

The social conflicts resulting from these events put an end to consensus historiography.[20] The battle profoundly influenced the study of the church's role in the past. Whereas the traditional historians had taken pleasure in depicting the French-Canadian habitant as obedient to the morality taught by the priests, the new generation of scholars shifted their focus to less docile peasants. The new trend is best exemplified by Robert-Lionel Séguin.

In the fifties, Séguin began to write essays questioning the high degree of "moral hygiene," as Canon Lionel Groulx put it, of the *habitant canadien* in New France. Three of Séguin's works that should be mentioned in this connection are *La Sorcellerie au Canada français du XVIIe au XIXe siècle* (Montreal: Ducharme, 1961), *Les Divertissements en Nouvelle-France au dix-septième siècle* (Ottawa: Musée national du Canada, 1968), and *La Vie libertine en Nouvelle-France au dix-septième siècle* (Montreal; Leméac, 1972). In the first book, Séguin demonstrated that there was superstition and sorcery in New France, whereas previous writers had stated that the colony's Catholicism had been uncontaminated by such unorthodox beliefs and practices. In *Les Divertissements*, the French-Canadian of the seventeenth and eighteenth centuries dared to break the rules of the church by drinking and dancing, despite the warnings of the curé and the bishop. In *La Vie libertine*, the habitant violated the marriage laws of the Catholic church, apparently without remorse.

Originally, *La Vie libertine* was a doctoral dissertation presented at the University of Paris. Although Séguin's thesis obtained for him the distinction *summa cum laude*, one may question the degree to which it really contributed to a better understanding of the society of New France. In general, the book did not add up to much more than a collection of facts. Séguin made no effort to measure the degree of sexual license among the habitants. Moreover, the periodic interjection of value judgments weakened his case. At one moment, the author seemed rather amused that a peasant should make love to his neighbor's wife, while at another he denounced homosexuality or bestiality. It is obvious that Séguin did not pay much attention to the critical tradition of historiography. Nor was the statistical treatment of the facts in the last part of the book of any redeeming value, as in fact it constituted a very poor example of quantitative history.

What, then, is the significance of the book? Its contribution to genuine knowledge is quite slim. However, Séguin's desire to prove that French-Canadian mores in the seventeenth century were different from those propounded by the church and praised by traditional historians puts him squarely in the new secular camp. Such histories are therefore useful for the study of "liberalism" in contemporary Quebec, but because they do not attempt to distinguish "normal" from "marginal" behavior, they do not lead to any deeper understanding of the Old Regime.

Other books have been written expressing similar views. Micheline Dumont-Johnson's *Apôtres ou agitateurs: La France missionnaire en Acadie* (Trois-Rivières: Boréal Express, 1970), belongs in the same category. The apostles so dear to traditional historiography were suddenly accused of political agitation and (to contemporary secular minds) betrayal of their specific role of preserving faith and morality. Like Séguin's work, *Apôtres ou agitateurs* is useful primarily as a reflection of secularization in contemporary Quebec.

Despite the increasingly secular mood of recent years, the area of religious history has continued to attract many historians. For the English-speaking reader, H.H. Walsh's *The Church in the French Era, from Colonization to British Conquest*

(Toronto: Ryerson Press, 1966) is a useful recent survey. Dr. Lucien Campeau has undertaken the publication of documents and narratives on the Jesuit missions in New France,[21] although his article about Bishop Laval does not provide much new insight.[22] Pierre Hurtubise is the only historian in a century-old tradition who has attempted to understand the controversial bishop within the context of his times.[23] Of the few doctoral theses on the religious history of New France written during recent years, one by Noel Baillargeon has been published in Canada,[24] while another by Guy Plante was published in Europe.[25] Parts of the two others have been published by Jean Blain and Cornelius Jaenen.[26]

Amerindian studies have traditionally been popular in North America, and thanks to anthropologists such as Bruce Trigger[27] and historians such as André Vachon[28] and Cornelius Jaenen,[29] the tradition has recently been revived. Jaenen has recently published a book consolidating the results of his long-term research in the field.[30]

The liberal mood in historiography is also exemplified by recent studies of the judicial practices of New France, which assume that the forms of punishment in the colony were very cruel.[31] One wonders, however, to what extent such anachronistic assumptions are really valid and whether the historian is in fact justified in making this kind of judgment.

Toward a More Scientific History

In recent years, a new historical school has emerged in Quebec in opposition to positivist traditions and present-minded historiography. As one might expect, the new approach did not originate in Quebec, but was imported, chiefly from France. During the last fifteen years, French historians such as Robert Mandrou, Georges Duby, Pierre Goubert, Fernand Braudel, Ernest Labrousse, Pierre Vilar, Albert Soboul, and others have been visiting professors in many French-Canadian universities. Moreover, some Canadian historians acquired their degrees in Paris, so that the influence of the *Annales* School has played an important part in recent revisionism.

It is unnecessary to describe here the essence of the French approach, which has been ably summarized for the North

American audience by Professor Isser Wolock, who refers to it as "the French school of history."[32] In a 1972 issue of the *Journal of Modern History*, John Hexter has given a detailed presentation of "Fernand Braudel and the *Monde Braudellien*..." for the American reader. In fact, the following summary does not apply only to the French historians. What is now called the New History in the United States as well as in the United Kingdom has spread throughout the West. What is specific about Quebec is that historians of New France have learned it from the pioneers of the New History: the French.

Let me simply recall here that quantification (the study of social groups through systematic inventories of series of documents such as notarial or judicial records) is used to reconstruct the daily life of both elite groups and the common man. Great events dominated by prominent individuals are no longer the historian's major preoccupation. Investigation of the *longue durée* replaces the old chronicles. Although much attention is devoted to the slow process of structural change, the new historiography is also concerned with more short-term matters like fluctuations in prices, profits, and wages, the indicators of economic conditions (depression, inflation, etc.) or, as the new historians say, with cycles or the *conjoncture*. The ultimate ambition of the new approach is to examine the totality of a society, therefore preventing the historian from the more or less arbitrary choice of one aspect of it. Hence the classical organization of the French thesis: geography, demography, economy, society, mentality. Although the French historians themselves are modest about their claims to achieve what they call *histoire totale*, they have nonetheless initiated an important movement toward a more scientific study of the past. Before attempting to establish whether the most recent essays on New France conform to these criteria,[33] I should point out that this type of historiography is quite different from what has been called interdisciplinary history.[34] Based as it is on theory derived from the study of contemporary societies, the latter variety of history is prone to all types of anachronisms, and is, to say the least, not always very historical. In fact, it is a rather North American way to practise the New History.

As Jean Blain has remarked, the new economic and social

history had not yet taken hold in Quebec in the 1950s.[35] At that time, the canons of critical historiography were either imported from the United States, or were the remnants of an older tradition which would soon cease to be of great interest to the majority of professional historians. Historical works written under the influence of this tradition took the form of descriptions and/or narrative accounts of New France in terms of the actions of great men and great events; the *Annales* School called it *histoire evénémentielle* or *histoire historisante*. Even in the early sixties, this style of historical writing was still very much in evidence in Canada, and indeed, the majority of historical works over the last fifteen years have followed in this tradition. It is by no means my intention to detract from the value and merits of the older generation of historians. In fact, the new variety of history has been made possible by the narrative and institutional history of the colony, and the works of such historians as Gustave Lanctôt, W.J. Eccles, and Marcel Trudel thus remain essential contributions to the knowledge of the past.[36] Their critical general histories are the starting point for more specialized studies. Moreover, Trudel and Eccles have shown in their recent writings that they are fully acquainted with the new history.[37]

Others who have attempted this shift of historical method, however, have had less success. In *La Civilisation traditionelle de l' "habitant" aux 17e et 18e siècles* (Montreal: Fides, 1967), Robert-Lionel Séguin tried to make use of some of the new kinds of sources (notarial deeds), but was unable to classify his evidence according to social strata. M.E. Arthur wrote about the book:

In the first place, the heavy reliance upon notarial documents—agreements, inventories, and so forth—is dictated by the decision to concentrate upon social history. In dealing with these documents, Dr. Séguin sometimes blurs the lines between country and town dwellers on the one hand and between social classes on the other. One is often led to question whether the "habitant" of the title was exclusively the "type terrien bien particulier" [the actual farmer] or any inhabitant of the colony, irrespective of his residence or rank in society. The inclusion of catalogues of goods owned by various seigneurial families and by scarcely typical bourgeois...suggests a greater affluence among the *censitaires* and a greater fluidity in social classes than may have existed. Only rarely, as for example in the discussion of the wearing of mourning, is the point made explicit that a custom belonged principally to one class.... The feeling of uneasiness increases as lists of luxury goods belonging to seigneurial and bourgeois families are examined. Then appears the conclusion that the *habitants* spent a disproportionate part of their income on wearing apparel.[38]

Cameron Nish gave evidence of a very different problem in *Les Bourgeois-Gentilhommes*. Richard Colebrook Harris was correct in his comments on Nish's misuse of quantitative analysis:

His method is to amass data in support of a particular proposition, but not to give the data any quantitative measure. It is one thing to show that some merchants behave in a certain way, and quite another to show that the group with such behaviour was a certain percentage of all merchants.... In some cases, as when Professor Nish discusses the extent of intermarriage among the elite, his evidence is ample enough to be fairly convincing; in others, as when he compares the commercial vigour of Canada and the English colonies, the evidence is so thin and the many assumptions so tenuous that few readers will be convinced. Whatever the weight of the evidence, almost all of it appears to have been selected to prove a point.... The chapter on the seigneurial system is a good example of the basic problem. It is true, as Professor Nish points out, that in the 1730s, 1740s and 1750s a sustantial group, most of whom had interests in commerce, government, or the military, received seigneuries; but it is equally true that almost all of these seigneuries were entirely unsettled and, even at the end of the French regime, furnished no revenue for their seigneurs. Professor Nish demonstrates that some seigneurs held more than a single seigneurie; true enough, but many more held only a fraction of one. Some seigneurs undoubtedly lived in the towns, and Professor Nish has listed some forty who lived there in 1744. At this date there were over two hundred rural seigneuries. Is one, therefore, to conclude that 80 percent of the seigneurs did not live in towns, or that the list is seriously wanting? Some seigneurs did sell their seigneuries, but in relation to the number of seigneuries, sales were strikingly few and far between. In short, a few examples do not make a case.[39]

These remarks by Cole Harris (who himself made such successful use of statistical analysis in his masterly work, *The*

Seigneurial System in Early Canada: A Geographical Study),[40] could apply to many other recent essays. Not only do some historians misuse the tools, but many of them fall into what the American sociologist Sorokin has called "quantophreny." In fact, the French School of historians has had a great many poor imitators on this side of the Atlantic. The many volumes and booklets published by Roland Lamontagne since 1962 are a most striking example of yet another such failure. Nish and Séguin were not disciples of the French School, but Lamontagne has laid claim to this prestigious title, his supposed master being none other than Fernand Braudel.[41] The work of this self-proclaimed disciple of Braudel has created confusion and doubt about the real possibilities of the new history, to the extent that some historians trained in the traditional pattern have, not surprisingly, questioned its validity altogether.[42]

Economie et société en Nouvelle-france, published in 1960 by Jean Hamelin, was the first essay written by a historian[43] using the French methodology. The conclusion of the book relates to the ideological controversy on contemporary Quebec, as we have seen in chapter 1, but the study as a whole raised relevant questions about the past. The inaccuracy of some of Hamelin's conclusions in the essay was largely a result of the type of evidence on which the study was based.

Reviewers accustomed to the old ways of writing history failed to grasp the importance of Hamelin's revisionism. Having studied at the Ecole pratique des hautes études in Paris, the author was a foreigner among his Canadian peers. Of the latter, William J. Eccles praised the new approach as a means of producing "a clear picture of Canadian society, in any period,"[44] but on the whole, the most favorable and sound reviews were not published by historians.[45]

As a result of Hamelin's study, there was a perceptible shift of focus among professional historians. One of them had learned to work through hypotheses rather than being "blindly" guided by primary sources. Hamelin's survey dealt mainly with *structures*; however, one chapter was devoted to *conjoncture* (the other favorite concept of the new historians)[46] through an analysis of series of wheat prices. The purpose of the book was to explain the failure of economic development in New France. Statistical information combined with analysis of administrators' correspondence showed that a lack of currency, capital, and skilled manpower[47] had precluded a "take-off" in the colonial economy. The methods Hamelin used to estimate the quality of manpower were particularly novel. Of course some of Hamelin's generalizations were weak, but nevertheless, the scientific spirit had invaded the field of historical studies. Systematic explanation had replaced implicit or explicit value judgments. The generous use of evaluative terms would no longer suffice as the stuff of history.

During the last twenty years, the economy and society of New France have been subjects of increasing interest to many historians. André Vachon's *Histoire du notariat canadien, 1621-1960 (Quebec: PUL, 1962)* combined the traditional with the new approach, while a number of short essays by younger historians were more obviously products of the new history. André Lachance's article, "Le Bureau des pauvres de Montreal, 1698-1699: Contribution à l'étude de la société montréalaise de la fin du XVIIe siècle," *Histoire sociale-Social History* (Nov. 1969): 99-110, is a good example. In the field of social history, the most valuable example of the new historical mode was *L'Hôpital général de Québec, 1692-1764* (Montreal: Fides, 1971) by Micheline D'Allaire. However, neither Lachance nor D'Allaire went beyond the level of institutional history and made virtually no attempt to refer to the social structure of the colony. Their studies can be considered to offer only a partial view of what is, in the full sense, social history. There remains much to be done in the reconstruction of social strata before institutional history can be placed in its proper social context.[48]

A number of studies in the history of commerce and industry are worth mentioning in this connection. J.F. Bosher,[49] James Pritchard,[50] and Jacques Mathieu[51] have already offered glimpses of the results of their long-term research and of their prospective publications.

The social history of political life has been initiated by Jean-Claude Dubé's very thorough biography: *Claude-Thomas Dupuy, intendant de la Nouvelle-France, 1678-1738* (Montreal: Fides, 1969). Using the methodological principles formulated by French historian Roland Mousnier, Dubé is currently working on a history of the office of the intendant during the entire colonial period.[52] His biography of Claude-Thomas Dupuy is a good example of the way in which the new economic and social history can transform the biographical approach to history. Dupuy is examined in the context of the French *intendance* and, through his connections in society, is established as representative of a particular social "type" in the colony. By comparison to Dubé's biographical approach, the limitations of the heroes of Thérèse Prince-Falmagne,[53] Antoine Champagne,[54] and Maurice Filion[55] are particularly apparent, although Champagne's work is in any case only partly a classical biography and in equal part panegyric. Filion, on the other hand, shows signs of adapting to the new history. In fact, the new trend is now so well established that recent works following the traditional pattern are occasionally reviewed in terms of the canons of the new historical science.[56]

Louise Dechêne of McGill University is the only Canadian historian who has fully applied the best of French methodology. In 1971, she challenged traditional interpretations of the seigneurial regime in a short essay, "L'Evolution du régime seigneurial au Canada; Le Cas de Montréal aux XVIIe et XVIIIe siècles."[57] The notion that the seigneurs were agents and entrepreneurs of settlement was claimed to be proven false. So too was the "frontier thesis" as an explanation of the distinctive features of the institutions in New France; in fact, the Sulpicians, seigneurs of the Island of Montreal, managed their fief in the traditional French manner. Nor did the presumed friendship between seigneurs and censitaires correspond to the facts. As for the notion that the intendant was an arbitrator whose role was to protect the censitaires, Louise Dechêne showed that, in fact, the intendant was consistently on the side of the seigneurs. The generous concessions of land allotted during the founding of the colony were quietly replaced by contracts in which obligations and constraints became increasingly burdensome. During the eighteenth century, contracts tended to be two or three pages long, whereas intitially one page had sufficed. And the habitant reacted against these increasing restrictions, belying the traditional image of the peasant as an independent, prosperous, and happy farmer. As Dechêne remarked, "The habi-

tants complained about levies being too onerous; they accused
the seminary of enriching itself at their expense, and considered the burning of their mills providential."[58]

In 1973, Dechêne's essay, "La croissance de Montréal au
XVIIIe siècle"[59] offered a few hints about her forthcoming
book. Some elements of the article should be noted here. Prior
to the publication of this essay, historians had generally believed
that the colony was characterized by rapid urban growth, basing
this assumption on the intendants' denunciation of poverty
and idleness in urban areas. However, through analysis of
census records, Dechêne demonstrated that "ruralization"
rather than urbanization characterized the evolution of the
colony. The tiny city of Montreal, for example, was a source
of recruits for land settlement.

This short essay, which dealt with demography, occupations, economy, and way of life, was but a small-scale sample
of Louise Dechêne's subsequent book, *Habitants et marchands
de Montréal au XVIIe siècle* (Paris and Montreal: Plon, 1974),
based on her doctoral dissertation defended at the University
of Paris. In the latter work, Dechêne adopted the traditional
organization of French theses devoted to *l'histoire totale*: geography, demography, economy, society, world view, and *mentalité* (i.e., the study of beliefs and cultural values as revealed by
the organization of families, etc.). Following the French methodology and focusing principally on the rich but not easily
elicited evidence offered by notarial documents, she chose to
study a small area, the island of Montreal, over an extended
period of time. She compiled and computed her evidence with
an unusual degree of precision and was then able to compare
the behavior of the different social groups in that part of the
colony with that of their counterparts in France. For the most
part, she was successful in reconstructing the process by which
the social structures of France were transplanted and/or
adapted in Montreal, and, in some cases, throughout the whole
St. Lawrence Valley. She pointed out in her introduction that:
"Step by step, we must follow the evolution of a society that
has left traces other than the impressions of a handful of
administrators, memoir-writers who paid little attention to
everyday life, or visitors in search of the picturesque—impres-

sions which are repeated over and over again, arranged to suit the purposes of whomever is writing" (p. 7).

This program was indeed an ambitious one, to say nothing of its implied condemnation of the work of most of her predecessors! However, she was correct to the extent that previous writers were not, in fact, much concerned with observing the structural *process*. When they did attempt to describe patterns of daily life, they tended to take snapshots based chiefly on impressionistic views, or on the comments of politicians, clerics, or "tourists."[60] As the psychology of testimony and the sociology of knowledge tell us, diaries rarely give accurate views about behavior, influenced as they are by the values, prejudices, and limitations of their authors (p. 299). As for the correspondence of governors, intendants, and the like, it, too, tends to reflect the preoccupations, fears, and aspirations of those of their own status, rather than the ordinary behavior of different social groups (see, for example, her comments on Jean Talon, the "Great Intendant," p. 302, n. 8). In short, therefore, while all these testimonies are useful in the study of the opinions and thought processes of a minority in the top social strata, they are frequently of no value for understanding the life of the common man. Moreover, because historians have, until recently, observed the French colony through the eyes of its rulers, they tend either to endorse or condemn the prejudices of those rulers. Liberal historians thus identify with such writers as the famous Baron de Lahontan, while the conservatives are inclined to prefer the impressions of missionaries and the like. Prior to the publication of *Habitants et marchands*, these types of primary sources were the substance from which historical portraits of the habitant, the trader, the seigneur, and so forth had been drawn. Little wonder that such histories have repeated the same old clichés about New France from generation to generation throughout the last century of historiography.

Dechêne's book divided the history of the settlement of New France into three major elements: (1) the motives of emigrants for leaving France; (2) the geographic and social origins of the settlers; (3) the structure of the colonial population, and the pattern of its growth. Most of the settlers in New France had suffered hardships, chiefly economic ones, prior to emigrating from France. However, there was no clear indication that they were driven from France by an actual economic crisis, as Robert Mandrou suggested in 1959.[61] The small number of immigrants (10,000 for the whole colony up to 1760), was not surprising as, at the time, France was a highly "populationist" country.

Louise Dechêne devoted particular attention to those settlers referred to as *engagés* (pp. 50-77). No idleness was permitted these quasi-slaves, she emphasized. After studying their working and living conditions, she rejected "the idyllic image of old and new *engagés* working side by side, eating at the same table, with no barrier to the new arrival being integrated into a family" (p. 62). Through an examination of judicial records, she showed that severe punishment threatened those (they were too poor to pay fines) who failed to fulfil the duties prescribed by their contracts (pp. 69f.).

Little was said about female immigration. Dechêne suggested, however, that on the whole, women settlers were far from the "call girls" Lahontan depicted. On the other hand, she judiciously noted that there were two sorts of women immigrants: those destined for marriage to the common settlers, and those intended for the military officers. "There were two parallel immigrations, of which contemporaries were well aware" (p. 80).

Dechêne's study of the military establishment followed the approach suggested by W.J. Eccles.[62] She focused particular attention on the proletarian status of soldiers working for officers as *engagés*, under the benevolent eye of the colonial authorities (pp. 85-88). The chapter on immigration ended with an analysis of the distribution of population according to geographic origin and rate of illiteracy (p. 95f.). In a chapter on the structure of the population, Dechêne dealt with various aspects of historical demography. But here, as in the case of many other realms of social life in that pre-statistical era, quantitative data had proven difficult to collect. Some of her more interesting findings in this area should, however, be mentioned. Administrators (and therefore historians relying on the records of this group) repeatedly observed that the natural growth of the population was inhibited by the substantial number of *coureurs de bois*. By studying the seasonal birthrate in the colony, however, Louise Dechêne disproved this notion:

> The fact that children were conceived between April and August refutes the widely held view that the habitants abandoned their land to be *coureurs de bois*. The journey west took place mainly between May and August, and it is clear that the large majority of married men were co-habiting with their wives [p. 114.].

In fact, the figure given on page 113 indicates that the level of fecundity tended to be higher or at least as high during the very months when the men were supposedly in the wilderness.

According to some superficial observers cited by Dechêne, such as the intendant Desmeules and Marie de l'Incarnation (p. 115), high death rates did not appear to have been a problem characteristic of New France. Even demographers have underestimated the situation by failing to take into account the large number of deaths which were not recorded at the time.[63] Despite the problem of collecting adequate data, Dechêne argued, through an ingenious process of calculation, that one quarter of the newborn died before their first birthday.

The chapters devoted to commerce began with a study of the elements of the market economy as exemplified in the colony. Many of the assumptions made by Jean Hamelin in *Economie et société en Nouvelle-France* were shown here to be rather weak or clearly obsolete. For example, Dechêne showed that, contrary to Hamelin's point of view, the currency in New France was not overvalued in order to keep a sufficient supply of money in circulation,[64] but rather to increase the profits of merchants (pp. 131 f.). In another instance, the *Compagnie des Indes occidentales*, concerned with its monopoly position and the duties collected on fur exports, had requested Frontenac's permission to search every household in the colony for hidden beaver pelts. Hamelin (p. 32) had assumed that Frontenac's action in refusing permission for the search implied that peasants were, in fact, hoarding pelts. By examining a significant number of inventories taken after death, Dechêne suggested that this assumption was false. Furthermore, the "courtier governor," as Eccles called Frontenac,[65] wished to "prevent the Company agents...from seizing the skins which several merchants, including his own associates, were smuggling to Europe" (p. 135).

One further insight in Dechêne's analysis of commerce in New France related to the level of profits from the fur trade. In reality, as she showed through a careful analysis of net return, profits were not as high as most historians, Hamelin included (*Economie et société*, pp. 51 ff.), have calculated, but actually averaged between 10 and 15 percent on invested capital.

In a chapter entitled "Production Relationships" (pp. 171-230), Dechêne analysed the relationships among the groups of participants in the fur trading economy. Here, too, her emphasis was on social and economic structures. Beginning as a random process, the commercial activity of the colony gradually acquired a structure by the end of the seventeenth century. At that point, the roles were well defined along capitalist lines. Professionalism had become the rule: the *coureur de bois* was replaced by the professional *voyageur*, while merchants, allied with and protected by the *gentilhommes*, had taken control of the whole process of production. The fortunes of the entrepreneurs, as revealed by twenty-one inventories taken after death between 1679 and 1712, consisted of a small amount of currency, between one-half and two-thirds pelts in stock, and various accounts owing, divided into good and bad debts. The *voyageurs* and *engagés* (the white manpower involved in the fur trade) represented only a small minority of the working population of New France (pp. 220 f.) and were often the products of families which had been exclusively involved in the fur trade for generations. They worked hard for a modest earning (pp. 226-239): "It was a hard trade, which did not employ very young men and scarcely provided enough income for early retirement."

According to Dechêne's account, therefore, the traditional portrait of the *coureur de bois* as a social type belonged to fiction. "For the historians of New France, massive participation by the population in this activity is taken for granted, as well as certain characteristic behavior usually associated with it, such as leaving the land, poor farming habits, insubordination, and immorality" (p. 217), and to these traits we can add their supposed tendency to spend money without stint (Hamelin, 57). As Pierre Goubert wittily remarked in a review of *Habitants et marchands*, Dechêne's thesis suggested that the historians who wrote about them were perhaps more numerous than the *coureurs de bois* themselves.[66]

In the conclusion of her analysis of commercial activity, Louise Dechêne questioned the validity of the famous "staple" theory as a tool for explaining the development of New France.[67] In fact, the fur trade involved only a small proportion of the colony's labor force, the majority of which was isolated from the sphere of international trade and absorbed in the founding of a largely self-sufficient agricultural society.

Following a study of the seigneurial regime on the island of Montreal, Louise Dechêne carefully examined the habitant on his land. She argued that the accepted portrait of an improvident, careless, and independent peasantry, spending lavishly and improvising farming methods, was a product of romanticism and liberalism, rather than an accurate description of the farm economy.[68] Bringing land into cultivation was a long and arduous task. Once the habitant was ready to sow a part of his lot, he followed the traditional pattern of French agriculture (pp. 303 ff.) which he had brought with him from the Old World. The fact that he did not grow large quantities of wheat was not, however, the result of poor agricultural methods. There simply was not a market for a substantial surplus production. Moreover, the superficial observations of the Swedish traveler Pehr Kalm in 1749, and of historians who relied on him, have led to the conclusion that crop rotation was unknown to Canadian peasants. Dechêne attempted to show this assumption to be false by examining a significant number of farm leases (p. 303). Robert-Lionel Séguin, basing his conclusions on the declarations of politicians, created the impression that the number of horses per farm was rather high in the colony.[69] As usual, his somewhat random quantitative documentation failed to give a correct account of the situation, and he took for granted the supposed accuracy of the intendants' observations on the subject. In the specific case of Montreal, Louise Dechêne calculated that, in fact, the number of horses per farm was not particularly high. Indeed in the late 1730s, the number of horses per habitant was still below the quota imposed by Raudot in 1709! The supposed "conspicuous consumption" was thus not evidenced by the numbers of livestock, despite the fact that administrators were shocked: "Here are these peasants, mounted like only officers used to be" (p. 319).

Dechêne's study of agricultural productivity (pp. 324-330) was intended to demonstrate that, in the Montreal area, it was comparable to average farm productivity in France. In effect, she aimed to destroy "the stereotyped image...of the irresponsible settler, who had only a secondary interest in farming, and who passively accepted the land offered, ruined it through negligence, and abandoned it at the first opportunity to become a *coureur de bois*.[70] Some may indeed have fitted this description, but there were many who were busy taming the countryside, building a family asset, and recreating a more or less familiar way of life, if possible, in the hope that the old habits and work patterns would bring security" (pp. 269f.).

Going beyond the occupational distribution of the population, Dechêne reconstructed the class structure of society. The seigneurial system, which began merely as a form of organization imposed on the settlement, gave birth to a seigneurial class (the Sulpicians in Montreal) whose increasingly high rents provided an economic foundation for their status and power. Indeed, if there was any "conspicuous consumption" in New France, it was an indulgence of the nobility rather than the habitants as so many historians have thought. The evidence provided by inventories taken after death indicates that the nobility was, in fact, the only group in the colony which indulged in the purchase of luxuries. The records show that the merchants, by contrast, owned no expensive furniture, nor in fact any possessions beyond the requirements of comfort (pp. 390 f.). It thus appears that, contrary to the view of Cameron Nish, it was necessary to distinguish between bourgeois and *gentilhommes* in New France, in so far as the records of their way of life and their habits of saving and expenditure would indicate.

At the opposite extreme, the peasantry lived in small cabins of 18 by 20 feet, "space necessarily being sacrificed for warmth" (p. 400), and in general, had a very modest standard of living. The habitant's furniture and clothes were scarcely adequate, still less luxurious (pp. 400 f.). His supposed delusions of grandeur appear to be a figment of the imagination of some historians.[71]

Dechêne's brief examination of craftsmanship (pp. 392-394) referred to some sound research undertaken by Peter Nicholas Moogk.[72] Her conclusions on social mobility suggested that in the Montreal area, such mobility was high, although generally directed *down* the scale of social strata rather than upwards. In this context, she also argued that purchasing land was not a source of social prestige for merchants, as so many historians from both France and Canada have thought; it was, in fact, viewed merely as a business operation (pp. 410 f.). The last two chapters of *Habitants et marchands* dealt with the family and religion, and here, too, Dechêne offered new insights to whet the historian's appetite.

It was unfortunate that the book had no index, as it will undoubtedly serve as a fundamentally important study of New France for many years to come. For Canadian historians, the publication of Dechêne's work was a turning point comparable to what has been called the "Ouelletist revolution," which began with the publication of Fernand Ouellet's masterly *Histoire économique et sociale du Québec—Structures et conjoncture* (Montreal: Fides, 1966). In so far as methodology and new evidence are concerned, *Habitants et marchands* is among the most genuinely original historical works produced in Canada in recent decades. Its overall impact has been to cast serious doubt on the validity of such widely held theories as the "frontier thesis" and the "staples approach."

If I had to summarize the orientation of *Habitants et marchands*, I might suggest that it could be considered a slightly Marxian response to the dominant liberal interpretation in Canadian historical writing. Unlike many North American historians, however, Dechêne does not treat Marxism simply as an ideology, and indeed, her work bears no resemblance to that of Marxist historians who speak the language of politicians. Instead, through careful analysis of a rich body of evidence, she renews the exploration of the relations involved in the process of production, an exploration which distinguished Marx himself as a social scientist.

Dechêne's criticism of liberal historiography can be characterized by a few examples. There was little industrial development in New France, which was primarily an agricultural and commercial colony. While liberal historians held mercantilism and the nature of colonial government responsible for retarding "development," Louise Dechêne pointed out that, in fact, merchants in the colony had established their fortunes in international trade, and thus had little incentive to encourage the growth of domestic industry. Some historians[73] have tried to account for the lack of industrial development in New France by distinguishing between two categories of merchants, the French and the Canadians, and by arguing that competition from the former inhibited the capital accumulation necessary for industrial growth. This nationalist and liberal account does not appear to correspond to what actually occurred in New France, or at least, in Montreal, in the seventeenth century. As Dechêne pointed out, the merchants of the island of Montreal had no such liberal and national consciousness. Most were capitalists whose activities were based on a market that spanned the Atlantic.

Some historians have stressed the importance of state controls on the economy, exercised through the granting of monopolies and trade licences, as well as through the participation of public officials in the fur trade. However, following the recent interpretation of J.-F. Bosher,[74] Dechêne argued that "it is irrelevant to denounce the 'corruption' of this or that official; what is important is a closer examination of the administrative structure of the Old Regime, where private enterprise progressed alongside and merged with the public sector" (p. 174, n. 4). Whereas such state intervention as price controls on bakers, butchers, and the like has been denounced as inconsistent with the liberal principles of a market economy, Dechêne pointed out that consumer protection was an established responsibility of the state under the Old Regime (p. 394).

Similarly, the law of primogeniture did not exist in New France, where the principle of equal portions for all children ruled inheritance. Liberal historiography has condemned such practices, holding them responsible for poor agricultural productivity because of their tendency to promote the fragmentation of farms. Dechêne noted, and implicitly praised, the egalitarian character of such customs. However, she proceeded to show that while every descendant had the right to claim his share, in fact only one member of the family continued to exploit the farm, paying his due to his brothers and sisters (pp. 294-298, and the chapter on the family). The only disadvantage of this practice was that the peasant of each new generation was saddled with a heavy burden of debt for many years of his working life.

Among the many reviews of *Habitants et marchands*, those by Fernand Ouellet and Hubert Charbonneau were particularly articulate.[75] Their criticisms may be summarized, like the book itself, under the headings of population, economy, and society.

Both reviewers argued that the number of *coureurs des bois* in the colony was probably much higher than Louise Dechêne's estimate, and Charbonneau's statistical argument seemed particularly convincing.[76] As for Fernand Ouellet, he contended that notarial deeds were not a useful indicator of the number of *voyageurs* and *engagés*, and his own figures seem to confirm that Dechêne may have underestimated the proportion of the population involved in the fur trade. Ouellet pointed out two other weaknesses in Dechêne's demographic calculations: the fact that the size of the total population remains unknown renders statistics on births, marriages, and deaths virtually meaningless; and the fact that the population was, in any case, a constantly changing and unstable one falsifies her analysis, since the classical demographic methodology she employs is only applicable to stable populations.

In the area of economic life, Ouellet contradicted Dechêne's thesis about the wealth of the habitants. Both historians relied on inventories taken after death to prove or disprove that the *censitaires* possessed currency. Four habitants cited by Ouellet did in fact possess large amounts of currency at the time of their deaths (about 1760). As for agricultural techniques, Ouellet argued that the fact that crop rotation was explicitly stipulated as a condition of farm leases proved that such practices were not, in fact, common.

Ouellet cast doubt on Dechêne's description of social classes in New France. According to him, the bourgeoisie were greatly influenced by aristocratic values and imitated the nobility in the consumption of luxury goods as in many other ways. Nor did he accept Dechêne's description of habitant life:

This is an almost idyllic picture.... This traditional habitant, no worse than elsewhere, experienced an egalitarian way of life...and his practices for handing on property breathed generosity.... But the author does not bring out this aspect, which contradicts the idea that "time is a leveler in rural society"[p. 485]. Even if society was becoming more and more rural, the rural world in the eighteenth century was increasingly diversified as a result of the commercialization of agriculture. The presence of merchants in rural areas, the increasing number of villages and craftsmen, all these things figure in a long-term context that created inequalities, even within the peasant group.... Rural society tended to stratify, making such egalitarianism a mere figure of speech.

Ouellet also pointed out that, for the colony as a whole and in the *longue durée*, the notion of a rural society based on uniform, small land holdings was entirely false, partly because—and here he agreed with Dechêne—land was not divided through the inheritance process. In the long run, "landed property was not destined to remain in the same hands, was not equally divided between individuals and...was subject to movements that created inequality, and that would give priority to grouping property at one moment, while at another deciding to parcel it out."

On the whole, Ouellet's review was harsh, but many of his criticisms were sound, rooted as they often were in his own impressive command of primary sources. But the ideology implicit in his convictions about the backward agricultural methods of the habitants, their way of life, and their relation to commercial activity in New France, placed him squarely in the old liberal tradition of historiography.[77] Therefore, it was not surprising to discover that he himself described writers like Louise Dechêne as the spiritual heirs of the old nationalist-agriculturalist ideology. In 1975 he wrote:

> Can one go so far as to say that nationalism has been rooted out of the historian's work? One need not look far to find new and unconscious idealizations. When, for example, in reading some of the recent studies by either amateur or scientific historians, we find an almost uniform picture of the oldtime habitant emerging—independent, no worse than elsewhere, aware of the market, egalitarian, tolerant, free-thinking, and revolutionary—then we know that such writers are not advocating an old-fashioned return to the soil; rather, it reveals the existence among us of petit bourgeois who have adapted to urban living but find the noise and pollution distressing, and who feel a nostalgia for the rural life, expressed through their ideologically biased reconstructions of the past.[78]

Nevertheless, if the history of New France is to be fully reexamined, it is undoubtedly sources like notarial documents[79] that offer the present generation of historians the greatest opportunity to grasp the reality of the daily routine of life among the different social groups, in terms of the value system prevailing at the time. It currently appears that Montreal will be singled out for this kind of systematic inquiry.[80] Before Louise Dechêne, Marcel Trudel had already examined marriage contracts in the Montreal region as a basis for his essay, "The Beginnings of a Society: Montreal 1642-1663."[81] In the same manner that ordinary behavior may be revealed by notarial records, the judicial records of the colony should permit an accurate understanding of crime considered in sociological terms, that is, as the nonconformity to social norms. Such articles as those of Jacques Mathieu (see n. 21) and John A. Dickinson[82] suggest the possibilities of exploration in the area. Beyond the period under study here, two scholars have published one book each in the field: André Lachance, *La Justice criminelle du roi au Canada au XVIIIe siècle* (Quebec: PUL, 1978); John A. Dickinson, *Justice et justiciables, La Procédure civile à la prévôté de Québec, 1667-1759* (Quebec: PUL, 1982). Despite the sharp distinction that I have drawn in this chapter between "scientific" historians and more present-minded ones, the historical profession in Canada is not really divided into such opposite camps. Besides, it must be remembered that classical training in the critical tradition was a prerequisite for what I have identified as the new scientific spirit. If I have drawn the reader's attention to the achievements of the second variety of history, it is because I firmly believe in the future of history as one of the social sciences. I remain conscious, however, that classical scholarship, as applied to the study of prominent figures, will survive alongside enquiries into social groups involving the analysis of large quantities of numerical data.[83] History is not art, nor science, but a combination of both.

The whole debate over the existence of a bourgeoisie in New France is a good example of the hybrid nature of history. The question was originally raised by historians in response to a contemporary controversy concerning the causes of the economic inferiority of the French in Quebec. But if Nish's conclusions, for example, have proven partly false, the reason is not simply the distortions introduced into the process of historical interpretation by current political and intellectual debates. Faulty historical methodologies are equally to blame for dubious conclusions. In the end, books written by historians like Nish or Robert-Lionel Séguin may belong to scientific literature, but they are vulnerable to the distorting influence of contemporary ideologies, because of their authors' lack of adequate methodological tools. For historians like Louise Dechêne, on the other hand, a comparison with the Jean Rostand case referred to at the beginning of this chapter seems more appropriate. Her analysis of the social structure of the island of Montreal in the seventeenth century is very successful, but her emphasis on the common man and her criticism of political leaders are inspired by a purely twentieth-century fascination with ideas like participatory democracy. Could it be that works like *Habitants et marchands* herald a general embrace of socialism by Quebec intellectuals?

IV

The Relationship Between Ideology and Method

Fernand Ouellet in

Economic and Social History of

Quebec (1966) and

Lower Canada (1976)*

Fernand Ouellet's *magnum opus, Economic and Social History of Quebec*, won general critical acclaim when first published by Fides in 1966, despite the attacks of nationalist historians. The work bore the stamp of a fresh methodological approach that overshadowed its underlying political stance. There is no doubt that the acclaim was justified. A new type of history was taking root in Quebec soil, based on the relational or dialectical method introduced by Jean Hamelin. Factual economic description gradually gave way to analyses of slowly changing social, political and economic organizations, or *structures*, and of short-term economic or social trends called *conjonctures*. Serial history—the study of "the repeated element...which can be integrated into a homogeneous series" and the phenomena of the *longue durée*, encompassing "structures" or "civilizations," developed by the *Annales* School—began to find a place

---

*The English versions appeared in 1980, and are here abbreviated as *ESHQ* and *LC* for page references. In *Lower Canada*, Patricia Claxton's translated adaptation, certain words and phrases quoted in this chapter do not appear, in which case reference is made to the original *Bas-Canada*.

81

in Quebec historiography. Imported from Paris as a result of exchanges and studies abroad, it progressively challenged the homegrown brand of historical writing.

Economic and Social History perhaps had some of the faults of the novice, and these were soon spotted by those working in a more advanced historiographical tradition.[1] Nevertheless, it marked a watershed in Quebec and Canadian historical writing. People spoke of a "Ouelletist revolution," a change comparable in scope to that brought about by the work of Herald Innis in English Canada. Its impact was overwhelming. Pierre Savard's cautionary remark fell on deaf ears: "One cannot but regret the broad generalizations unaccompanied by examples or any indication of sources."[2] Ouellet wrote with great assurance. It seemed unlikely that his intuitive deductions could be unfounded, or that they could be influenced by a modernistic, or more precisely, liberal ideology characteristic of some contemporary studies of the past, present, and future of the Quebec people. With the passage of time and subsequent developments in historical scholarship, it is now easier to recognize the "present-minded"[3] bias of what is, in other respects, an authoritative work. According to one view of the psycho-sociology of knowledge, all method is intentional. If so, the relationship between ideology and method is not as tenuous or incompatible as might at first appear. To begin with, however, let us see whether style and the obvious features of Ouellet's work indicate a partisan stance.

Style and Ideology

The experienced reader of history will immediately notice that Fernand Ouellet's narrative contained certain pecularities of style rarely found in contemporary work. Elementary semantic analysis shows how ideology has discreetly slipped in behind a screen of words, turns of phrase, and circumlocutions unusual in modern writing.

To appreciate Ouellet's originality as a narrator, one must understand his temperament. He is quarrelsome, passionate, and polemical, as his many trenchant book reviews indicate. His fondness for debate is no secret. Indeed, his debating skill is surprising in one who has consigned political history to a lesser place. He uses this skill both to cross swords with colleagues and to heap invective on the illustrious dead of nationalist persuasion. The result is a fairly politicized discussion in which twentieth-century Quebec, as perceived by the narrator, is seen as being collectively in hot pursuit of the remembrance of things past. The presence in the narrative of the historian-as-man, with his attendant prejudices, political choices, and social projections, is revealed by his frequent use of the perfect conditional tense or the speculative "might have." This outmoded device consists of asking, while positing various possible answers, what would or might have been the consequences of an option *not* taken by various historical agents, or of some alternate course of action. Although perhaps unaware of doing so, the historian thus reveals the desires, hopes, and regrets of the man. In a manner of speaking, he substitutes himself for the actual participants, making choices that they did not—choices which, in his opinion, would have been right in the circumstances. Actually, the perfect conditional still occurs in highly sophisticated contexts. In recent years, for example, American historians have asked whether economic growth would have been the same if the American Revolution, the transportation revolution, or Roosevelt's New Deal had not come about. For the most part, however, researchers rest their case on statistical calculations, which Ouellet did not. His traditional use of the perfect conditional as a literary device created subtle anachronisms, and constituted an error in method that betrayed an ideological stance. The poet Paul Valéry considered that reasoning based on the conditional "brings to the study of the past the anxiety and expectations with which we view the present. It endows history with the power of novels and short stories."[4] In short, the historian, while aware of the future of the past that he is analysing, tries to imagine an alternate, unreal past in order to influence the course of events according to his desires. He indulges in wishful thinking, taking desires for realities. Consequently the use of the perfect conditional confers considerable power on him: he becomes judge, arbiter, and moral censor of prominent individuals and groups.

Ouellet's use of the perfect conditional in the two works

discussed here somewhat approximated the moral judgments of our early historians. Rather than being offered an explanation of causes, the reader was obliged to make do with the information that other courses of action would have been preferable for the good of the community. It would be a highly revealing exercise to list how often and in what context the prepositional phrase "instead of" has been used throughout his work. For the present, let us look at other ways in which Ouellet expressed his desires.

Ouellet's major preoccupation was with the 1837 rebellion. Although this consisted of localized uprisings quickly put down, he treated them with the prominence given by nationalist historians. Unlike them, however, he refused to consider the rebellion as a short-lived attempt to remove the colonial yoke, seeing it instead as a sort of miniature French Revolution that went the wrong way and failed. Had the Patriotes emerged the victors, it would have been disastrous: "Independence, since it would have destroyed the two most viable sectors of the economy, namely the trade in grain with the west and the lumber industry, would have condemned Lower Canada to several decades of serious underdevelopment and would have strengthened the seigneurs and the clergy" (*LC*, 324). As we all know, the rebels were vanquished, the decades rolled by, and the clergy enlarged its material and symbolic power in Quebec. Meanwhile the seigneurs met the fate prophesied by Ouellet in the event of a rebel victory. Incidentally, in his opinion the upsurge of violence in 1837 could have been avoided for the greater good of all concerned, if only the French-Canadian petite bourgeoisie had agreed to work within the mercantile capitalist system and to cooperate with the key figures of the almost exclusively British politico-military structure. If they had, communications, as well as economic and social institutions that favored the uninterrupted development of the capitalist economy, would have been modernized. He frequently expressed regret that Quebec of the 1830s did not experience a fiscal revolution such as that of August 1789 in France—a regret shared by the radical minority opposed to Papineau within the Patriote party. A meaningful revolution in 1837, therefore, would have abolished the seigneurial system and clergy tithes, and brought about organizational changes likely to encourage the expansion of a market economy. Normally, a historian would attempt to explain why the rebellion was directed against the English-speaking bourgeoisie rather than the clergy and seigneurs. Ouellet merely decried French-speaking petit-bourgeois class interest, with its selfish distraction of the "rural masses" from the "real problems." But might not the rebellion's nationalist bias be partly explained by the fact that the habitants of nineteenth-century Lower Canada had a far lighter tax burden than the French peasants of late eighteenth-century France, their social counterparts? To my mind this would be the more scientific approach, more comparative in scope and less emotionally charged. By resorting to the conditional and musing about the "good fight" that 1837 might have been, Ouellet avoided examining the actual causes of the rebellion.

In the years preceding the riots at St. Denis, St. Charles, and St. Eustache, the business sector "saved the British regime," in Ouellet's words, by developing the forest industry. This industry supplied jobs for perhaps 5 to 10 percent of the population, according to some estimates. Therefore the halt in forest development following the international financial crisis of 1837-1838 might well have triggered rural unrest. Ouellet would not entertain such a hypothesis, however, because he could not admit that the bourgeoisie or the market economy system with its specific crises was in any way linked to the uprising. In this respect, his reading of the Canadian "revolutionary" phenomenon differed widely from Albert Soboul's examination of the French Revolution. Even so, in *Lower Canada* Ouellet considered the French Revolution the right way to change the course of History with a capital H.[5]

The narrator's involvement was further revealed by the use of the adverb "fortunately" or its antonym. As with the perfect conditional, this sort of individual approach was once the salt of historical discourse, although it is almost never found in current scholarly writing. Ouellet used adverbs to express both good and bad fortune and, if my impression is correct, did so more frequently in *Economic and Social History of Quebec* than in *Lower Canada*—the reverse of his tendency with the perfect

conditional. Unlike the latter, however, the adverbs "fortunately" and "unfortunately" were not prophetic; instead, they
gave the impression that Ouellet disapproved of the way things
were going. He was generally pleased when the market economy prospered, although not necessarily displeased when
"business" was not doing well. On two or three occasions he
let slip an "unfortunately" in talking of the strategic errors of
the rebels.[6]

A third clue to Ouellet's presence in the narrative was the
frequent use of the negative. All historians use the negative,
of course, but rarely as often as Ouellet. The device is
frequently designed to contradict an interpretation or "revelation" put forward by a predecessor. A reader unaware of
our domestic quarrels might wonder what the writer was talking about when he said, "Land speculation was therefore not,
as has been asserted, confined to the Eastern Townships" (LC,
35). In his 1966 work, the early nineteenth-century seigneurs
were regarded as niggardly in granting land, but he did not
object to clergy and crown reserves (28 percent of the Townships' surface area), or to gifts of enormous estates to private
parties such as senior officials and British businessmen. In
fact, he said nothing, whereas historians like Ivanhoe Caron—
not necessarily fervent nationalists—had severely condemned
land speculation in the Townships. At a time when the image
of the "good seigneur" as a colonizing agent was prevalent,[7]
Ouellet was in fact making a point of denouncing the seigneurs' shortcomings. In another negative statement, he
remarked that government seizure of the Jesuit estates "did
not really harm the church's financial state" (LC, 4l). The reader
deserves to know more in this instance, since the seizure
involved over 40 percent of the seigneurial estates held by the
church under the French regime, although Ouellet did not
say so.[8] The fact is that during this period even the bishop
did not possess a personal income equal to that of parish priests
with the best livings.

An even more explicit example of Ouellet's method of side-
stepping issues that might force him into painful "admissions"
was his treatment of the debate on allowances for members
of the legislative assembly. He stated that such allowances would

probably not have materially altered the assembly's social makeup (*LC*, 188). The reader accepts this apparently commonplace prediction without realizing that behind it lies an important political debate over an issue supported by the Canadian party, which in the 1820s became the Patriote party. The petit-bourgeois members of this party, less well-off than their counterparts in the party of business and capital, demanded a parliamentary allowance for expenses incurred in representing their constituencies, since they found the cost of travel and lodging during the session in Quebec City fairly onerous. The demand was urged on democratic grounds, and rejected, according to Henri Brun, "due to the skilful use of demagoguery. The opposition was led by a generally wealthy English minority and was inevitably seconded by all those members who already received government stipends for judicial, governmental, or administrative services".[9] The granting of parliamentary allowances was delayed until 1836, and their advent made a considerable difference to the petit-bourgeois Patriote party. The point to make was not whether earlier approval of this measure would or would not have changed the social makeup of the assembly, but that it was demanded for "loss of income and expenses incurred" for the session.[10] Ouellet's negative statements, in short, sometimes amounted to a calculated silence or a hidden rebuttal. In his polemical style he made abundant use of negative statements to emphasize the general stagnation and unimportance of events prior to the beginning of the nineteenth century. This was a way of pointing out to "nationalist" historians that the Conquest did not have the effect claimed by them. The excessive use of "not" in summarizing the latter years of the eighteenth century in his introduction to *Lower Canada* had another motive. Ouellet was about to ring up the curtain on the "drama"—as the French edition put it (*Bas-Canada*, 244; cf. *LC*, 156)—of agricultural crisis and demographic pressure. These sources of rural unrest were swept under the carpet by the French-Canadian middle classes, he said, in the interest of their struggle against English capitalism. There was evident dramatization in his exaggerated portrayal of economic and demographic fluctuations designed to highlight the tragic aspect of the rebellion and what he considered the "turpitude" of its promoters.[11]

The leading actors in this social drama were considered as providing a particularly weak leadership. Ouellet's portrait of Pierre Bédard, first leader of the Canadian party, produced a shower of negatives. His marriage "was not a success" and "his contemporaries were not impressed by his physical presence" (*LC*, 84). He "was never a republican or a democrat" (*LC*, 87), but then neither were the Fathers of Confederation, as Stanley Ryerson pointed out.[12] In fact, it is a trait common to the political tradition of all bourgeois societies. Ouellet, however, limited his censure to the Patriote party in his discussion of the nineteenth century, while remaining silent about the political conservatism of the great merchants of the St. Lawrence commercial empire.

Other aspects of Ouellet's individual style deserve mention, since they constituted a challenge to previous interpretations. The use of repetition as a stylistic device in *Economic and Social History*, for example, was not simply due to the chronological organization of the work, as Pierre Barral would have it.[13] Ouellet employed it as a pedagogical tool. Another device was the frequent use of such phrases as "it seems that," "one has the impression that," and "everything occurred as though." In a review of the French edition of *Lower Canada*, Pierre Tousignant took exception to the statement "as though French Canadians were being systematically blocked from the higher echelons of the civil service" (*LC*, 63), remarking wryly that English power was real, not a mere figment of the imagination. It hardly needs to be pointed out that in 1834 there were 45 French-speaking civil servants out of 1,600, whereas only 12 percent of the 600,000 people in Lower Canada were of British origin.[14]

Despite a colossal amount of personal research, Ouellet's work failed to synthesize the results of ten or twenty years of collective effort in the field, as has now been done in France and elsewhere. Instead, he supplied an outline based, at times, on somewhat meager documentation, and attempted with rather indifferent success to fill the gaps in his knowledge with assumptions. His temperament is such that he tenaciously upheld the hypotheses of *Economic and Social History* that he himself said would "age quickly" if the book achieved its goal (*ESHQ*, xxiii). Beneath the cosmetic coating of Ouellet's stylistic devices, these hypotheses were in fact a challenge. We should examine their substance, for if, as Jean Hamelin has suggested, Ouellet is a sort of giant, "axe-hewn from a squared log,"[15] it is important to get at the heart of his work. As a historian, Ouellet has paved the way for a transition from an ethnic to a social reading of the past.[16] Let us therefore take a look at social classes as understood by him.

Social Classes and Power Relationships

Total history such as Ouellet proposed must be studied through social relationships, the usual perspective in economic and social history. Since he did not use any very strict class definitions, it will be as well to clarify current terminology in reference to various social strata.

In the context with which we are dealing, "dominant classes" refers to the seigneurial class, which lived on income from landed property. The dominant position of this class was threatened by the rise of the bourgeoisie, and thus the social relationships of the Old Regime were gradually replaced by the capitalist social relationships that emerged in the wake of the expansion of the market economy. This is the most significant structural change of the period, and one that Ouellet has not sufficiently highlighted. This rising dominant class of bourgeois capitalists naturally included his great English-speaking merchants. "Intermediate groups," "middle classes," and "petite bourgeoisie" are all, in my opinion, synonyms for the following socio-professional categories: retail merchants, artisans, and members of the professions, this latter sub-group being associated with the clergy by reason of its intellectual training. Doctors, lawyers, and notaries were in fact products of a scholarly tradition, as were clerics. The classifications are not exclusively based on material considerations, although these are fundamental. The clergy, for example, formed a separate group because of the source of its income, as well as its considerable symbolic power. Artisans, whose skills placed them in the working-class culture, were also linked to the middle classes in terms of income and life-style. The urban and rural popular classes were more easily definable, and included landowning and tenant farmers, and wage-earning day laborers in the towns, sawmills and lumber camps. Concession road, village, river, and forest were the familiar environment of most, the rural-urban ratio having increased from 75:25 to 80:20 between the end of the eighteenth century and the 1830s.

Aristocracy and Seigneurs: A Dominant Class in Decline

In the 1960s, the image of the "good seigneur" as a colonizing agent drawing modest rents was still widespread among historians. In *Economic and Social History* Ouellet took a very different stand, devoting numerous pages to the profiteering nineteenth-century seigneurs who took advantage of the increased demand for land to raise rents, withhold land concessions, tax new products, augment land reserves, and engage in other speculative activity. Ouellet decried their boundless arrogance (*ESHQ*, 124) at the time of the American Revolution, while explaining, excusing, or simply summarizing the opinions of merchant capitalists of questionable loyalty, given the context. As in traditional liberal historiography, the seigneurial class was depicted as a parasitic group exacting a heavy toll on crops to support an extravagant way of life (*ESHQ*, 136). For French-language Canadian historiography, however, this was a fairly innovative view. Until then, a nationalist and conservative approach had prevailed in discussing the seigneurial class. Ouellet was less insistent on seigneurial shortcomings in *Lower Canada*, or so it seemed, perhaps because he did not cover the periods 1760-1791 and 1840-1850. Nevertheless, he mentioned the arrogance of agricultural landlords at the end of the eighteenth century, stating, "When they [the aristocracy] deplored the lot of the peasantry, their concern was really for their own future" (*LC*, 13). Ouellet reiterated his earlier views on the seigneurs' reactionary attitude and the crisis in the system during the early nineteenth century (*LC*, 180ff.), implicitly contradicting Maurice Séguin's theory that the seigneurial regime was "the shield of the French-Canadian nation" (*LC*, 140). Instead, Ouellet saw it as a burden on agricultural producers and capital investors alike, with the exception of the few capitalists who had acquired seigneuries of their own. In *Lower Canada,* however, he was less categorical about the selfishness of the seigneurial class, pointing out that land speculation was also current practice in the Eastern Townships, outside the seigneurial zone. He even went so far as to admit that this practice discriminated against the French-speaking population (*LC*, 38), which for him was quite an ideological shift.

The Bourgeoisie: A Rising Dominant Class

Stanley Ryerson took the bourgeoisie severely to task in *Unequal Union*, first published in 1968. In his view, it had formed a conspiracy against a "race," as well as against rural dwellers and the proletariat. A surplus of capital and labor in Great Britain led to the export of these resources to American colonial possessions. It was important to prevent the new arrivals from acquiring landed property, in order to maintain an abundant and cheap labor force for large-scale public works or future industrial projects. In this way, a reserve army of workers was created in the St. Lawrence Valley. Wage laborers stimulated "the universalizing of commodity production" and, "with the break-up of the old, self-sufficient, 'natural economy'" in the countryside (p. 36), habitants became consumers of goods manufactured by British workers. The capitalist conspiracy developed into the Confederation scheme. Such were the Marxist views on the British regime.

Ouellet's bourgeoisie, in contrast, offered the rural and urban working classes a much better social deal than the Old Regime. The masses were not mere tools. Reviewers of both *Economic and Social History* and *Lower Canada* criticized his image of the benevolent capitalist. Hilda Neatby took exception to the "honest egotism of big business"[17] in the former, while Allan Greer, in his review of the English edition of *Lower Canada*, remarked even more pointedly that "the accusation of concealing class selfishness under lofty ideals [referring to the French-Canadian petite bourgeoisie] might just as easily have applied to the merchants of the 'English Party.' "[18] Historians generally concede that bourgeois class interests, like others, are screened by ideological arguments every bit as convincing as those of the French-Canadian petite bourgeoisie. The ways in which bourgeois ideology was formulated have been documented by André Lefebvre in *La Montréal Gazette et le nationalisme canadien, 1835-1842* (Montreal: Guérin, 1970), although his nationalist bias has distorted his understanding of the class consciousness involved.

Ouellet's capitalists had nothing to hide. They were the instruments rather than the promoters of the "laws" of supply and demand. Putting men, goods, and services into circulation was not primarily a source of profit but a way of promoting universal good. One gets a picture of a hardworking bourgeoisie, guardian of the common weal; Adam Smith, or any other economist concerned with the theoretical and "scientific" justification of the rise of the bourgeoisie, could hardly have done better. Ouellet did mention a few ill-gotten fortunes among his bourgeois, it is true. These were described as *fortunes nauséabondes* in the French edition of Economic and Social History (45), although the English rendition of "sickening misfortunes" (*ESHQ*, 46) gave quite a different impression. At any rate, he contradicted the popular dictum about success smelling sweet—at least in so far as army suppliers (Michel Brunet's millionaires) were concerned. Such upstarts were weeded out at the beginning of British rule after the peace treaty of 1763. The conquering bourgeois cherished "dreams" and "hopes" of making their fortunes in a peacetime economy (*LC*, 21), and of employing their imaginative and aggressive qualities (*LC*, 62) in the fight against injustice (by which was meant the restricted frontiers of 1763) and government intervention, which increasingly hampered the free play of market forces (*ESHQ*, 112).

Ouellet's sympathies were well illustrated in his treatment of the jails dispute. This involved the debate over whether the building of jails should be financed by a land tax or by an increase in customs duties. He described two groups, the first composed of French Canadians belonging to the liberal professions or the petite bourgeoisie, including a few influential habitants with seats in the assembly, the second composed of English merchants. These two groups were opposed, "the one *claiming* to be protecting the interests of farmers and land-holders" against the English-speaking bourgeoisie, "and the other, in the name of commercial interests, *seeking* a more flexible distribution of the tax burden" (*LC*, 82; italics mine). Briefly put, Ouellet considered the burden on land excessive when discussing tithes, seigneurial *rentes*, and other forms of Old Regime dues, but legitimate when it came to taxing real estate wealth in order to stimulate imports and consumption. On one hand, "the English merchants...were particularly sensitive" to the increased tax on imports, while on the other "the peasantry" manifested a "*hyper*sensitivity" (italics mine) to land taxation (*LC*, 82).

In *Patronage et pouvoir au Bas-Canada* (Quebec: PUQ, 1973), Paquet and Wallot maintained that British merchants bene-fited from sizable supply contracts, implying that patronage filled other pockets than those of the "millionaires" of the Seven Years' War in North America. Ouellet believed that the merchant bourgeoisie's wealth resulted from hard work, not favoritism.[19] He described the cornering of markets in a given territory or sector as a "natural monopoly" (*ESHQ*, 167), which was the direct opposite of Ryerson's self-sufficient, "natural economy."

Writing in the liberal tradition, Ouellet linked "progress"[20] with growth in trade volume, and saw opponents of bourgeois activity, the middle classes of the Patriote party, as victims of fear and "the anxiety felt in the face of the demands of prog-ress" (*ESHQ*, 441). They failed to understand that moderni-zation schemes such as a St. Lawrence River canal system or the creation of banking institutions would benefit the popu-lation as a whole. He challenged the kind of historiography that had depicted capitalists as "base materialists, forgetful of collective values in favour of narrowly selfish views.... The promotion of economic interests, even if it serves vested inter-ests, can be the necessary point of departure for genuine prog-ress"(*ESHQ*, 217). In a word, the bourgeoisie exemplified what Maurice Crubellier called "Franklin's morality": a taste for hard work, thriftiness, and moderate aspirations.[21] Ouellet quoted L.-R. Masson's account of the Beaver Club (*BRH*, 1898, 216f.) and the businessmen of the North West Company: "Like all men who have suffered long and worked hard to reach a comfortable position, these bourgeois were impatient to enjoy their wealth and proud to display it, even at the risk of seeing this affluence, bought at the price of so much suffering, disappear in a few years." Ouellet added that "this adventurous bourgeoisie, while apparently enamoured of luxury and prestige, was not entirely given over to extravagant consumption. Many of its members reinvested the profits made in the West in other sectors of the economy," thus becoming agents of long-term growth (*ESHQ*, 145). But it was not only the bourgeois work ethic that Ouellet admired. He felt that producer-consumer relationships in a market economy did not generate the same social inequalities as the seigneurial system, in which "inequality was inherent" (*LC*, 151). This was why he emphasized the effects of the land *rente*, which undermined agricultural production for the benefit of seigneurs and clergy (*LC*, 128), whereas he presented forest development as a source of income distribution through jobs. Ouellet's lumber barons provided earnings and thus stimulated imports (*LC*, 128), improving the standard of living of the common habitant.

Ouellet's prepossession in favor of the bourgeoisie can also be inferred from his strategic silences. We learn that in 1831 John Neilson "disassociated himself from the [Patriote] party over the parish councils question" (*LC*, 230). How did it happen that this Presbyterian petit-bourgeois, who sympathized with French-Canadian nationalist sentiment, now sided with and was firmly supported by the Catholic clergy? (*LC*, 232.) The parish councils bill was a democratic measure proposed by Patriote members and quashed by English Protestants. It aimed at "giving representatives of local property owners a part" in choosing the wardens who administered the parish council, when as a general rule these officers were elected by the outgoing wardens. If Thomas Chapais's account was correct, Neilson's reason for defecting was that the bill was legally indefensible; parish councils were corporations administered by legally recognized officers, no more subject to interference than banks. Council funds came neither from taxes nor assessments, but from voluntary contributions.[22] Ouellet never spoke of bourgeois initiatives blocking popular power, but was quick to denounce the "mean-spiritedness" of the middle classes in their demands for democratic institutions. He also evinced surprise at other petit-bourgeois initiatives that aroused panic in capitalist circles in the 1830s, apart from the parish councils issue. In 1831, John Richardson opposed the incorporation of the city of Montreal. Ouellet commented that Richardson "was alarmed at the thought of the administration of Montreal and all the local institutions falling into the hands of the *patriote* party," then referred to an account in *La Minerve* stating Richardson's fear that "there seemed to be a...determination to gather all the power of the country to the popular branch." In other words, added Ouellet, "it was not the peasants and working classes but the French-Canadian middle classes which the English milieu dreaded finding in control of all the real political power" (*LC*, 264). The use of the negative was meant to put the reader on his guard against the democratic appearance of the measure. Instead of simply saying that the Patriote party was petit-bourgeois, Ouellet preferred to "enlighten" his readers, informing them that it was *not* a popular party—as though they might imagine citizens' committees springing up in a small North American city at the beginning of the nineteenth century. This is a perfect example of the kind of implicit anachronism that can slip into present-minded discussion of the past.

There does seem to have been a tendency to panic among the minority controlling international trade, key administrative posts, and the decision-making apparatus of government such as the legislative and executive councils. The circumstances surrounding the closing of assembly schools in 1836 illustrated this admirably. I shall not labor the point, however, except to say that Ouellet persisted in portraying the bourgeoisie as being opposed to the demagoguery and blind incomprehension of the petite bourgeoisie.

Why, one asks, were French Canadians so conspicuously absent from the bourgeoisie? Ouellet's often-stated and characteristic approach was that it was not the result of discrimination. "Lucid observers" supported this view (*ESHQ*, 378), explaining that the success of the English-speaking element was due to the formation of business partnerships and the diversification of interests. The idea that French Canadians may have displayed dynamism, but were pushed to one side by their rivals, was viewed as a nationalist thesis that did not fit the facts. Ouellet therefore rejected Michel Brunet's theory of the "decline" of the French-Canadian bourgeoisie being a result of the Conquest. That the Conquest may have caused a long-term alteration in investment patterns, as José Igartua suggests,[23] could not explain the "exclusion" of French Canadians. They excluded themselves because of their hostile attitude to bourgeois values; consequently French-speaking entrepreneurs soon succumbed to the English competition. This psychological and culturalist explanation was repeatedly used by Ouellet and served as an argument to refute the work of Tulchinsky, who considered that a dynamic entrepreneurship had really existed among French Canadians.[24]

Ouellet's interpretation was not surprising, considering that he was challenging the hypothesis that colonialism was responsible for the low proportion of capitalists among French Canadians. In his view, they lacked the capacity to participate. Unlike Brunet, he did not feel that the Conquest had "decapitated" the French, removing their economic elite. Easterbrook and Aitken, writing on the fur trade, saw the division of labor between the two founding peoples of Canada as a desire for "collaboration," resulting in English-speaking entrepreneurs and French-speaking wage-earners: "The English-speaking traders...took over almost without change the trading methods which the French had evolved, and relied upon the French Canadians, with their indispensable knowledge of rivers and canoes, to serve as *voyageurs*, interpreters, and guides." This division of labor along ethnic lines, they added, consummated the "marriage of British capital and enterprise with French experience and ability...an outstanding example of cooperation between the two nationalities after the conquest."[25] Ouellet maintained an analagous position. Referring to the late eighteenth century, he wrote: "Although British capital gained ground continually in the beaver economy, the French-Canadian contribution was no less impressive. We must first point out that the manpower was almost entirely French-Canadian.... The French-Canadian population also supplied the majority of *coureurs de bois*.... At a higher level, we encounter the clerks and the explorers.... Finally, French-Canadian society supplied a very significant proportion of the fur traders" (*ESHQ*, 108). In a 1967 essay, Ouellet hammered home the absence of any "disastrous" effect with a large, two-column table showing the ethnic distribution of fur traders. In 1769, 70 percent were French-speaking, as against 30 percent English-speaking; a year later, the percentage ratio was 76 to 24.[26] Here was a fine example of statistical reasoning for more or less conscious ideological purposes. In reality, the disappearance of French Canadians from the capitalist class was a long and gradual process, and such short-term fluctuations were statistically meaningless. Furthermore, the British merchants' preferential trading position vis-à-vis suppliers throughout the empire gave them a long-term, exclusive advantage in transatlantic commerce.

Ouellet portrayed capitalist expansion by the major traders within the Atlantic network as a series of struggles. The capitalists were up against petit-bourgeois opposition to the colonial system. The former were defending "vital" interests by opposing free trade, however, since differential tariffs enabled Canadian lumber to compete with forest products from the Baltic at the beginning of the nineteenth century (*LC*, 160). Ouellet felt that the introduction of free trade would have closed off the British market and brought poverty to Lower Canada. He concluded that petit-bourgeois ideology was somewhat inconsistent, or else influenced by some sort of masochistic instinct. According to Nicole Gagnon's interpretation of Ouellet's views, cutting off lumber-workers' income by advocating abolition of tariffs was an "absolutely suicidal...political goal."[27] However, the political acts and arguments of the Patriote party are more comprehensible when we realize that a group of small manufacturers produced goods that had to compete with imported products, as illustrated by Ryerson (*Unequal Union*, 37-41) and Tulchinsky. This group of small entrepreneurs did not figure in Ouellet's picture. Only the spokesmen of the petite bourgeoisie, "blinded...by their fear of the English-speaking bourgeoisie" (*LC*, 173), and given over to the ruralist myth, appeared. These petits bourgeois, while hypersensitive to capitalist measures, "underestimated" the power and influence of the Catholic clergy (*LC*, 173, 175); instead, implied Ouellet, they should have blamed this group for blocking the march of progress.

Intermediate Groups: The Clergy

The clergy formed a special sub-group by virtue of the fact that it drew its livelihood from agricultural produce in the form of tithes. Yet Ouellet had little to say about this aspect, limiting himself to discussion of the clergy's economic and cultural power. We would have liked to learn more about the actual basis of such power. Since the lay sector of the petite bourgeoisie was presumably incapable of correctly estimating the power of the priesthood, we would have expected Ouellet to examine and estimate the revenue produced by tithes and other emoluments, as well as the income from productive real estate under ecclesiastical management. Clergy estates constituted one quarter of the acreage held in seigneurial tenure at the end of the French regime, of which nearly half passed into the hands of the state at the death of the last Jesuit at the turn of the century. What, for example, was the revenue of seigneuries held in mortmain by nuns' orders in return for educational and nursing services, the rest being under the management of the Quebec and Montreal seminaries? If a detailed study were not possible, Ouellet could have referred his readers to contemporary estimates, as did Gustavus Myers in his early twentieth century study, *A History of Canadian Wealth* (Toronto: James Lewis and Samuel, re-ed. 1972, 68f., 106-113, 166f.). Milnes' estimate of the tithe in 1800, used by Myers and others, has been particularly singled out for study by critics of this church levy. Such studies may be partisan, but they provide some useful indications, nonetheless.[28] After various cross-checks, it seems that the acreage remaining in clergy hands after the government take-over of Jesuit estates in 1800 was greater than the proportionate amount owned by the church in France before the Revolution. On the other hand, revenue from tithes appears to have been far less here than in France, where, it is said, "the rates most frequently applied seem to have been between an eleventh and a thirteenth—

about 8 percent." This was twice the legal rate in Canada (a twenty-sixth of the harvest), which was almost as light a tax as the thirtieth and thirty-sixth sometimes customary in Brittany, where the parish priests were extremely popular with the faithful.[29]

The old social regimes of France and Quebec differed not only with respect to landed property and revenue, however. The general absence of comparative historical method made Ouellet too ready to equate the situations on either side of the Atlantic, and consequently undermined his argument. His discussion of the relative size of the clergy was a case in point. Mid-eighteenth-century Quebec had one priest for every 500 Catholics; between 1820 and 1830 the ratio was not more than one per 1,800. Yet Ouellet appeared to think that there was a high proportion of priests at the beginning of the nineteenth century. He used the rather facile method of estimating one priest for each average parish, forgetting that distribution was very unequal between town and country, both in France and Quebec. Between 1760 and 1840 the number of parishes rose from over 100 to roughly 200. With very rare exceptions, these parishes were mostly rural and always exceeded the number of recorded parish priests. Moreover, some parishes had no resident priest, while others had a curate—perhaps several curates in an urban parish. Lower Canada, in fact, suffered from a shortage of human resources, whereas France possessed a superabundance. Under the Old Regime the latter had infinitely more priests than places, as Bernard Plongeron and many others before him have pointed out. Before 1789, according to an 1818 statistic, there were 122,336 priests, or one for about every 200 inhabitants.[30] Nothing like this existed in Quebec during the years preceding the rebellion. In 1830, one priest for every 200 Catholics (403,572 in all) in Quebec would have meant over 2,000 priests. Records show 245: 160 priests serving 183 parishes, 42 curates, and 43 priests attached to seminaries or convents as teachers or chaplains.[31] In the light of these figures, the conclusion is obvious: the clergy here was not underemployed as it was in France. Prior to 1830 or even 1840, the bishop almost never had enough recruits to provide each parish with a resident priest. With about 300 priests available on the eve of the rebellion, one is hard put to imagine exactly what were the resources of this multitudinous and overbearing clergy that Ouellet implicitly compared to that of prerevolutionary France. An inventory of the material and human resources of the Catholic church in Quebec would have saved him from inferring similarities with Old Regime France where none existed. In the absence of a genuine comparative study, Ouellet gave us a sort of test-tube reconstruction—a curious procedure for a historian who professed to be antinationalist in outlook.

The clergy invented the myth about the Conquest being a stroke of providence, Ouellet implied (*LC*, 43), although Claude Galarneau has demonstrated that it was actually a senior British civil servant who first enunciated the idea. In the autumn of 1789, Chief Justice William Smith told the grand juries of Quebec that the French Canadians had been conquered, but by the grace of God were free men, adding that if there were any Canadian of old who lamented his separation from the parent tree, let him lift up his hands and thank heaven that "providence" had placed him under the benign rule of the British Empire.[32] This view was echoed by the colonial legislative council and Bishop Plessis. Indeed, the bishop's feeling of "horror" and "anathema" toward the French Revolution, an attitude shared by the lower clergy, led Ouellet to describe him as one who "persisted in seeing the parliamentary institutions of Lower Canada" in terms of the Old Regime social order—that is, "in the light of the philosophy of Bossuet" (*LC*, 67, 100). On the other hand, Ouellet was sympathetic to "a violent political sermon" (*LC*, 69) against the nationalist ferment of 1810. Plessis did not believe in the "Protestant peril," a phrase used in the French edition (*Bas-Canada*, 105). "His church was not in a state of servitude, he considered" (*LC*, 69). This satisfied the governor, who regarded the clergy as a reliable "counterbalance" to the growing influence of the French-Canadian professional and small retail classes (*LC*, 110). Ouellet could offer no firmer personal endorsement. But let a nationalist cleric appear on the scene, and Ouellet's historical objectivity was lost in a spate of pejorative adjectives. Bishop Jean-Jacques Lartigue, who early adopted ultramontane views and was sensitive to the national question, was described by Ouellet as "a worrier" as well as "doctrinaire and authoritarian" (*LC*, 168). "He remained unshakably convinced that the Royal Institution [for the Advancement of Learning] was the result of an ongoing Protestant plot against the Catholics" (*LC*, 169), an attitude based on what the French edition termed "suppositions" (*Bas-Canada*, 265). Ouellet portrayed Lartigue as suffering from a persecution complex, believing in plots, "Protestant machination[s]" and betrayal by the French-Canadian middle classes (*LC*, 169). Why, we wonder, did this "son of a farmer" (*LC*, 168) exhibit such petit-bourgeois distress at the spread of capitalist modernity in the towns? The fact is, Lartigue was born in Montreal in 1777, the son of a surgeon. Ouellet could easily have traced the urban, petit-bourgeois origins of Montreal's first bishop in old biographical dictionaries, even before the publication of Gilles Chaussé's *Jean-Jacques Lartigue, premier évêque de Montréal* (Montreal: Fides, 1980).

In discussing the geographic and social provenance of the clergy and the petite bourgeoisie, Ouellet appears to have originated one of the dominant features of the anti-ruralist myth: that is, the allegedly rural background of Quebec priests. The new middle classes of the 1960s embraced this myth when they finally chose to stop ignoring urban, industrial modernity and to hail it enthusiastically. In reality, the practising clergy at the beginning of the nineteenth century were mostly from urban backgrounds. Bishop Plessis and his coadjutor, Bishop Panet, were city-born like Lartigue. Apart from priests in Quebec, Montreal, and Trois-Rivières, three out of five of the 125 priests in rural parishes around 1810 came from Quebec and Montreal, the two cities possessing classical colleges, the *petits séminaires* that provided secondary education for future theology students. The Nicolet Seminary, which opened in 1803, had not yet produced graduates who could move on toward ordination. This is why priests with a rural background (twenty-eight priests, or 22.4 percent of the total) generally came from localities within a thirty to forty kilometer radius of the towns. Of the ten priests originally from France or the United States then working in Quebec, at least half were from an urban background, representing 5.4 percent of the total number. For those whose background was unidentified (fourteen priests, or 11.2 percent), one may safely assume that at least half were of urban origin, which means that about 70 percent of the working rural clergy were urban recruits. The majority of priests' families were city-dwellers, mostly from the upper and middle levels of society. When we compare this information with European studies, it is not suprising. Again, it is comparative history that enables us to see the phenomenon in accurate perspective. It was only between 1830 and 1850 that the Quebec clergy became mainly rural in origin. In France the clergy's background changed from urban to rural during the late eighteenth and early nineteenth centuries,[33] hence the Quebec phenomenon was part of a general Western pattern.

Intermediate Groups: The Secular Petite Bourgeoisie

Apart from the clergy, the petite bourgeoisie consisted of doctors, lawyers, notaries, surveyors, and retail merchants. Ouellet's historical reconstruction portrayed these middle classes as the great social novelty of the early nineteenth century. In a two-part section of *Lower Canada* entitled "The Birth of French-Canadian Nationalism, 1802-1812," he described this group as being related to the clergy, particularly on the cultural level. Both groups were educated in classical colleges, although they subsequently went their separate ways. In the French edition he had this to say of the early nineteenth-century clergy:

The new clergy emerging from the expanded classical colleges was not at all new in terms of background, and was probably closer to the lower classes than the clergy of the eighteenth century. The same was true of members of the professions [*Bas-Canada*, 111, cf. *LC*, 72f.].

In all probability Ouellet was about two decades too early in his pronouncements about rural recruitment to the petite bourgeoisie, since current research supports the view that the origins of the petite bourgeoisie and the clergy shifted at the same time.

It was at the beginning of the nineteenth century that the professional middle classes "concocted" the so-called myth of the agricultural "vocation of the French-Canadian nation," according to Ouellet (*LC*, 75, 76). In actual fact, he had been led to make unfounded assumptions about the geographic origins of the petite bourgeoisie. During the 1960s he produced a series of such statements. In 1966, for example, he wrote:

The majority of these professionals came from a peasant background. The family's hope of a priestly vocation for one of its sons, the desire of the clergy to ensure its growth and to recruit within the colony itself—these were the origins of many of these migrations of rural youth. (*ESHQ*, 209.)

The consequences were manifold. It was because they were supposedly "mainly from a rural background" that young professionals tempted by politics were incapable of adapting to capitalist-backed economic changes. In 1967 he stated that:

They not only shared certain well-established fears with the clerics and the habitants.... They became obsessed with the traditional distrust of capitalism.... To them the English, and even more the Americans, were promoters of a way of life hungry for material wealth and destructive of the older values.... They had idealized agriculture, the seigneurial regime...to such an extent that these institutions became, for them, the principal foundations of the French-Canadian nation.[34]

Thus was the spirit of nationalism born in the liberal professions, a nationalism depicted as the ideology of a "disfavored" sector whose members were increasing proportionately faster than the rest of the population. This accelerated growth in numbers and the corresponding crowding of the professions was a point frequently made (*LC*, 40, 71). Ouellet seemed less sure of his position in his 1976 work, however, although he had never done a quantitative study of the phenomenon. He wrote that "by 1825 there was talk" of the professions being overcrowded (*LC*, 171), and now discovered that professional men were just as numerous among the English minority. Closer study would probably have revealed that overcrowding was perhaps not as pronounced as Ouellet implied in his attempt to explain political crises, particularly that of 1810.[35] He showed the struggle by Bédard's party as a fight to obtain places for supernumerary professionals and not, as Wallot and Paquet had maintained, to find jobs for the less well-provided.[36]

Where did these petits bourgeois come from? Did they emerge from the new classical colleges in rural areas in the early nineteenth century, as Ouellet suggested? Considering what we know of the background of the working clergy in 1810, it would be surprising if the laymen who attended the same institutions came mainly from rural areas. Only Quebec and Montreal had classical colleges before 1803. The first rural college opened in Nicolet with hardly any students; further-more, the first students only graduated between 1810 and 1815. Consequently, the nationalist "aberration" of 1805-1810 cannot be blamed on the uprooted condition of its promoters. Interestingly enough, Ouellet's diagnosis rather resembled that offered by the new middle classes of mid-twentieth-century Quebec, based on their new-found knowledge of the social sciences, to explain and sometimes condemn the reaction of the "traditional elites" to postwar modernization in the prov-ince.

Once again we are confronted with the anachronistic reasoning caused by Ouellet's present-mindedness. In *Lower Canada*, although less sure of petit-bourgeois origins, he made the same assessment. Most French-Canadian professionals came from a society that was increasingly rural in outlook, he felt. "The French-Canadian professionals, even those born and raised in the cities, even the sons of craftsmen, profes-sionals, or merchants, were deeply imbued with the values of their overwhelmingly rural society; with perplexing [for whom?] facility, peasant atavism seems to have suffused the entire class" (*LC*, 71). In other words, attendance at the *petit sé-minaire* had produced misfits indoctrinated with anti-Enlight-enment philosophy. Such petits bourgeois must undoubtedly have been the sons of rustics, or at least rustics at heart, to foment the political crisis of 1810. Unsure of their origin, Ouellet confined himself to the remark that, in any event, their view of the world was "ruralist." Ouellet's middle classes were not only suffering from bucolic neurosis, however. As Allan Greer remarked, "much of this book [*Lower Canada*] reads like an indictment of the *patriotes*." The picture painted by

Ouellet was so overstated that the translator adapted the original text in order to tone down its polemical nature. As a result, Greer added, "Papineau and the *patriotes* are made to appear far less Machiavellian than Ouellet portrayed them in the French version".[37]

In the original *Bas-Canada*, Ouellet mounted a full-scale attack on his sworn enemies, the nationalists of yesterday and today, and the historians who promoted their views. In 1975, Ouellet categorically denounced fellow historians who differed with him. They too had fallen into the abyss of the ruralist dream. As always with Ouellet, these "strayings" were explained as aberrant nationalism, not as environmental consciousness or a new set of universal values. In addressing the Royal Society of Canada he stated:

> Can one go so far as to say that nationalism has been rooted out of the historian's work? One need not look far to find new and unconscious idealizations. When, for example, in reading some of the recent studies by amateur or scientific historians, we find an almost uniform portrait of the old-time habitant emerging—independent, no worse than elsewhere, aware of the market, egalitarian, tolerant, free-thinking, and revolutionary—then we know that such writers are not advocating an old-fashioned return to the soil; rather, it reveals the existence among us of petits bourgeois who have adapted to city life but find the noise and pollution distressing, and who feel a nostalgia for the rural life, expressed through their ideologically biased reconstructions of the past.[38]

The small, intellectual portion of the new middle classes which constituted the brains trust of the Parti Québécois naturally regarded early nineteenth-century nationalist political groups as having objectives comparable to their own: that is, to make Quebec an independent French state. Similarly, the size of the English population could not be too small for those historians who were sympathetic to nationalist feeling and who promoted Quebec sovereignty. They saw the English minority of yesterday or today as a threat to the cultural fabric of the majority. Ouellet would certainly not have supported the Parti Québécois's unilingual language policy if called upon to comment on the political choices of the late 1970s, for he wrote in 1966 that English immigration was "clearly insufficient" at the end of the eighteenth century. He took no account of the burden of colonial status, and later stated somewhat naively in *Lower Canada* that "it is apparent that the English minority had begun to see the precariousness of their position in a colony where they were overwhelmingly outnumbered" (*LC*, 63). This English minority was defined in *Bas-Canada* as predominantly "merchants, professionals, civil servants, and to a lesser extent, day laborers, artisans, and farmers" (p. 97). In an attempt to evoke the uneasiness of the minority, Ouellet adopted its state of mind. He went even further. Since the presence of the English minority was a guarantee of prosperity, it was therefore beneficial to the French majority. What would become of an independent Quebec? He answered this question in a chapter on colonial independence in *Economic and Social History*, with a quote from an English resident's letter written during the rebellion years:

The independence that one would like to see them achieve would be for them rather a misfortune than a blessing.... Before thinking of independence the French Canadians must educate themselves, become serious-minded, develop into business men, [*sic*] learn for the common good how to suppress or silence selfish and individual pretensions. Even if Lower Canada became independent today, it would have only conquered a future of misfortunes. You would see anarchy here [*ESHQ*, 332].

This quotation typifies the imperialist's view of the colonial; it is the same whatever the context, whether nineteenth-century Africa, or the whole present-day southern hemisphere in relation to modern northern economic imperialism. Since Ouellet's perspective was more or less that of his British correspondent, we can understand why the middle classes found so little favor with him, either in 1966 or 1976. He depicted this group in a succession of uncomplimentary phrases: "hypersensitivity to immigration" (*ESHQ*, 215), "vulnerability," "narrow...in outlook" (380), and "obsessive fear" (379, 385). Their vision of the world was a reflection of the future, an "idealized and bucolic vision," variously described as "wild" and "romantic"; "the land above all stood for refuge" (*ESHQ*, 385). This type of description was a further implicit indictment of the traditional elites; moreover, for the mid-twentieth-century reader it emphasized urban and industrial modernity and the need to adjust and develop. Ouellet transferred this perspective to the early nineteenth century when he wrote, "with a spirit of compromise on both sides, the system could have operated in an acceptable manner," or "merchants and professional men could have joined together for a total reform of the institutions of traditional society" (*ESHQ*, 387, 208f.). We get the impression that if only Ouellet had been there, things might have been different. What his compatriots needed was "a business bourgeoisie which, in the face of the prevailing *conjoncture*, would have been able to rally the population around realistic objectives" (*ESHQ*, 379). Lower Canada's problems "were, above all, due to its economic, social, and mental structures," and "to search for a political solution" to the ills of the early nineteenth century was to look backwards, "to cling to the past, to take refuge in romanticizing its misfortunes" (*ESHQ*, 31). This is not the way to write history. Ouellet's own idealistic vision in fact took the place of a comprehensive discussion that would have enabled his reader to understand the gulf separating the groups in question.

Louis-Joseph Papineau, whom Ouellet saw as a man of words when action was needed, incited a peaceable population to armed insurrection (*ESHQ*, 217, 219, 364). The rare economic initiatives taken by the French-Canadian middle classes did not produce the dynamic thrust he desired, being the result of a persecution complex rather than entrepreneurial endeavor. This was the case of the "group of French Canadians" who "set up the Banque du Peuple, whose initial object was to serve their compatriots who had ostensibly been mistreated by the English banks" (*ESHQ*, 388). In *Lower Canada*, he reiterated this generalization concerning the petite bourgeoisie, adding some new and cutting comments. His condemnation of this middle-class group was consistently based on its refusal to compromise, thereby creating an ethnic split and destroying "efforts at building class solidarity" (*LC*, 179). The reader is left with the impression that in *Lower Canada* seigneurs and habitants had been pretty well pardoned for their misconduct, whereas the middle classes had attracted the jovian thunderbolts of a merciless critic. Perhaps this was an

emotional reaction to the rise of Quebec's sovereignty aspirations. However this may be, by shifting the odium from the
habitant to the petite bourgeoisie, Ouellet certainly appeared
to have moved to the left.

In *Lower Canada* the harshest criticism was directed toward
the middle classes, sometimes simply by the use of an exclamation mark, although this stylistic device tended to be edited
out of the English edition (cf. *Bas-Canada*, 417, and *LC*, 272).
Occasionally he accused the nationalists of barefaced double-
dealing. Not only were they misjudging the current of history
and ascendant capitalism by attempting to achieve "political
transformation without social revolution" (*LC*, 176, 182); they
were furthering class interests by "preventing" and "blocking"
modernization, the source of working-class well-being. True,
petit-bourgeois vision was always "obscured" by fear of the
English-speaking bourgeoisie, but the "image of the ideal seigneury as an instrument of national survival had only one
purpose, and that was to prevent the rural lower classes from
questioning an institution which served the interests of the
French-Canadian middle classes and, in particular, the leaders
of the *parti patriote*, that company of starry-eyed lovers of landed
property" (*LC*, 151). Ouellet's approach was now sociological
rather than psychological, as in the 1960s. This time the
nationalist debate was explained by "class interests" rather than
the "vulnerability" that continued to cause supposedly
unfounded concern (*LC*, 76). In the 1976 version, the Lower-
Canadian petite bourgeoisie deliberately "obscured the real
root of the French-Canadian problem, namely the old social
regime" from the rural population (*LC*, 76). Ouellet took it
upon himself to expose their duplicity, writing of "the evolution from nationalism in liberal and reformist guise [cf. *masque*
in *Bas-Canada*, 347] to a democratic and republican nationalism (dedicated, for all that, to the seigneurial regime and
French customary law)" (*LC*, 224). "Revolution in legal guise"
is what they were aiming for (*LC*, 282), and Patriote party
radicals were "anxious to denounce" Papineau, who would not
support abolition of the seigneurial system (*LC*, 325). By using
the familiar didactic methods of repetition and negation,
Ouellet hoped to convince his readers. The petite bourgeoisie

was "a class aspiring to power for itself, but on behalf of the 'nation' " (*LC*, 84); however, the party it controlled was not a party of the people, and had no desire for universal suffrage (*LC*, 212). The nationalism of "Papineau and his followers did not attempt to set the peasants and urban rural proletariat against the clergy and seigneurs," but it "anaesthetize[d] the social aspirations of the masses" (*LC*, 197). That a petit-bourgeois party did not represent the working class was hardly a revelation. Where Ouellet's argument really lacked coherence, however, was in asking us to imagine the rural and urban proletariat—lumberjacks and urban day laborers—pitted against groups with which it had no labor relations.

The Patriote party that grew out of the Canadian party was "hungry for patronage" (*Bas-Canada*, 387), while at the same time viewing the British bourgeoisie as "A minority spawned by political patronage" (*LC*, 249). Ouellet did not say whether the incumbent powers did in fact abuse patronage. The troubles of 1837 were a fruitless venture planned by incompetent leaders; indeed, he qualified the "revolutionary leadership" as "glaringly deficient" (*LC*, 326), effectively damning the political path taken by the middle classes, "obsédés par la question nationale" (*Bas-Canada*, 485; cf. *LC*, 324). He made no bones about the fact that "the rebellions of 1837-1838 were the culmination of a nationalist movement instigated and guided by and for the benefit of the French-Canadian middle classes" (*LC*, 323). The political elites fed on their fear of the supposedly dramatic and irresistible rise of English-speaking economic power. The rebellion was a popular uprising instigated by the middle class, a pointless undertaking for which the rebel leaders alone were responsible. Nowhere did he hint at provocation by the executive, military, or economic powers. The rebels' failure, he remarked, "can certainly not be laid to the crushing might of the British army, which itself was hardly a model of seasoned discipline" (*LC*, 326). If we want a more precise interpretation, we must consult early writers such as Gérard Filteau and Duncan McArthur, who revealed how extraordinarily unequal were the opposing forces, particularly at St. Eustache. Numerical strength was not the only factor, however. Even with insufficient training, an army was still an army, and had an initial advantage over a makeshift combat force.[39] But in any case, politico-military commentary was something of an aside in a work primarily devoted to socio-economic development. The basic elements in Ouellet's picture were class, class consciousness, and ideology. As a liberal historian, he conceded "a certain liberalism" to the petite bourgeoisie "in that they believed in such things as freedom of the press and education of the masses" (*LC*, 102); but in the main he condemned a form of political thought and action that he considered prejudicial to the "popular" classes. The petite bourgeoisie was censured for not allying itself with merchant capitalism, and accomplishing a bourgeois revolution through the abolition of social relationships founded on seigneurial ownership and land rents.

The Biographical Approach

There is a further aspect of Ouellet's work that conceals a subjective thrust, and this is the use of selective biographical detail to describe various key personalities. In Canada, as elsewhere, biography is a controversial historical genre, deplored by some for its so-called humanist emphasis—a polite way of criticizing it for being unscientific. The anti-biography camp favors a more systematic reading of history, by the use of theory and statistical reasoning to formulate general statements. Whether or not it actually achieves anything, quantitative analysis at least rids historians of their inferiority complex vis-à-vis the synchronic sciences. The "biographiles" maintain that their work is both an art and a science, comparable to psychological or psychoanalytical case studies. Scientists may claim to explain everything, but biography finds its ultimate justification in the recognition of individual freedom of choice.

Eminent Canadian historians have given biography credibility as a field of scholarly research. Donald Creighton and Maurice Careless demonstrated the genre's potential for the younger generation of writers. These and other biographers treated their subjects—mainly politicians—with the attention and sympathetic understanding that Henri Marrou considered one of the virtues of the art. Attitudes or behavior generally considered abnormal, such as Sir John A. Macdonald's alcoholism, Mackenzie King's spiritualism, or the neurotic excitation and schizophrenic withdrawal of Louis Riel, were dealt with leniently by writers like Creighton, Blair Neatby, George Stanley, and Thomas Flanagan. Ouellet, although a social group historian, made use of biographical techniques, and he can justifiably be compared to the Canadian writers just mentioned. People tend to forget that before publishing *Economic and Social History of Quebec* Ouellet gained considerable notoriety with his portrait of Louis-Joseph Papineau in *Julie Papineau, un cas de mélancholie et d'education janséniste*,[40] a biographical essay removed from circulation by court order. Legal entanglements would appear to have deprived us of a substantial Papineau biography.[41]

The sympathetic warmth between biographer and subject is felt in a work like Jean-Louis Roy's *Edouard-Raymond Fabre libraire et patriote canadien (1799-1854)*. With respectful discretion, he revealed the private life of this petit bourgeois, who sheltered and financed the *patriotes* right up to the most critical moments of 1837-1838. Without passing judgment on his protagonist, Roy disclosed the rationalizations and contradictions arising from the conflicting claims of family feeling, political involvement, and the business commitments of his publishing ventures. Fabre, for example, advised his own son not to enter the priesthood, and yet, although anticlerical, numbered the clergy among his best customers, despite their disloyal habit of bringing back books from their European travels and thus reducing his sales. Imbued with the spirit of the Enlightenment, he nevertheless imported a cultural product that consolidated conservatism and clerical power. Although a nationalist, he worked with English-language publishers, subordinating politics to business. We like Fabre because his biographer respected his "hero." Ouellet, on the contrary, tended to treat his subjects unsympathetically. Perhaps he may one day write with compassionate understanding of some great and successful entrepreneur. So far, however, his choice has fallen on nationalist leaders whose ideology he abhorred.

Who can forget Ouellet's 1960 version of Papineau? Unfit for action, preferring the comfort of his library, this armchair politician nevertheless convinced himself that he had a vocation, an inescapable mission, and should enter the public arena. Hypersensitive, inconsistent, proud, he grappled his way to the top of the party hierarchy, only to lead it into the cul-de-sac of rebellion. *Economic and Social History* revealed the Patriote party leader as having "a doctrinaire spirit" compounded by "an obstinacy which knew no limits" (*ESHQ*, 383). "The almost mythical and obsessive value...attached to political action" made him "avidly" seek "the possession of power." Opposed to the idea of "progress to replace the automatism of tradition," Papineau was touted as a die-hard conservative who refused to have anything to do with the bourgeoisie (*ESHQ*, 384). The Papineau of *Lower Canada* had not changed one iota, "offering himself as the sacrificial lamb on the altar of *la patrie*" (*LC*, 186), yet leading his supporters to the slaughter without having the courage to share their fate. Ouellet had transformed his psychological approach of the 1960s into a defensive, ideological critique.

In 1966, Ouellet had little to say about Pierre-Stanislas Bédard, although he attributed the 1810 political crisis to agricultural problems and to the "hypersensitivity" of "personalities like those of Craig and Bédard" (*ESHQ*, 205). In 1976, however, Bédard, Papineau's predecessor as leader of the nationalist party, became a main character in the historical drama.

Previous historians had projected a fairly favorable image of Bédard. Primarily, they showed that, as a nationalist party leader supported by the newspaper *Le Canadien*, he had virtually demanded responsible government. This in fact meant control of the executive branch, since the cabinet would have been made up of members of the majority in the assembly. The governor, unable to silence the demands and fearing popular sympathy for a politician whom he considered a demagogue, suspended freedom of the press and imprisoned Bédard, one of the owners of the paper.[42] Bédard was a successful politician; his constituents reelected him during his incarceration, placing Governor Craig in a highly awkward position.

The Canadian party leader was held for over a year. A clever tactician, he demanded trial by jury, which he presumed would clear him of all suspicion of treason or the seditious activities of which he stood accused. Craig, however, wanted him to ask pardon for a crime that Bédard, a political prisoner, felt he had not committed. Bédard was released unrepentant, much to the governor's confusion. He retired from politics and was named a judge in Trois-Rivières, reportedly taking with him an unpleasant reminder of his cell in the form of a disease from which he never recovered. Such is the version supplied by traditional historiography.[43]

In Ouellet's version, one soon realizes that "nationalist" predecessors misled their readers. He skimmed over the circumstances of Bédard's "retirement from public life" (*LC*, 85) to enumerate character defects and unedifying details of his private life, in order to provide fertile ground for discrediting his political actions. Bédard's marriage "was not a success" and "his contemporaries were not impressed by his physical presence" (*LC*, 84). "Introverted, inhibited, awkward," this timid man also displayed "ineptitude in handling his own affairs." "No doubt alcohol helped him overcome his social inadequacies," but "behind his inferiority complex" lay a sense of "superiority" (*LC*, 85). Like an able psychoanalyst, Ouellet drew his subject into admissions that gave the ring of authenticity to his description. For example, in 1814, almost four years after his release from prison, and by then a judge in Trois-Rivières, Bédard wrote to his confidant John Neilson about his low self-esteem:

I have not the talent to impress anyone.... I am in no way great or amusing...people take possession of the space around me; they trespass.... I am so small.... A man incapable of exercising the least authority,...of playing the husband, of being the master, in short a man incapable of playing the man's role with other men [*LC*, 84, 85.].

At the age of fifty-five, Bédard continually belittled himself, shaken by the painful memories connected with the end of his political career. He was depressed "to the point of feeling removed from the abode of the living" (*LC*, 85). He had already been in a bad way in his early forties when, in debt and without a livelihood, he confided to John Neilson that "they affect my illness to be a nervous illness, which is a polite way of saying that I am odd" (*LC*, 86). Having thus introduced us to this ninny, Ouellet finally moved on to discussion of his public life. If performance in private life were any guarantee of effective political action, we could not expect much of the Canadian party leader. One wonders whether the historian and jurist, Henri Brun, was misleading his readers when he described Bédard as both an able tactician and a remarkable political theorist.[44]

Ouellet stated in *Lower Canada* that Bédard was "intellectually...unquestionably the leader among his confrères of the professional class" (*LC*, 87). The man must have been a fairly able political theorist, since he had formulated a theory of responsible government that "had not yet even been formally defined in England" (*LC*, 90). However, while conceding that "the theory...took form in Bédard's mind," Ouellet hastened to add that "the Canadian party's adversaries quickly grasped the disastrous consequences" it implied regarding their control of key political appointments and the colonial economy (*LC*, 89, 90). "Implementation" of responsible government, a French-Canadian nationalist device, "was unthinkable in the circumstances" (*LC*, 90). It would in fact have led to Quebec independence, a goal that Ouellet opposed in the interests of the French-Canadians themselves, in order to protect them from "a minority which was using nationalism and liberalism for its own ends," since "professional men and lesser merchants would clearly have been the first to benefit from the changes his party was advocating" (*LC*, 88). The middle classes were therefore seeking to control patronage so as to corner civil service jobs. Here as elsewhere, Ouellet hammered home his point, asserting with convincing frequency that the petite bourgeoisie was working for class interests, and not for the masses that it claimed to be "liberating." His section on the rebellion ended on the same note, exposing middle-class double-dealing:

In the absence of vigorous direction from the elite, the popular elements might have taken control and pursued the cause toward their own objectives. If they did not it was because they were lacking a class consciousness of their own, the conservative nationalists having long made so much of the perils hanging over the entire "nation" and of the protection inherent in the seigneurial regime [*LC*, 327].

Ouellet's psychoanalysis of Bédard, Papineau, and the middle classes generally, was made possible by the extensive and varied qualitative source material available.[45] Ouellet felt he had evidence of "abnormal" behavior and attitudes derived from contemporary accounts. For example, although the interdependent Quebec and Ontario economies urgently needed improved means of communication to stimulate trade, the "elites" refused to grant funds, preferring an "isolationist" withdrawal into their traditional territory. Moreover, they suffered from a persecution complex revealed in public debate or confidential remarks, which showed their sense of being victims of discrimination. They had become detached from reality, Ouellet argued, and this accounted for their taking refuge in the mythical dream of maintaining outmoded institutions. Despite these psychological aberrations, the middle classes cleverly camouflaged their real interests by instigating an ideological debate on the national peril. Taken together, these attitudes and forms of behavior, as determined by Ouellet's psychological and sociological analysis, accounted for the major anomaly that occurred at the end of the period, to wit: the popular uprising was not an anti-fiscal revolt in the style of Boris Porchnev's French peasants of the seventeenth century.[46] In other words, the petit-bourgeois leaders had deflected the revolutionary potential of the lower classes toward a false target: the bourgeoisie.

Ouellet's successive *tableaux* of social minorities, either in power or aspiring to it, raise a number of questions about methods and sources. Nicole Gagnon pointed out in her review of *Bas-Canada* that Ouellet was "somewhat cavalier about the basic principles of historical criticism," as his portrait of Bédard amply proves. Generally speaking, Ouellet did not distinguish clearly between public discussion that was tactical, strategic, or ideological, and the very different nature of confidential remarks or writing, or of sources that had been kept private voluntarily since their inception. He responded indignantly to one of Bédard's political arguments as follows: the acceptance of responsible government "would imply a concentration of power in the hands of a French-Canadian middle class dedicated to the preservation of traditional heritage and opposed to capitalism and English-speaking immigration. And Bédard was preaching elimination of ethnic distinction!" (*LC*, 90.) Ouellet's exclamation mark does him no credit as a critical historian; rather, it is a sign of his subjective opposition and personal immersion in the stuggles of the early nineteenth century. The role of the historian was to ascertain Bédard's function, which was to provide an ideological statement of class rationale. The concept of ideology could then have been used for purposes of historical criticism. Ouellet, however, was not generally inclined to conceptualize. In her assessment of *Bas-Canada*, Nicole Gagnon emphasized his confusion of psychological and sociological concepts such as "perception," "representation," "ideology," that is, the kind of self-serving argument that disguises social class interests by identifying various social or political goals with the common good.

Ouellet's analysis of middle-class ideological reasoning was obscured by his frequent interpolations of value judgments, even though one still got a fairly clear idea of the drift of class debate. But every story has two sides. Where in this work do we find any mention of bourgeois class interests disguised by ideological discourse? Ouellet ignored this aspect of the question; and yet research in the English-language press of the period or in private business documents would have revealed the existence of plans and strategies on the part of those whom Ouellet so uncritically admired. One might well ask whether it is possible to consider bourgeois ideology without a strong subjective bias, either for or against. Furthermore, one must tread very carefully when evaluating traditional qualitative sources. Marc Bloch and Louis Gottschalk, in the light of research into experimental psychology, and more particularly into the psychology of personal and hearsay accounts, have warned historians against accepting rationalizations or statements made in good faith, which more refined critical methods would be likely to expose.[47] Personal accounts can at most reveal little more than highly subjective perceptions or depictions of reality. In the view of some Marxist critics,[48] when such individual accounts are used to characterize the perceptions or ideological statements of classes or groups, about the most one can do is to indicate the subjectivity of the groups in question.

A less critical view was expressed at the St. Cloud colloquium.[49] It was suggested that ideological debate could be used to indicate group subjectivity in much the same way that anthropologists use life stories to analyze actual experience. Such a suggestion is acceptable, on condition that the scholar limit himself to defining the history of class subjectivity, and not superimpose his own subjectivity on that of his sources. This was a serious defect in Ouellet's work, since it obscured the logic of class relationships and their corresponding "ideological" justification. Ouellet identified with the past to the point of assuming a participating role that interfered with his appreciation of what really happened. If, on the contrary, he had adhered to a dialectical analysis of group subjectivity, we could have had an excellent empirical study of class conflict.

V

Ideology and Quantitative Method

The Rural World of Fernand Ouellet

In *Les Canadiens après la conquête, 1759-1775* (Montreal: Fides, 1969), Michel Brunet attacked Fernand Ouellet's use of quantitative method in *Economic and Social History of Quebec*, issuing a warning to historians and readers "fascinated by the claims of quantitative history." The ebullient Montrealer observed that "too often they forget that great discoveries generally arise from the patient observation of a few dominant factors rather than the compiling of incongruous and undigested data. Columns of figures, graphs...and tables...may be a useful adjunct to a work of history, but they can never replace the historian, who must keep in mind all dimensions of collective activity" (p. 13). Brunet's book, categorized by Pierre Savard as part of the "stormy debate" surrounding the significance and consequences of the Conquest, rejected some of Ouellet's hypotheses. The criticism was possibly inopportune. Nevertheless, he maintained that some interpretations put forward in *Economic and Social History* were "farfetched," and that statistical reasoning "cannot replace the carefully thought out evaluation of the determining forces" shaping group destinies. Brunet reiterated his thesis that the Conquest caused the decline of the French-Canadian bourgeoisie, and that to deny it would be to opt for psychologism. In his opinion, the usefulness of a history of group attitudes in explaining and assessing business activity was doubtful (p. 109, n. 9).

Some of Brunet's footnotes read like a settling of accounts, questioning Ouellet's sincerity (p. 166, n. 4), or indulging in sarcasm: "Professor Ouellet may rest assured that no one will accuse him of partiality toward the French Canadians, since he reserves it entirely for the conquerors" (p. 171, n. 25). To the repeated accusation of treason was added that of being a "moralistic historian" (p. 209, n. 33). Ouellet's great error, Brunet felt, was to have misconstrued the extent to which Canadians under the French regime "possessed collective freedom and autonomy," which was lost in the course of the Seven Years' War (p. 284).

A more substantial refutation of Ouellet's work was Maurice Séguin's La "Nation canadienne" et l'agriculture, which, as mentioned in chapter 1, appeared in 1970 although originally written during the 1940s. His attempt at economic analysis, while somewhat naive, had the merit of providing a more solid ground for criticism. In one sense, Brunet's position was based on purely ideological assumptions.[1] Ouellet was well-advised to answer him on the grounds of method. To the accusation of "traitor" he replied that Brunet's work was "tainted with racism," and justified his own statistical reasoning as follows: "The quantitative method, totally dependent on the historian's exactitude, no doubt has its advantages; but it can also have its disadvantages, especially when used to support a purely ideological approach.... Both methods (quantitative and qualitative) demand exactitude and self-discipline."[2] At the time, historians were moving toward a general acceptance of the statistical approach to history, with événementielle or event-oriented history gradually giving way to the economic and social history of the masses. Brunet was in fact fighting a rearguard action.

The historian in search of total history finds himself in a difficult position. He has ample qualitative material with which to reconstruct the progress of the dominant classes and intermediate groups. However, when it comes to the diachronic analysis of the illiterate masses, that is, comprehending the underlying factors affecting their long-term development, he must look elsewhere for information. Synchronistic social sciences can use the interview as a means of exploring the lives of the silent majority, otherwise coded and classified by statistics-hungry researchers. Historians working in fields that predate the invention of sound recording do not share the advantages of present-day anthropologists and ethnologists, however. They find themselves up against an apparently inert mass, and are only too glad to uncover the rare expository work written from a rural or working-class viewpoint. Statistical analysis, therefore, offers one of the few available methods of understanding the lives of the majority of human beings. Such information has not passed through the prism of interpretation by the governing classes, but is based on indicative records—a source in which our "quantophrenic" mentality generally places a high degree of reliance.[3]

The problem with Ouellet's use of serial, quantitative methods was his profuse accompaniment of psycho-ethical discussion, particularly his moral portrait of the rural population. It is this portrait, as it appeared in *Economic and Social History* and *Lower Canada*, that I should like to outline before assessing his statistical spectrum of rural life. His discussion was mainly concerned with landowning agricultural producers. Vague references to a rural proletariat in the French edition of *Lower Canada* dealt with ill-defined groups (e.g. *Bas-Canada*, 185; cf. *LC*, 120). If he meant young men in search of land or jobs, these were not members of the proletariat, strictly speaking, but young vagrants forced to leave home because of lack of family resources. If he meant seasonal forest workers employed for felling and loading, these were indeed wage laborers. In any case, this small group of landless men represented a tiny proportion of all rural households, with or without servants.

In his 1966 work, Ouellet depicted the habitant as tied to routine and insensitive to the marketplace, a poor agricultural producer and a spendthrift, more interested in acquiring consumer goods than the equipment and skill needed to increase productivity. Rather like the clergy of the period, he decried the habitant's luxury-loving habits and improvident nature (although in the interest of increased productivity rather than moral salvation). These characteristics had been discussed early in his career, in a 1956 article.[4] Inherited from New France,[5] the "widespread taste for luxuries" was initiated by the presence of pedlars as middlemen (*ESHQ*, 7). These traveling salesmen "excite[d] the covetousness of the habitant" (*ESHQ*, 170). As villages developed, country storekeepers further encouraged the "lavish spending" that he held partly responsible for "the impoverishment of the agricultural class"; these expensive habits were apparently repressed with success after 1815, only to resurface in the 1840s (*ESHQ*, 463, 482).

Finally, the material considerations of everyday rural life were affected by the direct relationship between fluctuations in the forest industry and consumer spending. In *Lower Canada*, Ouellet wrote that for the years 1802-1812, "since part of the wealth generated [by lumber] found its way [through wages or other forms of income] into the hands of the population in general, it was also a major stimulant to...consumption.... Soon there was a sawmill in every parish that could claim a favourable location" (*LC*, 59). The role of the major bourgeois entrepreneurs engaged in the import-export trade was to create jobs and redistribute part of the profits, thus providing purchasing power. As long as the demand for lumber was high on British markets, this meant a rise in exports and consumption. Indeed, in 1976 Ouellet seemed fairly inclined to accept André Garon's concept of the consumer-habitant.[6] Since writing *Economic and Social History* ten years earlier, he had divested the habitant of the 1960s image of an improvident spendthrift with luxurious tastes, a waster of money and farmland. Why? Did Ouellet's general argument in favor of the benefits of capitalism seem inconsistent in the presence of this wasteful rustic? Perhaps. Ouellet wrote in 1966 that "the excessive textile imports" sometimes "encouraged the rural consumer to buy more than he needed" (*ESHQ*, 466-467). Whatever the reasons for his shift in attitude in *Lower Canada*, the bourgeoisie was clearly no longer suspected of encouraging wholesale self-indulgence. Habitants as farm producers did not always respond to the need for more productive methods, however (*LC*, 122). They resigned themselves to poor conditions in times of crisis, unmoved by the information campaigns conducted by agricultural societies, apathetic, and overcome by the pervading "resistance to change" (*LC*, 122, 123). But this time there were no gibes about a supposedly immoral lifestyle. Ouellet was too preoccupied with his own views to answer his critics concerning the existence of an agricultural crisis in the early nineteenth century. Instead, he directed his fire at Wallot and Paquet, whom he accused of having elaborated "farfetched" theses to show rural sensitivity to domestic market conditions (*Bas-Canada*, 191)—an accusation that has been tactfully softened in the English version (cf. *LC*, 119).

Hilda Neatby, in reviewing the original *Histoire économique et sociale du Québec*, admonished Ouellet sharply: "Quantitative history seems to be almost as provocative as qualitative."[7] She was referring to the polemical nature of the work, which trumpeted the virtues of a more accurate history, on the assumption that statistical reasoning had at last freed the discipline from the "impressionist" versions of earlier writers, blind to the subjectivity of their sources. Neatby was fairly clear about Ouellet's tendency to arrange statistics to corroborate his views.[8] Nicole Gagnon also drew attention to Ouellet's "almost fanatical respect" for quantitative demonstration in *Bas-Canada*. She warned readers that some tables were either puzzling or useless, and very often unsubstantiated. The tables, in addition to being badly placed and organized, had headings that were frequently misleading. Some series proved almost impossible to check.[9]

Ouellet's questionable passion for figures arose from his ultimate desire to discover the reasons for the 1837 uprising. If the rural population answered the call of the nationalist elites, it was not solely in response to a convincing ideological appeal. He wanted to show the existence of objective conditions creating discontent. He therefore discovered the existence of a crisis in agriculture accompanied by severe demographic pressures, these being two factors that combined to trigger the political crisis and armed insurrection. Ouellet backed up his highly dramatic picture of conditions preceding the political crisis (*LC*, 75, 76) with apparently objective, quantifiable information in his subsequent discussion of these two factors. At times, however, he compiled superficial results based on unreliable or insufficiently examined sources.

The spread and refinement of quantitative methods now make it possible to appreciate the unsubstantiated nature of

Ouellet's statistics. He had to rely mainly on arbitrary samplings from very incomplete series of data, and all too rarely advised the reader of their undependability. As economic historians have frequently remarked, it is very difficult to carry out quantitative studies for the early days of statistics or for preceding periods. As we shall see, in *Lower Canada* Ouellet relied too readily on contemporary statistics that called for close scrutiny. His cardinal sin, however, was to generalize continually from the particular—a methodologically indefensible form of reasoning for which Cameron Nish's *Bourgeois-Gentilhommes de la Nouvelle-France* (see chapter 3) was criticized, and which Ouellet himself condemned in Tulchinsky's study of early nineteenth-century businessmen.[10] Ouellet was far too concerned with *conjonctures*, that is, short-range economic changes, and not nearly enough with *structures* and institutions. For example, he failed to provide details such as the total number of seigneuries or parishes in Lower Canada. Furthermore, the reader would like to judge the relative importance of the various economic and social sectors on the basis of figures showing how many people belonged to the seigneurial class, their "ethnic" distribution, and extra-seigneurial occupations. Ouellet provides no classifcation of seigneuries by acreage, soil type, extent of settlement and development, or analogous categories. The institutional dimension of the seigneuries is just one aspect that he neglected, however. When Ouellet illustrated a point with statistics relating to a single parish, seigneurie, riding, or "significant" region, how was the reader to know whether there was consensus on whether certain criteria defined any one area as representative? He gave no indication of whether the figures reflected widespread or merely marginal activity in the community as a whole. Was payment of rent in kind the normal form of income for a given seigneury? Or was it the exception, listed by Ouellet because the source was readily accessible or satisfied both wish and intuition? Why choose fifty-three parishes in the districts of Quebec and Trois-Rivières to estimate the extent of demographic pressure in the mid-1820s? How many were dropped from the list, based on what criteria? Why was no parish shown from the District of Montreal, the most densely populated area of Lower Canada? Were almost two-thirds of the parishes in the territory eliminated at random? And yet the one-third shown was too large for a mere sample. The same lack of critical selection was visible in his use of parish priests' income statements—a further example, incidentally, of his vagueness in assigning sources.[11] Presumably, he drew some of his figures from the Montreal archdiocesan chancery registers in which revenue statements were periodically cumulated. Tithe records furnish similar information. With perseverance and a little luck, one may occasionally find a parish record that was fairly systematically kept; generally speaking, however, the series contain chronological and geographical gaps, and Ouellet frequently overestimated their usefulness. Ideally, tables should show the reader these gaps in period and region, followed by a critical evaluation of the source. Only then can it be used to indicate production levels. The same holds true for the use of parish population figures to indicate demographic pressures.

Demographic Pressures

In *Economic and Social History*, calculations based on contemporary census figures showed that between 1800 and the middle of the century, most parishes did not achieve the same growth rate as the overall French-speaking population in Quebec. Ouellet wrote: "As for the parishes founded between 1760 [French edition gives 1765] and 1844, they were first populated very quickly, subsequently reaching a level beyond which growth became very difficult, if not impossible. It is significant that after 1822 many of these parishes record a decline in population" (*ESHQ*, 354). Having buttressed his argument with a short table, he then expressed reservations as to the validity of his calculations, adding that "these figures...are only provisional assessments subject to revision through more thorough inquiries within each locality" (*ESHQ*, 355). In *Lower Canada*, demographic pressures were again estimated, with fresh calculations based on the same contemporary census figures. After carefully going over Ouellet's method, I cannot avoid the conclusion that he has greatly overestimated demographic pressures. How could he have arrived at such mistaken results? We shall see.

Ouellet's conclusions were based on the simple but ingenious method of taking the parish population figures in the 1790 census, and adding the annual difference between recorded births and deaths (the natural growth rate) until the 1822 census (or the 1825 census, if figures for the particular parish were not shown in 1822). If the figures in these last two censuses were less than would be expected from his calculations for each parish, he deduced that it was due to emigration.[12] If, on the other hand, the 1822 or 1825 census figures were greater than the natural growth rate would justify, he attributed the difference to immigration (*LC*, 143, 356, 357). The following illustration will give some idea of his method.

The 1790 census listed 991 persons for the parish of Cap St. Ignace in 1790, and 1,565 in 1822. However, 991 plus the annual natural growth rate between 1794 and 1822 should give a population of 2,032. The difference between this figure and the 1822 census figure therefore represents a minimum estimate for emigration, in the absence of records for the four years 1790, 1791, 1792, and 1793.

Before discussing the validity of this method, I should point out that transcription errors make some results doubtful at the outset. For example, the first two parishes listed are given thus:

Parish	1790	1822	Emigration
Kamouraska	1,706	1,492	1,234
and			
St. André		1,784	

The population of Kamouraska between 1820 and 1825 was in fact about 5,000. Ouellet probably copied the error from a secondary source, possibly Ivanhoe Caron, adding a further twist of his own. Caron's transcription reads as follows:[13]

St. André	1,492
Kamouraska	(blank space)

Ouellet presumably inserted "and" between the two place names, and transposed the 1822 figure of 1,492 inhabitants from St. André to Kamouraska. Furthermore, his 1822 figure for St. André (1,784) was in fact the 1825 census figure, although this last figure has been corrected in the English edition. The 1825 census also showed Kamouraska with 4,964 inhabitants,[14] and this was the figure that should have been used, since the 1822 figure was unavailable. Instead of a minimum *emigration* of 1,234 people between the end of the eighteenth century and the mid-1820s, therefore, what we now have is an *immigration*, since the natural growth rate could not account for the population tripling within twenty-five years.

As the pioneers of quantitative history have taught us, statistical sources must be thoroughly checked with the usual methods of historical criticism, just as qualitative sources must. Take Ernest Labrousse, for example, whose works were considered a model of method by Ouellet in *Economic and Social History*. This French historian took a critical look at value and volume series in *Esquisse du mouvement des prix et des revenus en France au XVIII siècle* (Paris: Dalloz, 1933). In *La Crise de l'économie française à la fin de l'Ancien régime et au début de la Révolution* (Paris: PUF., 1944), 1:121 ff., he outlined the preparation and checking of statistics, setting forth the basic method of empirical research into pre-industrial socio-economies, still valid today. His works stressed how essential it was in quantitative history to test sources by cross-checking for conformity or consistency, depending on the origin of the source. Until this has been done, there is no hope of establishing the relative importance of data or the credibility of mere estimates for bygone eras. Cross-checking would clearly have saved Ouellet from a serious error regarding the Kamouraska population; if it only numbered 1,492 inhabitants in 1822, how could he account for the 256 births, 35 marriages, and 110 burials registered that year in relation to previous figures? Unless the parish was peopled by rabbits, not human beings... This was not the only transcription error: Ouellet gave the 1825 census figure for St. Pierre de Montmagny as 738 (actually the Berthier figure) instead of 1,124, and localities such as Nicolet need to be cross-checked.

Of course, errors in transcription were not the main reason for Ouellet's overestimation of demographic pressures. Despite his statement that "thus there was considerable movement" after 1800 (*LC*, 144), really severe pressures did not occur as early as he placed them. In order to appreciate where his argument went wrong, we have to understand the basic principles of method in serial history.[15]

Any series of statistics, whether chronological or geographic, should be uniform. A price series should show wholesale, middleman, or retail figures, but not a mixture of categories. Each price should be based on identical quantitative and qualitative units. Ideally, prices quoted should be from the same region, or else allowance should be made for regional variations. Aggregates of regional series make it possible to calculate national averages. When dealing with food prices it is essential to set guidelines for determining an annual price that levels out seasonal fluctuations, that is, a price per crop year based on the yearly average of quoted monthly prices of foodstuffs. In examining the economies of an earlier day, it is often difficult to eliminate seasonal fluctuations, although these do have their uses in short-term analysis. Frequently, a researcher will find only one or two pre-harvest prices for a given year, whereas the next year provides a fine crop of post-harvest figures. In practice so many variations occur that an accurate, perfectly uniform series is virtually impossible. Such are the working principles enunciated by Labrousse. It is to be hoped that Ouellet will follow his example and tell us some day how he prepared his price tables, instead of simply asking the reader to believe they are accurate. Although he admitted in *Economic and Social History* that some of his chronological series had gaps, he should have provided his readers with more information about monthly and regional fluctuations.

In an article published jointly with Jean Hamelin and Richard Chabot,[16] Ouellet challenged the soundness of Wallot and Paquet's price series for the turn of the nineteenth century. Despite repeated assurances, however, he does not succeed in convincing us that the "soundness" of his own tables "is beyond question" (p. 87). Readers should know the monthly distribution and provenance of each price, otherwise it would simply be an act of faith to accept the annual averages. Even without such a stringent requirement—and perhaps I am being overly strict—I find his general statements far from acceptable. The article says that sale prices for religious orders "are generally retail rather than wholesale or middleman prices," whereas the market prices are usually middleman and not, as Wallot and Paquet state, "retail prices" (pp. 90ff.). Hamelin, however, in *Economie et société en Nouvelle-France*, wrote that the book-keeping of religious institutions did not necessarily show retail prices, and that "the social status of the buyer can also distort prices. Some convent bursars were touched by their clients' poverty and reduced prices accordingly" (p. 15). In rural areas, Ouellet used the auction sales figures for the Quête de l'En-fant Jésus as retail prices. However, as anthropological and ethnological studies have shown, the fair market price was often exceeded at Quête auctions by buyers who sought pres-tige or wanted to show their wealth. Ouellet himself supplied a good example of how socio-psychological mechanisms inflate prices under such circumstances.[17] The sale of pews by auction was a perfect illustration of the unrealistic nature of prices at auctions for the church's benefit.

Quantitative volume tables present their own difficulties, although less complex, especially because equivalences of weights or measures are not needed. The rule of uniformity still applies, nonetheless, since comparisons in time and space would otherwise be meaningless. Take parish populations, for example. Ouellet established several chronological series based on the 1790, 1822, 1825, 1831, and 1842 censuses, in order to show an increase or decrease in each locality. As we saw when correcting the Kamouraska figure, this locality expe-rienced considerable demographic growth between 1790 and the mid-1820s. If Ouellet had included the next five years in his table, we would have seen a 30 percent drop (4,964 inhab-itants in 1825, 3,213 in 1831). What happened? Emigration was unlikely, or at least would not be enough in so short a time to account for a marked change unless some catastrophe had occurred. The drop was essentially due to the creation of St. Pascal on the southern boundary of the mother parish. To compare census figures between 1825 and 1831 would there-fore be totally unrealistic and contrary to the basic rule of uniformity. The best Quebec amateur historians have avoided this kind of pitfall,[18] whereas Ouellet imprudently charged ahead, perhaps only too delighted to discover a dramatic demographic crisis equal to his "spectacular" agricultural crisis. These must, he felt, be the reasons for the political crises of the time. To his way of thinking, popular unrest at the end of the eighteenth century and the political crises of 1810 and 1837 could only be explained by economic or demographic imbalance.

Among the parishes listed in the *Lower Canada* tables (356 ff.), several were subdivided between 1790 and 1822. If the 1822 or 1825 census did not show the figure expected (that is, the sum of the 1790 figure and the annual differences in births and deaths), it did not necessarily follow that the inhabitants had moved away—at least, not at the rate presumed by Ouellet. For example, the Charlesbourg of 1790, with 1,854 registered inhabitants, had different boundaries from the Charlesbourg of 1825, when the population numbered 1,417. Despite this, Ouellet concluded that over 1,000 people had moved away. Yet according to the historian Joseph Trudelle, in the autumn of 1796 Charlesbourg "gave birth to St. Ambroise" de la Jeune Lorette. Trudelle stated clearly in his monograph that St. Ambroise was composed "uniquely of Charlesbourg residents," a comment that would have to be verified in a systematic study of parish boundary changes.[19] For purposes of this discussion, however, the reader need only bear in mind that Ouellet, although perhaps unaware of doing so, in some instances more or less imagined the existence of demographic pressures, Charlesbourg being an extreme case. Incidentally, it happened to be the native parish of the Canadian party's first leader. Ouellet wrote of Pierre Bédard's birthplace: "In 1794 many parishes were already in a state of crisis. In Charlesbourg, for instance, the population dropped from 1,998 in 1784 to 1,854 in 1790 and to 1,417 in 1825, despite 1,354 births and only 735 deaths between 1794 and 1821, indicating demographic pressures and emigration" (*LC*, 47).

The first question to ask is whether this drop of over 10 percent between 1784 and 1790 was not due to error or some variable, such as the season at which each census was carried out. Were the Hurons of Lorette included? In both? Furthermore, until further information, we must assume that the drop in population between 1790 and 1822 was basically caused by the creation of St. Ambroise.[20] This was no minor amputation, since the population of St. Ambroise in 1825 was greater than Charlesbourg (1,512 as against 1,417). At the time of its formation, the new parish absorbed a considerable number of people along with its territory, as shown by figures such as 37 births and 34 deaths in 1795, 50 births and 24 deaths in 1796, and so on. The Charlesbourg curé registered 70 births and 24 deaths in 1794, and 47 births and 29 deaths in 1795. Obviously, one should not rely too heavily on such figures, as they have yet to be tested in a variety of future studies. Moreover, perhaps not all records of civil status for a given parish include parish members only. For the moment, however, suffice it to say that Ouellet's assumption that the population decreased stands on somewhat shaky ground. Why pick Charlesbourg as an example of early demographic pressure, in any case? Perhaps it is one of his characteristic methods of explaining a political phenomenon.

In the mid-1790s, the government adopted legislation to raise a militia, a levy that the rural population detested, especially since it had not been required since the French regime. Sporadic popular resistance to this initiative took place all over the countryside. Occasionally, discontent gave rise to violence. Charlesbourg probably offered the most spectacular resistance, with popular anger reaching a state of what can justifiably be called revolt and near riot. People gathered to prevent the drawing of lots for the militia levy. Historian Thomas Chapais stated that "over three hundred men of this parish and of Jeune Lorette (recently separated from Charlesbourg), armed with guns, pitchforks, hunting knives, crocks, and flails, patrolled for several days and nights, for fear of being enlisted," and that the resistance was put down by the arrest of two ringleaders.[21]

If we are to draw a legitimate comparison between census figures for the end of the eighteenth century and the 1820s, geographical criteria must apply, not only for Charlesbourg, but for all the parishes affected by boundary changes. Several of the localities in Ouellet's *Lower Canada* list had large portions removed. Rivière du Loup (Louiseville) boundaries were moved to create St. Léon in 1802, for example, with a population of 1,680 by 1825,[22] more than half the number of the former Louiseville (3,526). Whether 872 inhabitants moved away from Louiseville, as Ouellet stated, is open to question. St. Grégoire de Nicolet, founded in the same year as St. Léon, started off with 1,757 inhabitants.[23] By 1825 the parish, an offshoot of Bécancour, numbered 2,780.[24] St. Stanislas, where the parish register began in 1808, took territory from Ste. Anne de la Pérade and Ste. Geneviève de Batiscan. There are other instances, but it is obvious that in order to compare population figures given in different censuses, the geographical frame of reference must be uniform. There is an enormous amount of work to be done in this area, both by historians and geographers. Until such time, however, there can be no reliable comprehensive analysis.

The extent of Ouellet's errors in reckoning can be seen in his treatment of St. Eustache des Deux Montagnes, an area much favored by him, it being one of the centers of the 1837 uprising. One of the common features of the history of boundary changes was the subsequent, partial recovery of lost territory, or occasionally the acquisition of new territory and population from neighboring parishes when a portion was lost. The St. Eustache region, where political violence broke out at the end of the 1830s, was a typical example. Ouellet looked at demographic pressure between 1822 and 1842, and gave the following table for regional population growth (*LC*, 359):

Population Change, St. Eustache Area, 1790-1842

	1790	1822	1825	1831	1842
Ste. Scholastique	—	—	2,684	3,769	3,683
St. Benoît	—	5,609	4,115	4,431	3,010
St. Eustache	2,385	4,476	4,833	4,830	3,195
St. Hermas	—	—	—	—	1,382
Total	2,385	10,085	11,632	13,030	11,270

As was so often the case, Ouellet's remarks about this table were not clear, juxtaposing parish and region in the same paragraph. The reader who wished to reconstruct his method rather than take his findings for granted had difficulty. The significant point, however, is that Ouellet used this table to demonstrate emigration: "In the region of St. Eustache, to which there was a considerable influx for a time after 1790, a point of stagnation was reached by 1822; thereafter, despite much subdivision, there was an excess which drifted away" (*LC*, 156). In *Bas-Canada* (243), "despite much subdivision" is omitted. The next sentences point out that despite emigration, farm units continued to be divided into smaller portions of land.

A proper understanding of the demographic changes in the area can only be had by including other parishes in Ouellet's list. I have drawn up an amended list, giving fairly uniform geographical references, and showing the year in which parish registers were begun, in order to give a clearer idea of regional population growth.

Changes in the St. Eustache Region
(in the order given by Ouellet)

Parish	Registers Opened
Ste. Scholastique	1825
St. Benoît	1799
St. Eustache	1769
St. Hermas	1837
St. Colomban	1837 (not listed by Ouellet)
St. Augustin	1838 (not listed by Ouellet)

Let us now look at the boundary changes that occurred in this region between 1790 and 1842.[25]

St. Benoît, where the parish register began in 1799, was originally part of St. Eustache. It in turn lost land with the successive creation of Ste. Scholastique (1825), St. Hermas (1837), and St. Augustin (1838). We know that the new parish of St. Hermas absorbed two concession tracts from St. Benoît: St. Pierre (pop. 679 in 1825), and St. Hyacinthe (pop. 274 in 1825). Along with partition went annexation of land from other parishes. For example, the St. Joachim concession in the St. Benoît parish requested annexation to Ste. Scholastique, which took place in 1831. The St. Hyacinthe concession asked to be annexed to the same parish in 1818, but this request was refused and the concession later became part of the new St.

Hermas parish. A systematic study would probably show that new parishes not only acquired land from the mother parish, but from other localities as well. Ste. Scholastique (1825) lost land in the formation of St. Colomban, which also took in part of St. Jérôme. The latter had been a missionary offshoot of Ste. Anne des Plaines since 1832, and acquired its first resident priest in 1837. As a further complication, St. Augustin (1838) was not simply a part of St. Benoît, for a local history of Ste. Scholastique stated that, "In 1838, part of Des Anges et des Saints (pop. about 400) in the Ste. Scholastique concession went to St. Augustin."[26]

We now have a fair idea of the numerous boundary changes that occurred in various periods and localities. Ouellet was unaware of them, and therefore did not understand the significance of the information on which he based his discussion. Below is my reconstructed table for the St. Eustache region (in reality the seigneurie of Rivière du Chêne or Mille-Iles), including the parishes of St. Augustin and St. Colomban, with an estimate of parish populations made in the mid-1830s by the diocese of Quebec and published by the legislative assembly in 1836:[27]

Changes in Parish Populations for the St. Eustache Region
based on census figures

Parishes	1790	1822	1825	1831	1836	1842
Ste. Scholastique (1825)	—	—	2,684	3,769	4,395	3,683
St. Benoît (1799)	—	5,609	4,115	4,431	5,247	3,010
St. Eustache (1769)	2,385	4,476	4,833[28]	4,830[29]	5,710	3,195
St. Hermas (1837)	—	—	—	—	—	1,382
Total (given by Ouellet as 1842 regional total)						11,270
St. Colomban (1837)	—	—	—	—	673	(?)836
St. Augustin (1838)	—	—	—	—	—	2,080[30]
Total	2,385	10,085	11,632	13,030	16,025	14,186

This gives a far more accurate idea of changes in the region than Ouellet's table. To establish truly uniform geographical references, however, each figure should be checked out. It may well be that the population of the region actually increased, as calculations by Serge Courville seem to indicate,[31] although for the purposes of this discussion I will assume that the figures given here are fairly reliable. The drop in the St. Benoît population between 1822 (5,609) and 1823 (4,115) was probably due mainly to the creation of Ste. Scholastique, which by the mid-1820s had 2,684 inhabitants. The total population of the four parishes in Ouellet's table rose from 10,085 to 11,632 between 1822 and 1825. Between 1831 and 1842 the agglomerate population of Ste. Scholastique, St. Benoît, and St. Eustache decreased by about 30 per cent (13,030 to 9,888), which very likely accounted for Ouellet's comment that "a point of stagnation was reached by 1822; thereafter...there was an excess which drifted away" (*LC*, 156). But part of St. Benoît was taken to form St. Hermas (pop. 1,382 in 1842), and this accounts for much of the apparent population drop in St. Benoît in 1842. People had not actually moved away, therefore, and the extent of demographic pressure in the region was not nearly so great as Ouellet claimed.

Ste. Scholastique also suffered a "technical" drop in population with the formation of St. Colomban (pop. 673 in 1836), and a further drop as the result of at least two concessions (392 inhabitants) being taken for part of the new parish of St. Augustin in 1838. Since the population of Ste. Scholastique remained the same between 1831 (3,769) and 1842 (3,683), despite the fact that its area decreased, its growth was presumably normal. This could only be confirmed, however, if we knew whether the 1831 census took into account the transfer of the St. Joachim concession from St. Benoît to Ste. Scholastique that same year.

We are left with the "mystery" of St. Eustache, where the population dropped from 4,830 inhabitants in 1831 to 3,195 in 1842. No doubt the drop was partly the result of deaths and departures caused by the rebellion. Canadian government investigators wrote at the end of the 1840s that "the emigration began mainly after the insurrections of 1837 and 1838, and was strictly limited to the District of Montreal."[32] Adam Shortt probably got his estimate of early emigration in Lower Canada from this source when writing that "for the first time a very considerable number of French Canadians, chiefly from the districts involved in the Rebellion" left the country for the United States.[33] In *Le Feu de la Rivière du Chêne* (St. Jérôme, 1937, p. 219), Emile Dubois put the number of exiles resulting from the armed uprising at 400. Gérard Filteau estimated that between thirty to seventy patriots died in the fighting (*Histoire des patriotes*, L'Aurore, 1975, p. 366). A further 120 prisoners should be added to the unknown number of "voluntary" emigrants. Those who left for good did so not only because of repression, but because of serious material losses. "The church as well as the presbytery, the convent, the seigneurial manor, and over sixty dwellings... went up in smoke on the evening of December 14, 1837," according to another source.[34] Even so, the rebellion cannot explain a drop of 34 percent between 1831 and 1842, or of a hefty 44 percent between 1836 and the latter date, and boundary changes remain the most likely other cause of sudden fluctuations in population before 1842. C.-E. Deschamps wrote that the parish of St. Augustin (1838) was formed from the "concessions or *côtes* of Petit Chicot, des Anges north and south, of St. Henri, of St. Augustin, St. Louis des Bouchards, part of the côte St. Louis des Corbeils and part of the Petit Brulé, all from the parish of St. Eustache."[35] Three concessions from Ste. Scholastique, and two from Ste. Thérèse de Blainville, were also added to the new parish. Between 1825 and 1842 an estimated 1,000 people from the St. Eustache area became part of St. Augustin between census-takings. Clearly, then, estimates of parish populations drawn from the various censuses do not furnish adequate information about population movement.

Ouellet ignored the extent and number of boundary changes partly because he did not understand the bishop's reasons for subdividing parishes. How and why was this done? Boundaries shifted frequently, judging from the diocesan correspondence dealing with the annual distribution of appointments. The area of a parish served by one priest, occasionally with the help of a curate, depended on the number of settlers and how much land was cleared. When enough settlers were living too far from the parish church and felt they could afford to form another parish, they submitted a request to the diocese, which sent an investigator—usually a vicar-general—to see whether a clear majority of freeholders favored the project.

The bishop's emissary had to make sure that the population as a whole could support a priest and eventually underwrite the cost of building a church, even if petitioners initially were only asking for a resident priest officiating in a modest chapel, with one floor being used for living quarters. The bishop's answer was based on both human resources and the likelihood of raising enough tithes. If the total crop yield (the legal tithe was 3.84 percent of the gross) appeared unlikely to support a priest, the bishop would sometimes insist that the future parishioners sign a contract agreeing to provide a minimum income for the first incumbent. Before naming a priest, however, the bishop compiled a dossier on whether the parishioners had the actual material resources to provide a priest with a livelihood and living quarters, as well as a parish church and a cemetery. The extraordinary and considerable expense of buying or constructing buildings was underwritten by special taxes called *répartitions légales* (legal assessments), unless parishioners wished to adopt a scheme of voluntary contributions. Such contributions were occasionally complemented by a gift of land from some prominent figure. Current expenses were paid out of the ordinary receipts of the parish council (collection, pew rent, and a portion of the fees charged for acts of civil status such as certificates of baptism, marriage, and burial). Building costs were a heavy burden for newly-formed parishes, however. Compared to members of long-established parishes, those in a new parish were subject to double taxation. Parish boundary changes can only be understood in the light of such institutional details. It is even possible that this carving up of parishes may have caused popular unrest. We can well imagine the discussion over where to build the new church that would have to be paid for by both petitioners and those who opposed the project. The possible sources of conflict over such questions were many, and offered causes for unrest that were as important as "demographic pressures" or an "agricultural crisis."

The bishop made his parish appointments in the light of available personnel. A populous parish might need a curate, particularly if the parish priest were serving two or even three churches, or were ill. Because of lack of personnel at this period, old and ailing priests sometimes had to stay in harness until they died. If a parish were too small or deserved "punishment," the resident priest was sometimes removed. The loss of a priest through death meant delays in his replacement. The suspension of a priest for misconduct might mean a temporary setback in setting up a permanent parish. In general, because of the gap between population growth and the number of priests available, the least unforeseen event could affect parish organization and delay the formation of new parishes. In a word, the size and number of parishes depended on supply as well as demand. Usually, a former curate was first appointed to a new parish created through subdivision. Such a post obviously needed a young man, since it was poorly paid and sometimes isolated. The priest in the neighboring mother parish might have opposed the subdivision because it meant reduced income, although less work. When, however, a young priest was available and the faithful were willing to accept him, the bishop was inclined to deprive an experienced curé of part of his resources.

All this suggests the need for a dialectic approach to demographic and territorial changes, as well as a diachronic analysis of the available religious personnel in relation to the number of parishes. To state that each average parish in the 1820s had a priest, as Ouellet did, is not very enlightening, since it gives the impression that there were enough priests to go around. To begin with, the difference in the relative number of priests in urban and rural areas should be taken into account. The towns were far better served; furthermore, a considerable portion of those priests available for rural parish duties actually worked in rural colleges. Between 1800 and the rebellion years, the number of priests in the province rose from under 150 to over 300, and the number of parishes from 120 to over 200. The relative number of teaching priests was increased by the creation of six rural colleges between 1803 and the mid-1830s at Nicolet, St. Hyacinthe, Ste. Thérèse, Ste. Anne de la Pocatière, Chambly, and Assomption. In 1831, 160 parish priests and 42 curates were working in 183 parishes. Forty-three worked in hospitals or seminary-colleges. These colleges did in fact provide many recruits to the priesthood drawn from habitant families, but the results only began to be felt after the rebellion. The fact that parishes more than doubled in number between 1840 and 1867 must be attributed to the increase in clerical personnel.[37] Until we have more information, therefore, we must assume that the creation of a new parish normally implied the cutting up of old ones. The formation of a parish such as Ste. Eulalie before settlers actually arrived seems to have been the exception.[38] Such rare initiatives apart, this is why changes in parish populations offer, at best, a less than perfect gauge of demographic growth. Moreover, changes in parish boundaries, or merely the temporary joining of two parishes under a single priest, depended largely on how the bishop chose to manage his resources.[39]

Demographic pressures resulting in a rural exodus probably occurred far later than Ouellet supposed. He himself quoted contemporary evidence supporting this view in *Economic and Social History*. People were "compelled...to go to the United States...because of improper conduct,...to get away from apparently overly strict parents...or to escape their creditors," wrote Romuald Trudeau, a Montreal petit bourgeois, in the mid-1820s (*ESHQ*, 355). There might have been other motives for temporary or permanent departures, such as marrying without parents' approval. Debt and the lure of wages might also have influenced migration. In any case, there is no evidence of a marked and permanent migration before 1830, even in the Montreal region.[40] Ouellet also cited an 1836 comment in *La Minerve*, to the effect that French Canadians "are starting to emigrate" (*ESHQ*, 356). The date at which demographic pressures began to affect rural Quebec needs to be reconsidered, therefore, as does the period of agricultural difficulties. For the moment, however, it seems reasonable to assume that Ouellet exaggerated the seriousness of these problems, and that behind his superficially imposing scientific apparatus lay a subjective interpretation opposed to "nationalism." After all, he purported to explain the political crisis of 1810. Yet, rather than seeing it as the result of genuine cultural and political demands, or of the opposition between bourgeoisie and petite bourgeoisie, he preferred to fall back on the comfortable theory that men's acts are solely governed by material concerns. Current research supports the view that emigration to the United States, which was the eventual consequence of demographic pressure, actually started during the 1830s. The fact that the rates of births, marriages, and deaths showed no lasting changes seems to indicate that demographic pressures were not severe. Since birth and marriage rates remained steady, there must have been a fairly good balance between the population and its land or other resources. The abundance and availability of habitable land in this new country removed the threat of dangerous overpopulation such as pre-revolutionary France had known. In the ages of enlightenment and revolution, a teeming world was a phenomenon of Europe, not North America.

Ouellet's initial study of population changes on the Ile d'Orléans may have led him to generalize for the whole of inhabited Lower Canada. He gave a table for population growth on the Ile (*LC*, 355), just before his table listing some fifty parishes in the districts of Quebec and Trois-Rivières. The amount of available land on the island was limited in this case. Nevertheless, in his chapter on demographic pressures in the French edition, he stated categorically that "in general, the demographic situation seemed no less explosive than the economic" (*Bas-Canada*, 242). Yet, as we have seen, the growth rate and, in particular, the population density on seigneurial land were not as dramatic as Ouellet made out.

I would now like to turn to Ouellet's "agricultural crisis," in which "wheat production tended increasingly to fall behind a burgeoning population growth" (*LC*, 117), a discrepancy described in the French edition as "spectacular" (*Bas-Canada*, 175). Possibly this was another exaggeration, reflecting an intuitive explanation of a political crisis through dramatization of the material condition of the rural population.

The "Agricultural Crisis"

In *Lower Canada*, Ouellet questioned the findings of Wallot and Paquet, maintaining that their "price index increase...tells us nothing of the change in wheat production or peasant [i.e., rural] standard of living" (*LC*, 119), and that "the evidence in fact is contrary to the contentions of Professors Wallot and Paquet" (*LC*, 118). Their report of an "agricultural crisis" later than 1802 led Ouellet to seek further "evidence." However, since the publication of the work of Serge Courville, John McCallum, and Marvin McInnis,[41] it is difficult to believe in an early and widespread crisis of the catastrophic proportions described by him in both his 1966 and 1976 works.

Ouellet emphasized that "the average habitant was invariably vulnerable" (*LC*, 125) to the "convergent ill winds of falling agricultural production and a general decline in prices" (*LC*, 117). The French edition talked of the "violence" of fluctuations in wheat production (*Bas-Canada*, 179). He made these fairly exaggerated and dramatic statements in a relatively conscious effort to "uncover" the "basic" causes of the 1837 rebellion. He could not prevent his subjective involvement in the narrative, and being aware of the eventual outcome he unwittingly foreshadowed the tragedy in his discussion. The political crisis of 1810 was thus a sort of dress rehearsal for 1837; there must have been preceding economic unrest, he felt, and 1802 was as good a year as any to begin looking for it.

Research to date indicates that it was during the 1830s that falling agricultural production reached critical proportions, mainly as a result of climatic conditions and blight. Farmers may have become involved in other activities at the beginning of the century, but, as André Garon has pointed out, this was in response to a labor market generated by the development of lumbering.[42] Normand Séguin put forward the concept of an economy based on agriculture and lumbering.[43] This economy reflected the diversified occupations of the working population in newly settled areas, where the limited requirements of subsistence farming "liberated" people during the off season. This type of economy increased markedly in certain parts of Lower Canada, once protective tariffs offered investors the guarantee of Great Britain as a permanent client for Canadian exporters. Future research may show that whenever and wherever a high degree of subdivision of inherited farmland occurred, it was one of the many consequences of forest development in areas where agriculture was not the main occupation.[44] St. Eustache is an example. In such areas, a farmer-lumberjack needed less land for cultivating mixed food crops. Although Ouellet spoke of the period as one of agricultural crisis, commercial agriculture with apparently high yields was being practised along the St. Lawrence South Shore. Farming may indeed have been a productive occupation in well-cleared areas. This and other aspects of the agricultural question certainly bear looking into, with particular attention to environmental features and the variation in potential resources from one region to another. Anyone familiar with Quebec's geography would hardly be surprised that investors chose the St. Lawrence Valley as a source of wood supply for the British Empire: the network of rivers running at right angles into the St. Lawrence provided abundant water transportation for lumber. Being buoyant, it could simply be floated to cargo ports, thereby keeping costs competitive, irrespective of distance, in comparison with the heavily taxed lumber from the European Atlantic regions. As soil along the St. Lawrence lowlands became relatively exhausted, the cost of producing wheat increased. Lumber was therefore looked to as a substitute staple in the eastern end of the commercial empire of the St. Lawrence. In other words, falling crop yields (and these need to be reevaluated according to regional fluctuations) were only one of several factors influencing the decisions made by capital investors. Ouellet apparently forgot that the habitant was not part of the decision-making process in the Quebec economy. Numerous studies have shown that Quebec farming practices were in no way unusual in North America. I refer particularly to an essay by Jacques Boucher, which merits more attention than it has received heretofore.[45] Comparative history makes it clear that the type of farming carried out in Quebec was no more "backward" than elsewhere in the north-eastern Atlantic region.

Commercial agriculture aimed at the Quebec and imperial markets developed in Ontario because of its highly productive virgin soil and milder climate. By the same token, capital investors naturally passed over Ontario for lumbering development, in the early days at any rate, because of production costs. Ouellet took exception to the fact that Quebec depended on

Ontario for food produce (*LC*, 120). But considering the market economy that was gradually being built up, Ontario was a logical choice, since production costs were lower west of Quebec, and consumers got their goods at the best price. The cost-effective rationale also governed the choice of Quebec for forest development, a decision that was further influenced by the geographical features and the available manpower. Quebec produced young men at a great rate, as we know, and population growth meant finding new means of subsistence. The fur trade had made rural men familiar with a territory in which they could now find new resources. The creation of a proletariat was further assisted by dazzling the rural consumer with the abundance, variety, and novelty of British industrial goods. History repeats itself with a strange irony, for the fur trade had been similarly built up by whetting the appetites of the Amerindians with consumer goods.

Once the agricultural yield in the St. Lawrence lowlands had diminished, the requirements of a system based on profitable returns made it necessary to switch from growing grain for market to subsistence farming, mixed with hog and sheep raising, these animals being willing to eat almost anything. Nothing was more predictable, in fact. Susbistence farming actually went very well with intensive lumbering, since it guaranteed a family's daily bread and could keep the wage level down. This in turn could lower the many production costs involved in felling, floating, squaring, and loading the lumber aboard ships at Quebec City. It is hardly fair to blame the farmers for their incompetence in failing to change production methods, thereby causing a drop in farm activity (*LC*, 120). After all, they had no say in the market, and it was the market that decided such matters in the light of relative costs in various sectors of production.

Ouellet, along with his critics and commentators, concentrated too much on the social and economic aspects of one sector—agriculture—instead of discussing the relationships between the different sectors. He should have focused on the development of crops and livestock production in relation to lumbering and the equally lucrative import trade. Here again Quebec, with its far larger population, offered a much bigger consumer market than Ontario. If the farmers' conservative attitude caused the alleged wheat crisis, why was wheat production so high in the South Shore parishes along the St. Lawrence east of Quebec City? The answer is that the local Quebec City market stimulated producers to meet the demand. A parish like L'Islet did not merely "resist" the "collapse" in wheat. Joseph Bouchette, the official surveyor, wrote in 1815 from Kamouraska that "wheat and all varieties of grain almost always yield abundant crops.... This seigneurie has the best dairies in the province, and sends a continual and large supply of butter to Quebec, where it is preferred above all others."[46] Bouchette made virtually the same remark about the neighboring parish of Rivière Ouelle. There was no "structural" or organizational crisis to be seen in these parts, except for poor crops due to unforeseen bad weather or blight, as in the 1830s. On the other hand, Bouchette commented on how much lumbering he observed in touring the province. Although he gave no figures on workers, he noted the number of sawmills. The Lotbinière seigneury had six, in addition to five potash factories, even though only one-eighth of the seigneury was under cultivation. Vaudreuil had four; here, too, there was still relatively little farming because not enough land was cleared, possibly due to a lack of demand. There were three sawmills at St. Michel de Bellechasse and several at St. Vallier and St. Thomas de Montmagny. He saw others at St. Jean Port Joli, St. Roch des Aulnaies, Louiseville, Yamachiche, Nicolet, Terrebonne, Boucherville, Contrecoeur, Beloeil, St. Hyacinthe, Lachenaie, St. Sulpice, Lavaltrie, and elsewhere. Clearly, by the early nineteenth century lumbering had become more than just a way for farmers to earn extra money. Ouellet agreed with the stand taken by agricultural societies against clear-felling (*LC*, 122), an activity no doubt associated with the growing lumber market. It was something of an understatement to write that growth in the lumber business "was not seriously affected by agricultural deficiencies" (*LC*, 126). On the contrary, by 1831 Lower Canada had 727 sawmills—four times the number of parishes—and by 1844 it had 911 (*LC*, 128). Sawmills were just one of the many enterprises stimulated by the lumber trade. How many men worked at felling, floating logs downriver, and loading ships for the Atlantic crossing? According to an estimate cited in *Economic and Social History*, "one-eighth of the working population" was seasonally employed in lumbering (*ESHQ*, 408). Such figures make it plain that forest development had a considerable impact. The limited amount of farming took care of food and shelter, while earnings from lumbering and allied activities went, in part, to buy goods produced in British factories. Ouellet himself felt that the volume of imports was directly related to distribution of a proportion of lumber profits in wages (*ESHQ*, 406; *LC*, 60, 128). The drop in demand for wood resulting from the international crisis of the 1830s may well have been an equal, if not greater, cause of rural unrest than any "agricultural crisis." Indeed, Ouellet spoke of "the British regime" being "saved by timber" during the decade prior to the uprising (*ESHQ*, p. 395). If so, then the crisis in the lumber trade could have fanned discontent quite as much as rural overpopulation or poor crops. Lumbering gave the rural population access to the trade economy, and by offering his labor for hire, the habitant stimulated imports.

Capitalism not only welded new social bonds by displacing the seigneurial relationship based on the *rente*; it also set up new consumer relationships and a new cultural pattern. Many "new" economists have emphasized the role of psychology and culture in their approach; they have demonstrated how social influence spread from the production to the consumer sector through wage labor.[47] Rural people were strongly tempted by consumer incentives—the spirits and textiles displayed in the general store—a phenomenon which, as I remarked earlier in this chapter, Ouellet felt "excite[d] the covetousness of the habitant" (*ESHQ*, 170). The initial stimulus of wage labor created a solvent demand, and the habitant now had the means to satisfy his desires. However, in the 1836 industrial and financial international crisis, which resulted in the paralysis of Lower Canadian banks in the spring of 1837, people's livelihood was endangered. Indeed, a whole way of life in forest and village was threatened by shrinking credit.[48] Future scholars may turn up evidence showing that some of the 1837 rebels were actually unemployed laborers or men heavily in debt to the general store, distributor of the consumer goods on which the new culture was based.[49] Joseph Masson, a major potash exporter to Britain, ordered British merchandise worth 100,000 pounds sterling in 1836. He may have overestimated the solvent demand, apparently not for the first time. Shrinking credit was only one of the effects of the crisis in the imperial economy. Masson's biographer noted that business was slowing down in the colony, and that in addition to bankruptcies, imminent or real, wholesalers were putting pressure on small shopkeepers in cities, villages, and countryside, threatening them with ruin.[50] In order to satisfy their suppliers, country storekeepers in turn pressed their debtors. In *Economic and Social History*, Ouellet touched on the problem of rural debtors. He implied that their debts were mainly seigneurial dues (*ESHQ*, 472); but their creditors could well have been country shopkeepers in large part. He assumed that "the impoverishment of the agricultural class was not related to production deficiencies alone; it was also connected to habits of luxury" (*ESHQ*, 482). Ouellet's argument echoed that of the clergy of the time, but did not explain that the growth of this taste for "luxury" was promoted by importers of manufactured goods. The 1837 rebels looted general stores, destroyed the account books for fear of their land being seized by the storekeepers, and dreamed of confiscating bank funds and wholesalers' stock for the poor.[51] To my mind, these are the earmarks of a revolt against capitalism in crisis. Perhaps Ouellet's wished-for, "real" revolution against church and seigneurial dues did not take place in 1837-1838 for the very reason that the main source of social tension in rural western Quebec no longer lay in the relationships of the Old Regime. Ouellet himself indicated as much, as did Michael Cross and others.[52]

In the eastern part of the province, the crisis in the capitalist economy indirectly led to habitant unrest. In order to buttress his argument concerning habitant ineptitude, Ouellet cited a letter from Charles-Eusèbe Casgrain to John Neilson dated January 1, 1839:

We are here in [a] state of alarming poverty. The needs are such that I fear we will not be able to provide sufficient for the winter for all the poor who grieve us and sear our souls with their stories of hardship. The harvest has been so poor that a good half of the habitants will not have enough for themselves. Most of these are in debt and without [further] credit. The rest are little better in consequence of debts contracted in hope of good harvests which have been lacking for several years. It is a sad state of affairs partly the fault of the people themselves who have unwisely indulged in expenses beyond their means and conditions due to the excessive eagerness of merchants to make them advances and long-term credits which have brought if not ruin, at least great penury to many. To all I preach reform as much as I can to make them understand the necessity of denying themselves any object of luxury and of obtaining everything with the produce of their land and animals without turning to the merchants [*LC*, 279].

One couldn't ask for a better example of contemporary opinion corroborating the historian's ideology; the reader, unaware of the context, can only approve the argument. In the first place, however, C.-E. Casgrain was not a seigneur as stated in the index to *Bas-Canada* (a title removed in the index to the English edition). He was a lawyer turned gentleman farmer, very well-informed on the agronomy of his time and desirous of influencing his neighbors in order to make them more self-sufficient. He was a potato grower, and considered this crop especially suited to the needs of large, poor families. His brother, who inherited the family seigneury, was also a merchant. For a number of reasons the two brothers did not get along, and perhaps even detested each other. This ill-feeling may have been partly responsible for his criticism of the buying of British merchandise. In the passage quoted by Ouellet, C.-E. Casgrain was talking about a region with very little lumbering, but where capitalism influenced conditions in times of crisis, as much if not more than poor farming methods. The increase in goods offered, along with the availability of credit in a time of poor crops, further indebted the farmer. Are we looking at a subsistence crisis or a crisis in the market economy? It was probably a combination of both, but Ouellet only emphasized the former.[53]

The hypotheses mentioned here may one day be proved, at least for some regions, in which case the so-called ethnic aspect of the Montreal region uprisings and general discontent will figure less prominently in explaining the "revolution." Ouellet did not explore this possibility, however, and when writing *Lower Canada* merely expanded the explanation of the causes of the rebellion given in *Economic and Social History*.

Writing in the 1960s, Ouellet took for granted that there was an agricultural crisis in 1802. He based his view on indirect information such as fluctuations in the volume of wheat exports from the port of Quebec. Wallot and Paquet argued fairly convincingly that a crisis was unlikely at such an early date. When writing *Lower Canada* in the 1970s, Ouellet therefore made every effort to uncover new evidence. He believed the answer to his critics lay in papers such as tithe books and parish fundraising receipts for the Quête de l'Enfant Jésus. These discoveries may have satisfied his polemical leanings, but it is doubtful that they left us any the wiser concerning the social and economic life of nineteenth-century Quebec. As in the case of demographic pressures, Ouellet failed to abide by the accepted standards of historical criticism.

The Quête de l'Enfant Jésus was by far the most questionable of Ouellet's sources. The table listing the ten-year fluctuations in wheat donations to the Quête between 1773 and 1832 in St. Denis, Varennes, St. Marc, and St. Philippe de Laprairie (*LC*, 351) should have demonstrated a drop in wheat production, Ouellet's sign of a crisis. Even on the hypothetical assumption that none of these parishes was subdivided between these two dates, the table is still not convincing. The Quête in Varennes brought in the same amount of wheat for the decades 1783-1792 and 1813-1822, whereas annual contributions in St. Philippe increased from 54.8 to 70.2 minots for the same periods. It would be easy to give other examples; as the attentive reader frequently found, the tables given did not support the argument. More serious, however, is the inability of the actual source to withstand critical examination.

Unlike tithes, contributions to the Quête were voluntary, and could not therefore reflect fluctuations in production accurately. Either because of his economic determinism or a somewhat naive use of "scientific" methods, Ouellet failed to take into account the cultural aspect of the donations. The parishioners were inspired as much by their faith and confidence as by their wealth. What would we think of an economist who relied on the annual receipts of superlotos as a guide to business cycles? The buyer of a lottery ticket is often counting on chance to solve his money problems. His purchase is motivated by faith and confidence in his luck, which is why lottery sales can be stimulated by crisis or depression. A similar dynamic operates in societies imbued with religious faith. The parish priest of St. Charles sur le Richelieu wrote in mid-January of 1819, "The Quête de l'Enfant Jésus was fairly good, considering the poor year we have had." But in April he noted, "We are threatened with severe shortages. A parishioner who paid me sixteen minots of wheat last year has only given me three and a half this, being one of the hardest hit."[54] Thus, in societies of an earlier day where God was looked to for material solutions much as lotteries are today, the receipts of the Quête might well be in inverse proportion to resources. The generosity of the faithful during periods of shortages and high prices can be explained by their reliance on heavenly aid for pressing practical problems. This is borne out by the easily available records showing the number of requests to the bishop for permission to pray publicly for relief in periods of drought, frost, hail, or blight. The parish priest was often merely an intermediary for these requests, undertaken on popular initiative. The Quête receipts may well indicate fluctuations in zeal and piety rather than resources, since donations were a matter of choice, not necessity. The social analysis of donations cannot be made merely in terms of available assets.

In principle, the parish priests' tithe books ought to reflect resources more accurately than the Quête receipts. Ouellet assured us that the accounts were "far more probing" than previous indicators used in export and price tables (*Bas-Canada*, 181; cf. abridged text, *LC*, 120). Ostensibly, tithe books should indicate the relative volume of various crops that were taxed at a rate of one-twenty-sixth of the total harvest. The tithe requires close scrutiny as a source of revenue, however. Historians have quite rightly pointed out the inherent difficulties of this type of serial source. Some have adhered rigorously to critical standards.[55] Pierre Chaunu, in the first volume of *Séville et l'Atlantique* (Paris: Colin, 1955), provided an excellent illus-

tration of how to evaluate fiscal sources.[56] Since Ouellet cited
the inventor of the concept of serial history as a major influence on his method, he would have done well to reread
Chaunu's carefully argued history of Seville. In a commentary
on Ouellet's agricultural crisis, Timothy Le Goff remarked that,
with regard to tithes, series of volume statistics based on tithe
books and parish priests' periodic income statements appeared
to be more reliable in Quebec than in France.[57] He referred
his readers to the classic work in this field, *Les Fluctuations du
produit de la dîme* (La Haye, 1972) by Joseph Goy, Leroy Ladu-
rie, and others. Since no similar reference work was available
for Lower Canada, Le Goff put his faith in Ouellet's established scholarly reputation, and took him at his word. But was
this really the case? Let us look at how the tithe system worked
in Quebec.

Chronological series based on tithe books may reflect
production fluctuations in those rare parishes where no subdivision occurred. In theory, the tithe books could also be relied
upon for localities where subdivision took place without a
separate parish priest being named. This was possibly the case
in Yamachiche, which was subdivided to create St. Barnabé
in 1835.[58] As the original priest served the new parish with
the help of a curate, he retained the right to the tithes of both
parishes. Ouellet, in any case, felt that the Yamachiche tithe
book was a highly reliable source for the 1830s (*Bas-Canada*,
424-425; *LC*, 177-178, 386, mentions "a 6.3 % under-report-
ing in tithe receipts when compared to census data"). Let us
give him the benefit of the doubt.

Whatever may be true for Yamachiche, are we therefore to
conclude that parish bookkeeping was a reliable index of cereal
production for all Lower Canada? For one thing, the series
seem to have too many gaps in time and space to provide a
source as reliable as the census reports. Even though the latter
are not annual, or may reflect a particularly good or bad year,
they nevertheless offer a fairly consistent territorial survey.
The tithe books, on the other hand, have the advantage of a
more unbroken time sequence. Periodic tithe income statements introduce yet a further confusing variable for the
economic historian. These were prepared for the bishop's

pastoral visits, and covered the groups of parishes included in his tour. Consequently, they only provide figures for a limited number of localities within any given crop year.

The scientific method comprises more than just the historical evaluation of quantitative sources, as work being done in France well illustrates. A thorough knowledge of law is essential, this being a far more effective tool for interpreting the past than the concepts and theories of the "synchronic" sciences, as used or abused by various historians. Theory based on observation of contemporary societies is subject to a special kind of anachronism when applied to the past. It is one of the pitfalls of an interdisciplinary approach. A knowledge of legal codes and customary law, as well as of commentaries on individual statutes or various bodies of law, enables the historian to fill the gap between codified law and legal practice. In France, such documents are often used very effectively in understanding the socio-economic and socio-cultural aspects of the Old Regime. It is therefore imperative to evaluate sources before using series such as the tithes, if a similar standard of scientific knowledge is to be achieved.

Tithes were based on the gross harvest, which meant that villagers did not contribute. Ouellet, however, related the tithe total to the number of communicants in the parish. Such a method offers no sound basis for long-term study of parishes where villages formed rapidly.[59] A tithe/communicant ratio can lead to the gradual under-evaluation of production per farm. The subdivision of farm units may, as Ouellet insisted, indirectly "correct" the distortion caused by the appearance and growth of villages. But far more serious drawbacks invalidate the tithe as a source.

In modern parlance, the tithe was a regressive tax. The tithe owner, as the church was technically called, took no account of individual ability to pay. Furthermore the tithe was based on the gross product of the harvest, not the net—that is, before deducting seed grain for the next year. Paradoxically, those parishioners not subject to tithes were the very ones to profit most from the priest's services, since villagers lived close to church and presbytery. An émigré French priest, knowing that the tithe had been abolished by the Revolution in his native land, one day asked Bishop Plessis whether the parish clergy's mode of payment ought not to be reviewed, since it was such an issue. The bishop replied, "It is not as desirable as you think for the clergy to be independent of the people in temporal matters. Well-conducted and conscientious curés like yourself would benefit, it is true. But there might perhaps be a greater number for whom such independence would have unfortunate consequences" (April 17, 1807). This answer reveals an astute sense of management. If parishioners paid their dues faithfully to the parish priest for whose income they were responsible, but who himself was answerable to diocesan authorities, they would be more likely to consult the bishop if they felt they were being badly served. Conversely, should a priest consider himself poorly paid, the bishop had a means of inquiring whether the tithe income was affecting his performance. If the bishop were short of clergy and unable to meet the demand for resident priests, he might ask parishioners to undertake individual commitments to contribute to the curé's income. As it stood, the system probably had as many disadvantages as advantages. The poorest parishes might have no curé at all, or might find the one they had dissatisfied with his situation. Some priests were highly sensitive about the amount of their income in relation to services rendered. The following grudging comment was made by a priest in the Richelieu area upon handing over half his tithe revenue to his coadjutor—an arrangement made when he took over the parish: "I told him [the coadjutor] that he was appropriating half my tithes. Perhaps this was putting it rather strongly; I am prepared to moderate my language, as long as it conveys the fact that I am carrying the whole spiritual burden while he gets half the temporal revenue." This comment by the curé of St. Ours in October 1791 was not the only one of its kind. Generally, however, parish priests whose income was siphoned off to other beneficiaries made do without too much grumbling. In correspondence between the bishop and his parish clergy, the latter did not appear overly concerned about being fully paid for services rendered. In Canada, parishioners delivered their tithes to the priest, whereas in France such dues were exacted in the actual field. The Quebec priest could

not verify whether he received his exact portion of the crop—
and neither can the historian, for that matter.

On what crops were tithes based? In his *Receuil de notes diverses
sur le gouvernment d'une paroisse* (Paris, 1830), Thomas Maguire
reproduced the list established under Civil Law: "wheat, buck-
wheat, Indian corn, rye, barley, and oats." He noted that "tithes
are also paid in peas, although these are classed as vegetables.
I do not know whether peas, which are becoming a field crop
in some areas, are subject to tithes."[60] His article on tithes
ended with the remark that "tithes are payable within the year,
and cannot legally be recovered after the prescribed limit."
We are dealing here with the legal definition of tithes. In
practice, the bishop advised his clergy not to sue for payment.
Anxious to avoid discrediting Roman Catholicism in the eyes
of the Protestant population, he favored settlement out of
court. The bishop's realistic and prudent attitude reflected
the presence of a considerable non-Catholic population in the
diocese of Lower Canada. It amounted to between 15 and 20
percent, although unevenly distributed. The church had its
own means of disciplining recalcitrant parishioners, however,
and could apply powerful symbolic sanctions. No tithe, no
Easter; hence no absolution of sins between the seventh and
ninth month following the harvest. Delinquents would therefore be denied the sacrament of burial if they died indebted
to their curé. Naturally, the bishop reserved to himself the
power of absolution for such a sin. The very severity of this
episcopal discipline suggests that tithes were not paid conscientiously. Nevertheless, it was possible to negotiate with the
curé for deferred payment beyond the Easter term. This means
that any systematic attempt to define a single crop year in the
tithe books becomes fairly difficult. How are we to know
whether arrears were posted for the year in which they were
due or the year in which they were paid?

We now know which crops were legally subject to tithes, and
what legal or symbolic power the parish priest could exercise.
The next step is to ask whether the parishioners paid them
conscientiously. Tithes were, after all, moral rather than legal
obligations. Ouellet did not ask this question, and yet, from

the standpoint of historical criticism, tithes cannot be considered a credible source unless it is answered.

The bishop's correspondence reveals a hiatus between principle and practice. As with religious sanctions, such as refusing the sacraments to defaulting parishioners, so with legal sanctions. Compared to the norm, the correspondence shows a wide divergence in practice between regions, parishes, and even individual curés. When naming a priest to a parish, the bishop made sure that the faithful could and would provide lodging and livelihood. At this juncture, the crucial factor was a guaranteed minimum income. The bishop had to satisfy himself that the tithes would support a priest, and possibly a curate in the event of the parish increasing rapidly, otherwise parishioners would have to contract legally to pay a fixed minimum. In 1805, the farmers of St. Eustache agreed to pay the parish priest 300 minots of wheat if the tithe fell short of this amount. Of course, should tithes exceed this limit, the priest had a right to the whole. The villagers in the parish agreed to pay a cash supplement. In 1831, the farmers of Ile du Pas contracted to pay their tithes in potatoes. These are just two instances; I could easily cite twenty. The bishop held a strong negotiating position, as he almost never had enough priests to go around and could always remove a priest from one community to satisfy petitioners elsewhere. There were cases where it might be assumed that tithes were paid punctually, since a third of the tithe revenue was deducted to provide an annuity for a retired predecessor. However, the correspondence mentions priests who defrauded their pensioners, and quite probably parishioners did likewise on occasion. On the other hand, we can reasonably assume that parish priests would willingly forego a portion of their tithes when crops were poor, thus leaving families with enough to see them through. When all these variables are taken into account, can we really believe that tithe series indicate violent fluctuations or agricultural crisis, as Ouellet so unhesitatingly did? As with the parish census reports, in reality tithe books (all too rarely preserved in local archives) and periodic revenue statements submitted to the bishop are more useful in reconstructing clerical life than in producing agricultural statistics.

Fresh from the seminary, a young recruit to the priesthood finished his training under an experienced parish priest who needed an assistant, usually in a well-provided parish. The small salary paid a curate was thus no great burden on the priest. The novice was gradually initiated into the difficult arts of preaching and hearing confession, in addition to the less demanding activities of his ministry, such as celebrating mass and teaching catechism. If the young priest should prove to be a poor preacher or confessor, he would eventually move into a teaching career. Although the pay was significantly less, he would be among his fellows, and not isolated with an unappreciative rural flock. If, on the other hand, he was good at pastoral work and showed a liking for it, he was considered an early candidate for parish priest. An "old" curate, as young priests with three to five years' experience were called, stood a good chance of being given a parish, unless it were particularly prosperous. In this case there was little chance for him, except if he were heavily in debt or perhaps a member of some "respectable" family. Occasionally, a priest who had worked in a college for many years might be offered an important parish. Such livings rarely went to young priests. An active priest could very well end his career as head of a lucrative parish, unless he were guilty of some sexual sin or other infringement of diocesan rule, in which case he would be demoted to a curacy or banished to a seminary, there to mend his ways. His last parish would have to provide sufficient income for savings; these, added to the annuity it would pay him on retirement, would support him until his death. A number of curés actually left considerable estates, and college authorities were ever hopeful of bequests to subsidize their institutions or to set up endowment funds for needy students. Often this was how colleges found the means to recruit and educate a future priesthood.

The permutations and combinations of pastoral life were many. A priest might find himself serving two, or occasionally three, churches, or caring for two half-settled parishes and a distant mission. Under such circumstances, the faithful might feel justified in paying half the legal tithe for half-time services. If, on the other hand, the tithes were considered insufficient, the bishop could authorize tithes based on potatoes, cod (in the Gaspé Peninsula), or the oil of the white beluga whale (in Charlevoix county), tow, tobacco (Ile du Pas), or any other product deemed necessary for maintaining the priest's livelihood.

It should be noted that letters from parish priests dependent on rural labor never criticized their parishioners for poor farming habits.[61] Correspondence dealing with crop yields gave the impression that the varying good or bad years were the result of weather or other vagaries of nature. Bishop Panet wrote to console a disgruntled priest in 1828: "You may well have received only 240 minots of wheat this year, less the portion that you pay in annuity to Monsieur Keller [retired]. But you will agree that such adverse conditions have not occurred for a long time in the District of Montreal." This priest served a newly developed parish, it is true; but what is worth noting is that the bishop clearly felt that really bad crops were not common in the Montreal region as a whole. These examples are not important in themselves. The point is that a systematic geographic study should indicate which regions were newly pioneered and which had been settled for a century. In January 1809, for example, Bishop Plessis consoled the first parish priest of Joliette for his meager 400 minots of wheat from 1808 by remarking that "the parish is likely to increase considerably in the near future," either by the clearing of new land or by an imminent realignment of boundaries. Other sources would probably support McCallum's hypothesis that we are dealing with agricultural fluctuations caused by weather and blight. Ouellet paid little attention to this possibility; if he had, he would have been obliged to reconsider his view of the habitant, among other things. McCallum actually cited a passage from *Economic and Social History* to prove his case for the state of farming in Lower Canada. According to Ouellet, "This traditional type of agriculture, whose prosperity was based on the opening up of new areas of cultivation, not on technical progress, was dependent in the highest degree on climatic variations. With drought, excessive rains, or an early frost destitution could immediately waylay the farmer" (*ESHQ*, 115). McCallum went on to say,

Thus, the 'inadequate' crop of 1804 arose partly from an 'unpropitious season'; crops were mediocre in 1805 yet exceptional in the following year; in 1812 damage was inflicted by late frost and a cold August; in 1814 the wheat crop was destroyed by dryness; and in 1815 and 1816 very severe damage was inflicted by frost in August and September. Also, the Hessian fly was a serious problem between 1805 and 1816. Consequently, while downplaying the role of weather conditions in his conclusions, Ouellet demonstrates their central importance quite effectively.... Where to this is added the possibility of a population shift from farming to forestry...there is no reason to believe that the causes of the periodic crop failures between 1800 and 1815 were different from the causes of the six crop failures in the 1780s.[62]

In the course of their observations on Quebec agriculture, parish priests remarked on the habitants' methods, and appeared to find nothing "scandalous" in their farming practices. Some, on the contrary, implied that the habitants were well aware of the cost and yield of each crop. The parish priest of Sorel wrote in 1790:

In large parishes where the soil is good, this kind of tithe [Indian corn, broad beans, and potatoes] is rare, since wheat and other cereals grow very well. Here, however, the soil is so poor that wheat, or even peas and oats, will scarcely grow at all. The hardworking habitants know the nature of the soil and make use of the most fertile areas near their outbuildings; they put the necessary manure on land where Indian corn, broad beans, potatoes, and tobacco are growing, and do very well. Some habitants—quite a few, in fact—harvest forty to sixty minots of Indian corn, and between 300 and 500 minots of potatoes, thereby securing the means to barter for wheat. Especially since the recent bad years, they have really learned what their land will produce.

This letter presumably gives a realistic appraisal of the situation, judging from the fact that it informed the bishop, two or three months after the harvest, that most parishioners had refused to pay their tithes on the pretext that their type of crops were not taxed in several local parishes. Unlike the L'Islet priest, who suspected his parishioners of substituting non-tithable crops for wheat to escape their dues, the Sorel priest felt that resistance to tithes in the 1790s was due to a sudden wave of propaganda. Perhaps the presence of Protestants influenced public opinion. In any case, opposition to tithes took place after the poor harvests at the end of the 1780s, and the likelihood of cheating after mediocre harvests was therefore increased. On January 1, 1789, the curé of Ste. Marguerite de Blairfindie in the L'Acadie area wrote that he had only been able to raise "two thirds, and more often one half" of what was owed him, "the parish being afflicted by a great number of needy people." At Pointe du Lac in the same year, the bishop urged the parish priest not to dun those "whom poverty leaves penniless." The St. Ours parish priest, who had to pay half the tithe revenue to his coadjutor, wrote the bishop after the 1790 harvest, "Some have refused to pay the tithe, or at least have not come forward to do so, and others, despite promises, have only paid a portion. I took the liberty of ministering [the sacraments] to a few whom I considered insolvent." Six months after the 1815 harvest in St. Jacques de l'Achigan, the parish priest could not bring himself to demand the tithes due. "Last year I handed out on credit the small amount of grain received, but these poor unfortunates still cannot pay me....I live as the humblest among them...let alone give them relief." The account suggests to what extent lumbering or some other non-agricultural activity might in some instances compensate for crop failure. "Last year was very much the same, but money was available, whereas this year it is hard to come by and no one can find a job."

Occasionally "fraud"—although it is hard to believe we are dealing with a genuine fiscal document—was blamed on the habitants' lukewarm piety. On May 24, 1803, the parish priest of St. André de Kamouraska wrote, "Not only am I in dire need because the tithe is so low; but most of my parishioners are very hard, irreligious, and positively coarse in their dealings with me.... I believe I will be driven to sue sixty of them to get my tithe if I want to eat." A number of other letters could be cited to show that "irreligion" was a cause of defaulting on payments. "The tithe will be forthcoming when piety has taken root among them," stated the bishop to a Quebec missionary serving in New Brunswick in 1823.

The ill will to which parish priests ascribed the refusal to pay tithes was perhaps to be expected. In St. Athanase d'Iberville in 1825, the faithful asserted that the parish had not been legally constituted. Only between ten and twenty people bore the expenses of the parish and its priest. "It is absolutely useless to ask anything of the others," stated the curé. A year earlier in St. François de Montmagny, parishioners claimed that, as their pastor looked after two parishes, they only received half-time services and therefore would not pay the full tithe. This type of resistance embodied a logic found elsewhere. The faithful paid only for services rendered, and the absence of a resident priest "salved" their consciences. On the other hand, when the tithe was too modest and the bishop felt the parish-ioners were getting the required services, various supplements payable by the villagers or the parish council were arranged. We would have to check whether the priests' account books showed these sources of revenue before assuming that tithe figures are a reliable measure of production. For example, the curé of St. Césaire wrote Bishop Lartigue on April 16, 1823, "You requested an exact list of my receipts in tithes and offerings since Easter. The following is as shown in my account book: 56 minots of wheat, 26 1/2 of peas, 19 minots of oats, about 6 minots of Indian corn, and 5 or 6 minots of potatoes. This is the legal tithe. In addition, 20 minots of wheat were donated by the parish."

Whatever the explanation—poor harvest or "ill will"—parishioners varied in their tithe-paying habits. A curé might be considered unconscientious, particularly if he opposed part of his flock's desire to subdivide the parish, as occasionally happened. A priest who was generous or in easy circumstances would not trouble much about the income from his living, whereas another, perhaps in debt or of a parsimonious nature, might be more insistent. "A curé who does not demand his due always pleases the habitants, while one who is very strict automatically falls from their good graces," opined the Joliette priest when he announced to the bishop that he was "resolved to...pursue them...*with a sword at their backsides if need be,*" in his letter of October 1828. The priest of La Présentation declared that he had not been paid by some of his parishioners for upward of twenty years, and he was probably not the only one. Other firsthand accounts for parishes such as Bellechasse and St. Nicolas (1823 and 1825) show that the cereal tithe was not regularly paid. In 1792, the priest of St. Thérêse de Blainville stated that he was in dire poverty because his northern parishioners would not pay their proper tithes. The bishop accepted this statement and named him to the parish of St. Ours. In 1818 the priest of St. Eustache, and in 1822 that of St. Clément de Beauharnois, complained of similar recalcitrance. "The habitants of The Cedars have not improved: either they pay irregularly or not at all. This year, 110 have given nothing so far," stated a letter of September 11, 1825. Mention of the phenomenon occurs in every period. On his pastoral visit in 1868, Louis-François Laflèche, bishop of Trois-Rivières, noted that tithes were poorly paid almost everywhere.[63] Defaulting was not a phenomenon which grew up ten or fifteen years before the rebellion, as Ouellet assumed. In 1794, Bishop Hubert wrote to Rome that the habitants "default on tithes and seigneurial dues as long as they can get away with it."[64] It was not in the bishop's interest to hide the truth, as he received no portion of the parish revenue. Given so many firsthand accounts, can anyone seriously claim that the tithe was a reliable index of crop production and yields, or that one need only multiply the annual receipts by twenty-six in order to arrive at an estimate of the harvest? In his review of historical writing on the agricultural crisis, Professor Le Goff, although aware of the questionable reliability of such sources in France, accepted Ouellet's use of them, as mentioned earlier. So convinced was Le Goff by the author of *Lower Canada* that he wrote, "the solidity of these series seems better than similar records which have been used recently in France."[65] Actually, it may well be that the French series were more trustworthy than those of Quebec, because in France the clerical tax was exacted on the spot.

What useful purpose can tithe books serve? For one thing, they offer a basis for study of how the parish clergy were paid. True, tithes were not the only source of revenue. In extreme situations, such as in certain "missionary" areas of the Eastern Townships, the Maritimes, or Ontario, priests lived on payments from the clergy's mutual savings fund or on fees for providing dispensations to marry. Some priests, who served both whites and Amerindians, were paid in part by the colonial authority. But in general tithes remained the principal source of the rural parish priest's income. For this very reason the publication of the tithe series would be of vital importance to historical science, on condition that all the books kept were reproduced. In an article published between the original French editions of *Economic and Social History* and *Lower Canada*, Ouellet referred to series with numerous geographical and chronological gaps that did not always support his argument on the subject of the "crisis."[66] He offered them as proof of an even more serious situation than that outlined in his 1966 work. Before expounding such hypotheses, he should have tested the validity of his sources. In 1833, the parishioners of St. Antoine de la Rivière du Loup (Louiseville) reportedly gave 260 minots of wheat and 50 of oats in tithes. Multiplied by 26, these quantities would supposedly provide an estimate of the harvest: 6,760 minots of wheat, 1,300 of oats. Yet in the 1831 census, the same parish appeared as having harvested 32,149 minots of wheat and 48,658 of oats.[67] This enormous gap could either be the result of a poor harvest or a very partial payment of tithes. Until such time as these questions have been carefully researched, however, the reasonable assumption is that tithe records are not the most useful basis for writing a history of agriculture. Ouellet himself expressed his reservations before using this source:

There is no overall study at the present time on the habitants' attitude to tithes.... To what extent did they fulfil their obligations? There was definitely a chronic unwillingness to pay the whole, a tendency that might be accentuated in times of poor harvests. The second question deals with a period in which a habitant minority may have begun to question the actual institution.... It would seem that after 1830 there arose a significant rural minority that attacked the legitimacy of the institution.[68]

Having set forth this *caveat*, he nevertheless proceeded to use the tithe data as though it were an accurate reflection of production fluctuations.

Ouellet's polemical temperament and his tendency to dramatize were well illustrated by his style of quantitative analysis, in which he overestimated "demographic pressures" on the basis of parish census records, and placed too much emphasis on a drop in wheat production and yields, relying on a variety of secondary sources. A little less emotional involvement would have given us a work commensurate with his talent. Perhaps John Neilson's intuition was right in situating the rise of demographic pressures after the 1812-1814 war. In *Lower Canada* Ouellet tried to cover far too wide a spectrum, perhaps forgetting the adage about biting off more than one can chew. Total history represents an enormous undertaking, and a work such as Pierre Goubert's *Cent Mille Provinciaux*, covering the 100,000 French residents of the Beauvais region, was a remarkable achievement in individual research. But Ouellet's period of study began in the middle of the eighteenth century; the Quebec population had already exceeded 100,000 "provinciaux" in the 1780s, and numbered over 500,000 at the time of the rebellion. Furthermore, this population occupied an immense territory that varied widely in climate, agricultural potential, and forest resources. The task was clearly too much for one scholar, and Ouellet's inability to throw his net both wide and deep was indicative of a strategical problem faced by researchers.

The question is, should we keep churning out premature attempts at nationwide total history, or should we try to gain new understanding of the period through thematic or regional studies? The second approach seems to offer the only hope, given the current organization of historical research. The wide-ranging syntheses will come later, designed to weave individual research into a coherent whole rather than serve as an ideological vehicle. There is no doubt that works with an emotional content are captivating and make enjoyable reading, so long as one can distinguish the political obsessions of our time from what appears to be scholarly dissertation. Nicole Gagnon has described *Lower Canada* as an expression of "pro-federalist and pro-capitalist bias, based on what savors strongly of nineteenth-century ideas of progress."[69] In fact, historians are strongly influenced by their preoccupation with current problems. If we really want to push back the frontiers of knowledge, we will have to depoliticize professional history. Ouellet himself called for more regional monographs in 1966, but ten years later very few had actually appeared. To talk about "the rapid progress of research for this segment of Canadian history" (*LC*, xiv) showed a forgetfulness of the relative neglect of this period by the new generation of historians. Bibliographies of historical works for the last ten or fifteen years clearly indicate that far more and varied work is being done on New France than on the British regime.

Ouellet has made possible great strides in our approach to history. As founder of the journal *Histoire sociale*, he has significantly changed our historical perspective. In hailing the appearance of Ouellet's *Eléments d'histoire sociale du Bas-Canada*, Jean Paul Bernard paid deserved homage to the Canadian founder of social history: "Some who are either die-hard separatists, or who can't be bothered, reject his works out of hand without giving them the attention they merit.... One has only to attempt a similar type of work to appreciate how adept he is at doing more sophisticated research and writing than simple summaries of political debate."[70] With Jean Hamelin, he pioneered the quantitative serial method in this country, and there is no question that he opened up new avenues of research. And yet one cannot wholeheartedly endorse the unqualified praise accorded him by Michael D. Behiels, following the publication of the French edition of *Lower Canada*: "*Le Bas-Canada* achieves and surpasses the exceedingly high standards set by his *Histoire économique et sociale*.... M. Ouellet maintains the same quantitative methodological approach—refined and reinforced by a vast assortment of statistical data."[71]

Refinement of statistical methods, however, implies a critical examination of even the most official sources. We know, for example, that the 1844 census count was lower than it should have been,[72] and that the 1825 census was perhaps similarly inaccurate.[73] Census figures for parish sub-groups are even more suspect because of the formation of about seventy new parishes in Lower Canada between 1790 and 1840.[74] Because Ouellet did not take this into account, his rebuttal of Wallot and Paquet's view of demographic pressures rested on very uncertain ground.[75]

Ouellet's reading of history gives rise to more general epistemological problems, however. One of these involves the opposition between a soft determinism and a libertarian perspective. For over a century, Quebec historians narrated the story of a people programmed by the Great Beyond. This providential determinism gave way to a form of economic determinism, with Ouellet as one of its most highly respected exponents. Outside Quebec, where the swing has not been so great, this distinctive aspect of *Economic and Social History* caused a certain amount of comment. Claude Fohlen wrote in 1967 that this masterwork "might...give some readers the mistaken impression that an inflexible relationship existed among the various economic, social, and political components. Such an impression could perhaps have been avoided by a more comprehensive discussion of these relationships."[76] In other words, material considerations are not the only operative factors in history. Men create their own destiny to some extent. Their will, their desires, and their freedom of action release a specific energy that affects the evolution of the human species.

Conclusion

A Look Ahead

With few exceptions, the new generation of historians was born during the 1940s. Typical of this generation is its predilection for contemporary history, as exemplified by such scholars as Paul-André Linteau, René Durocher, and Jean-Claude Robert, the trio who wrote *Quebec: A History, 1867-1929*, tr. Robert Chodos, (Lorimer, 1983). Although there is still a great deal of research being done on New France and the first hundred years after the Conquest, the period most favored lies between 1850 and the present. Accustomed as we are to an all-pervading utilitarianism, we ask: What is the use of history, if not to understand the genesis of the present, and perhaps to shape the future?

Several new areas of study are evident, among them labor history and, more recently, the history of women. Urban history and the wider field of regional history also occupy a growing place. Such studies deal mainly with power structures, as well as socio-material and economic conditions. Economism, the dominant philosophy of our time, permeates all the major areas of study. It should therefore come as no surprise that so little cultural history is being written.

Actually, even histories of ideologies often serve to reveal "class interests." Are the human sciences, and history in particular, sacrificing man himself as a subject? Are we so convinced of his immutable relationship to material things that we see no point in studying his feelings, passions, tastes, imaginative qualities, and beliefs? That the history of Catholicism should today be a marginal genre in a land once noted for its piety shows all too clearly the process of "reification of derealization," or more simply, the creation of concepts that are out of touch with human life—that "anthropology without man"[1] which has absorbed us in the last few decades. Those who look

164

for a vigorous new cultural history should remember that in France, under the leadership of Fernand Braudel, the second *Annales* generation, as Philippe Ariès called it, first devoted itself to socio-material history. But historical anthropology, ethnology, and psychology, disciplines that were marginal before 1960, have come into their own during the last quarter of the twentieth century.[2] There is perhaps even a third generation of *Annales* historians, in Ariès view. Why, then, have Quebec intellectuals not followed the same path, since they are so powerfully influenced by French thought?

Until the mid-twentieth century, the young were taught by the priests, brothers, and nuns of Quebec schools that ideas ruled the world. Frugality, renunciation, self-denial: such were the moral watchwords broadcast by these men and women of the church to a world increasingly "hedonized" by consumer forces. Although this spiritual perspective still dominated Quebec historiography, it gradually gave way to a materialist approach to "national" development, in harmony with the growing consumer morality. According to the new historians, material considerations were what "stimulated" the dynamics of history. The settlers of New France had come to exploit the natural resources of the St. Lawrence Valley, not to bring the Word of God. As methods became more refined, the materialist interpretation, whether Marxist or non-Marxist, was reinforced by the spread of a sometimes excessive or mistaken reliance on quantitative techniques. Fernand Ouellet's work was a notable example. In history as in other social and human sciences, past and present human behavior was variously explained in terms of economic determinism, economism, or a quantophrenic scientism. Even such cultural sciences as anthropology and ethnology maintained that societies evolve in response to conditioning by their physical environment and social relationships. The materialist interpretation gained ground as the economy of (over)production and (over)-consumption grew. Current economic changes, however, have led to the appearance of new life-styles. Some unorthodox economists predict a possible return to frugal living, inspired by a concern for the environment and the quality of life, thus challenging the expansion of the wasteful consumer economy of the postwar years. Will the present generation of historians rewrite history in the light of the newly emerging values? Yes—if such values are here to stay.

But scientific history should also incite us to look beyond the present bounds of knowledge. Progress in method, and in particular a better division of scholarly labor, make it possible to hope for a better understanding of the past. Each generation of historians has a duty to push back the frontiers of knowledge. They need not repudiate their predecessors, who performed the same duty in their day. But those who take up the torch must make some distinction between what, in earlier research, appears reasonably close to reality, and what seems conversely to be the fruit of fantasy, fashion, or ideology. Scientific knowledge, whether in history or biology, moves forward because of research and refinements in method. These in turn depend on the funds and resources supplied by public agencies to various fields of research. Such funds and resources are distributed in accordance with the public's attitude to knowledge as a cultural asset—the public consisting of taxpayers and voters. In the last analysis, these are the people who decide how much support will go to the educational and cultural aspects of scholarship, and how much will be devoted to its so-called utilitarian, practical, and technical vocation.

NOTES

Abbreviations:

ACAM	Archives de la chancellerie de l'archevêché de Montréal
AE	*Actualité économique*
AN	*Action nationale*
BRH	*Bulletin des recherches historiques*
CHAR	*Canadian Historical Annual Report*
CHR	*Canadian Historical Review*
CJEPS	*Canadian Journal of Economics and Political Science*
DCB	*Dictionary of Canadian Biography*
ESHQ	*Economic and Social History of Quebec*
JHALC	*Journals of the House of Assembly of Lower Canada*
LC	*Lower Canada*
MG	Manuscript group
PAC	Public Archives of Canada
PAQ	Public Archives of Quebec
PUF	Presses universitaires de France
PUL	Presses de l'Université Laval
PUM	Presses de l'Université de Montréal
PUQ	Presses de l'Université du Québec
RAPQ	*Reports of the Archivist of the Province of Quebec*
RHAF	*Revue d'histoire de l'Amérique française*
RS	*Recherches sociographiques*
SCHEC	*Société canadienne d'histoire de l'Église catholique*

Foreword

1. There are praiseworthy exceptions such as David Carr, William Dray, *et al.*, *Philosophy of History and Contemporary Historiography* (Ottawa: University of Ottawa Press, 1982).

Introduction

1. Claude Galarneau, *La France devant l'opinion canadienne (1760-1815)* (Quebec: PUL, 1970). Jacques Monet, *The Last Cannon Shot* (Toronto: University of Toronto Press, 1969), published in French as *La Première révolution tranquille. Le nationalisme canadien-français, 1837-1850* (Montreal: Fides, 1981).

2. I will be discussing European influence later. French-Canadian works that influenced Hamelin, Ouellet, and others include Aegidius Fauteux, *Essai sur l'industrie au Canada sous le régime français* (Quebec: L.-A. Proulx, 1927); Ivanhoe Caron, *La Colonisation de la province de Québec. Débuts du régime anglais, 1760-1791* (Quebec: L'Action sociale, 1923), and *La Colonisation de la province de Québec* (Quebec: L'Action sociale, 1927).

3. Séraphin Marion, *Relations des voyageurs en Nouvelle-France au XVIIe siècle* (Paris: PUF, 1923). Gustave Lanctôt, *L'Administration de la Nouvelle-France* (Paris: Champion, 1929). Antoine Roy, *Les Lettres, les arts, et les sciences au Canada sous le régime français* (Paris: Jouve, 1930). Paul-Emile Renaud, *Les Origines économiques du Canada* (Mamers: n.p., 1928).

Chapter I

1. Denis Vaugeois, *L'Union des deux Canadas. Nouvelle Conquête?* (Trois-Rivières: Editions du Bien public, 1962), 127, n. 1.

2. Arthur Maheux, *Ton Histoire est une épopée* (Quebec, 1941), published in English as *French Canada and Britain: A New Interpretation*, tr. R.M. Saunders (Toronto: Ryerson Press, 1942). This is the text of lectures given at Laval University. Father Archange Godbout wrote a detailed survey of the controversy that followed its publication. Archange Godbout, «Les Préoccupations en histoire et les thèses de M. l'Abbé Maheux,» *Culture*, 4 (1943), 28-43. Godbout based his text on no less than 28 cited reviews and articles.

3. Arthur Maheux, *Pourquoi sommes-nous divisés?* (Radio-Canada, 1943), published in English as *Canadian Unity: What Keeps Us Apart?* (Quebec: Les Editions des Bois-Francs, 1944).

4. Ibid., p. 56.

5. Lionel Groulx, *Chez nos ancêtres* (Montreal: Bibliothèque de l'Action française, 1922), 12. This passage refutes the sermon preached by Monseigneur Pâquet in 1902, part of which was frequently quoted in the sixties to explain Quebec's economic lag. It has been referred to by Jean-Charles Falardeau, Roland Parenteau, Jean Lesage, Marcel Trudel, Michel Brunet, and Mason Wade, to name a few notable examples.

6. The theme of survival dominates English-Canadian historical literature, as can be seen in Ramsay Cook's "La Survivance. English

Canadian Style," *The Maple Leaf Forever* (Toronto: Macmillan, 1971), chapter 9.

7. Maheux, *Pourquoi sommes-nous divisés?*, 124.

8. A.R.M. Lower also supports this view in *Colony to Nation,* as do other Ontario historians. J.M.S. Careless, in *Canada: A Story of Challenge* (Macmillan, 1953), gives it as the explanation for the English Canadians' excessive zeal in rallying to the defense of the British Empire.

9. It should be remembered that in 1950, Abbé Maheux was co-chairman of a commission of the Canada and Newfoundland Education Association, which reached the conclusion that history textbooks throughout Canada should be revised to foster national unity. Commentary on this subject by some leading Canadian and American historians appeared in *AN* (May 1950).

10. Guy Frégault, "Le Mythe de M. le chanoine Groulx," *AN* (Nov. 1944): 163-173.

11. Michel Brunet, "French-Canadian Interpretations of Canadian History," *Rebuilding the Canadian Union—A Symposium of the Viewpoint of the French-Speaking Canadian* (Toronto: Public Lectures of the York District High School Board, 1964), 8.

12. Even though Frégault left Montreal in the late fifties, most of his work was published while he lived there. I feel that environment is significant in this respect, and therefore consider him a member of what I call the Montreal School of history. The same is true of Fernand Ouellet and Marcel Trudel with respect to the Quebec School; they left Laval University for Ottawa campuses during the mid-sixties.

13. In a parallel study of New France and the British colonies, Frégault found many striking resemblances between the two colonial empires. Frégault, *La Guerre de la Conquête* (Montreal: Fides, 1955), 17-100. This appeared in English as *The War of the Conquest* (Oxford University Press, 1969).

14. Guy Frégault, *Canadian Society in the French Regime* (Ottawa: Canadian Historical Association, 1968). It appeared in French in 1954.

15. Guy Frégault, *La Civilisation de la Nouvelle-France* (Montreal: Société des éditions Pascal, 1944), 280.

16. Frégault, *La Guerre de la Conquête*, 457.

17. This refers to statements in Frégault's article, "La Colonisation du Canada au XVIIIe siècle," *Cahiers de l'Académie canadienne-française*, 2 (1957), 51-81.

18. This diatribe concerns an article by Fernand Ouellet cited by Frégault: "M. Michel Brunet et le problème de la Conquête," *BRH*, (Apr.-May-June 1956): 92-104. Ouellet had questioned the existence of a business bourgeoisie in New France, alleging that the extravagant habits of the traders prevented them from amassing capital.

Frégault had more or less rejected Parkman's views in *La Civilisation de la Nouvelle-France*. One of Frégault's students at the University of Montreal, Rosario Bilodeau, defended a thesis on "La Liberté économique et politique des canadiens sous le régime français," summarized in *RHAF* (June 1956): 49-68. It was this kind of discussion that occasioned the polemical tone of Frégault's article.

19. I am aware of the lack of documentation regarding Maurice Séguin. His manuscript thesis, "La 'Nation canadienne' et l'agriculture, 1760-1850," although considered a remarkable work, was not published until 1970. The information given here is from a fairly substantial article, "La Conquête et la vie économique des canadiens," *AN* (Dec. 1946). To really understand Séguin's influence, one should read Denis Vaugeois, *L'Union des deux Canadas*. Even though the book is poor from the literary and technical standpoint, it provides a good survey of the development of Séguin's thinking. Indeed, Fernand Ouellet remarked of Vaugeois: "He is the avowed disciple of Professor Séguin and displays an embarrassing fidelity, to the point of reproducing course notes in his book. While adopting his master's categorical statements, however, he has not absorbed his method. According to Vaugeois, the merit of the book is entirely due to M. Séguin, although the latter might not care for the dubious honor of having fathered its contents." *Livres et auteurs canadiens* (1962), 68.

20. Vaugeois, citing Séguin, *L'Union des deux Canadas*, 16.

21. Séguin, "La Conquête et la vie économique des canadiens," 326. There appears to be an attempt to cope with the separatist movement by reminding French Canadians of their "revolutionary" history. The publication of Louis-Joseph Papineau's *Histoire de l'insurrection au Canada* by Editions Orphée (1963) is an example. The introductory remarks emphasize that the aim of this publication is to provide information for the current separatist movement. Numerous other examples could be given. Mid-twentieth-century French Canada was taking an unprecedented interest in this revolutionary venture.

22. Opinions about Michel Brunet are sometimes as excessive as his own writings. See Benoît Lacroix, O.P., reviewing *La Présence anglaise et les canadiens* (Montreal: Beauchemin, 1958), in *RHAF*, 12 (December 1958): 428-434.

23. Michel Brunet in his review of Marcel Trudel, *L'Eglise canadienne sous le régime militaire, 1759-1764*, vol. 2 (Quebec: PUL, 1957), in *RHAF* (March 1958): 583.

24. Michel Brunet, "Premières réactions des vaincus de 1760 devant leurs vainqueurs," *La Présence anglaise*, 37-48.

25. Michel Brunet, "La Conquête anglaise et la déchéance de la bourgeoisie canadienne, 1760-1793," ibid., 49-112.

26. Michel Brunet, *French Canada and the Early Decades of British Rule 1760-1791* (Ottawa: Canadian Historical Association, 1971). It appeared in French in 1962.

27. Michel Brunet, "Trois Dominantes de la pensée canadienne-française: l'agriculturalisme, l'anti-étatisme et le messianisme," *La Présence anglaise*, 113-166.

28. Ibid., particularly p. 256.

29. Michel Brunet, "Le Nationalisme canadien-français et la politique des deux Canadas," ibid., 233-292 passim.

30. Michel Brunet, "Une Autre Manifestation du nationalisme canadien: le Rapport Massey," and "L'Aide fédérale aux universités: les deux points de vue," *Canadians et Canadiens* (Montreal: Fides, 1954), 47-58, and 59-67.

31. Michel Brunet, "Centralisme et fédéralisme," ibid., 153-173. This was a critical review of Maurice Lamontagne, *Le Fédéralisme canadien: évolution et problèmes* (Quebec: PUL, 1954).

32. Michel Brunet, "L'Inévitable infériorité économique des canadiens-français," *La Présence anglaise*, 221-232, and "Problèmes contemporains de la société canadienne-française," *Canadians et Canadiens*, 107-118. The latter was a review of Jean-C. Falardeau, ed., *Essais sur le Québec contemporain* (Quebec: PUL, 1953), which included essays by Quebec scholars and two Americans, Mason Wade and Everett C. Hughes. The latter came through unscathed, but Brunet did not spare Mason Wade, the *bête noire* of the Montreal School. One of the articles of faith of the school is that no foreigner shall study French Canadians, and the same goes for French-Canadian researchers who borrow foreigners' conclusions or working hypotheses. English-Canadian historians also fall under this embargo, and get a grudging or sometimes acrimonious reception because they see the French-Canadian situation from the standpoint of pan-Canadian nationalism. My view is based on a thorough examination of reviews by Frégault, Séguin, and Brunet appearing in *RHAF*.

33. Michel Brunet, "Le Nationalisme canadien-français et la politique des deux Canadas," *La Présence anglaise*, 233ff.

34. This position taken by the Montreal School gradually separated it from Groulx.

35. Brunet, *La Présence anglaise*, 203.

36. Ramsay Cook, "L'Historien et le nationalisme—le cas Michel Brunet," *Cité Libre:* (Jan. 1965), 5-14.

37. Claude Galarneau, "Le Deuxième Centenaire du siège de Québec et le journal d'un curé:" *RS* (Oct.-Dec. 1960), 497.

38. *Champlain* and *Frontenac* contain a variety of documents with commentary, and are part of the Fides "Classics" series. For all practical purposes, Frégault's *Frontenac* is the same as W.J. Eccles's *Frontenac: The Courtier Governor* (Toronto: McClelland and Stewart, 1959). "L'Affaire Jumonville" was an article published in *RHAF* (Dec. 1952): 331-373. Trudel's intention was to refute statements about the "hero" of earlier works.

39. This tendency is well exemplified in Trudel's *L'Esclavage au Canada français. Histoire et conditions de l'esclavage* (Quebec: PUL, 1960), and all his works on the military regime.

40. Marcel Trudel, "La Nouvelle France," *Cahiers de l'Académie canadienne-française*, 2 (1957): 23-50. This is a description of the colony around 1750.

41. There seems to be a curious contradiction concerning Champlain's program of action. On one hand Trudel stated, "We are used to thinking of Champlain as having a whole agricultural program in view.... Actually, to find out what Champlain's program really was, we should read his two long memoranda of 1618. These constitute a veritable blueprint for colonization—commercial colonization, that is.... Champlain does not mention agricultural produce (this was France's main product), although he states elsewhere that the fertile land would be able to support the permanent population drawn to this country by commercial incentives, agriculture being merely a secondary activity in his program." *Champlain* (Montreal: Fides, 1956), 9ff. However, in the same year as the publication of *Champlain*, Fides brought out *L'Histoire du Canada par les textes* (Montreal, 1956) by Frégault, Brunet, and Trudel, containing the following commentary on Samuel de Champlain: the "fertile shores" of the St. Lawrence "could become the basis of an agricultural colony, an aspect with which Champlain was particularly concerned.... With a Frenchman's ingrained respect for the soil, he persuaded his countrymen to turn their backs on the riches of the sea, on fishing and trade, to build New France—which in his eyes was truly a *new* France—on the resources of the land" (p. 18). In the 1963 edition (1:18), these remarks were unchanged.

42. Marcel Trudel, "Le Séparatisme, solution de reniement," mimeographed text of a lecture given 11 Dec. 1961.

43. Marcel Trudel has made a study of the history of the Roman Catholic church, and recently concluded that the conscious isolation of the two ethnic groups in Canada originated in religious intransigence on both sides. The Catholic sectarianism of New France was followed by Protestant sectarianism. The unhappy marriage of church and state is seen as being partly responsible for the difficulties French Canadians have experienced in relation to both levels of government. As a remedy, Trudel has proposed a clear separation of civil and religious powers. Marcel Trudel, "A la Recherche d'une solution honnête," *Perspectives sociales* (Jan.-Feb. 1963): 8-12; "La Servitude de l'Eglise catholique du Canada français sous le régime anglais," *SCHEC*, transactions (1963): 11-33 passim.

44. Jean Hamelin, *Economie et société en Nouvelle-France*, Cahiers de l'Institut d'histoire, no. 3, (Quebec: PUL, 1960).

45. During the 1960s, the Ecole des hautes études commerciales had undertaken a study, based on new criteria, of the economic

development of New France. The controversy surrounding Hamelin's work produced two articles: Pierre Harvey, "Stagnation économique en Nouvelle-France," *AE* (Oct.-Dec. 1961): 537-548, and Cameron Nish, "Bourgeoisie coloniale en Nouvelle-France," *AE* (July-Sept. 1963): 240-265. The economist Harvey emphasized that New France was not alone in suffering from an absence of hard currency. The American colonies and even Europe had similar problems. The chronic trade deficit did not explain the colony's economic stagnation. All developing countries normally experience a similar situation. The margin of fur trade profits that remained in the colony would have been enough to make more than one millionaire, according to Harvey. He agreed with Hamelin regarding the labor force, although adding that the American colonies had the same difficulty. Harvey then formulated working hypotheses that had already been enunciated, either by Groulx or Frégault. For example, the choice of a site for the colony was in part responsible for the economic stagnation in New France. Furthermore, the growth rate was conditioned by the small population. How could there be a guaranteed turnover of industrial products in a country of some 50,000 inhabitants? Historian Cameron Nish, on the other hand, set out to prove that Frégault's views on the bourgeoisie were probably closer to the truth than Hamelin's. As Frégault had done in *The War of the Conquest*, Nish compared New France to the American colonies. He listed various definitions of the bourgeoisie and considered the question of whether New France had millionaires between 1729 and 1748. Nish took issue at the outset with a premise generally accepted in economic history, that is, that absolute monarchy hampered bourgeois initiative, whereas in democratic countries the bourgeois rise to power resulted in significant economic expansion. Parkman, Creighton, Lower, Ouellet, Hamelin, and many European and American historians share this view. However, a study by Arthur Lewis, *The Theory of Economic Growth* (London, 1956), has seriously undermined "this former axiom of progress." In the second part of his article, Nish analysed the period under discussion. Some of his observations are worth noting: marriage guaranteed links among rich families, some of which (such as the Vaudreuil family) were close to the seat of power; several entrepreneurs were quite ready to diversify their investments; the volume of exports in New France was sometimes comparable to that of the English colonies, relatively speaking; there was a great deal of real estate speculation, despite the Edicts of Marly, which the Superior Council refused to ratify for thirty years! Such examples of the way in which the interests of the business class figured in political institutions shed new light on New France's economic development. Nish developed his argument in his *Les Bourgeois-Gentilhommes de la Nouvelle-France, 1729-1748* (Montreal: Fides, 1968).

46. This final paragraph on Hamelin is based on the introductory chapter of Jean and Marcel Hamelin, *Les Moeurs électorales dans le Québec de 1791 à nos jours* (Montreal: Editions du Jour, 1962), which is a shortened version of his *licence* dissertation submitted to the Laval Institute of History in 1954.

47. See my survey of some thirty articles and book reviews by Ouellet in the *Bulletin de liaison de la société des professeurs d'histoire du Québec* (April 1965). Few references to particular articles have been made in the present text for this reason. In the mid-sixties, Ouellet's most recent syntheses all dealt with more or less the same material, as in "Les Fondements historiques de l'option séparatiste dans le Québec," *CHR* (Sept. 1962): 185-203, reprinted from *Liberté* (Mar. 1962): 90-112; "Nationalisme canadien-français et laïcisme au XIXe siècle," *RS* (July-Aug. 1963): 47-70; "Le Nationalisme canadien-français: De ses origines à l'insurrection de 1837," *CHR* (Dec. 1964): 277-292; "Le Clergé et l'échec des insurrections de 1837-1838," *Liberté* (Jan.-Apr. 1965): 42-49.

48. D. G. Creighton's *The Empire of the St. Lawrence* contains strikingly similar conclusions. Earlier, I mentioned the xenophobia of the Montreal historians; the difference between the Montreal and the Laval school is well illustrated by the fact that the latter are very sympathetic to English-language historians studying the history of French Canada. See *Aperçu sur la politique canadienne au XIXe siècle*; (Quebec: PUL, 1965) by Jean Hamelin, John Huot, and Marcel Hamelin. This is a synthesis of political histories by Careless, Creighton, Saywell, Neatby, Underhill, and others. The same could be said of American historians Mason Wade and Helen T. Manning, the latter having been frequently guided by Trudel in her *The Revolt of French Canada, 1800-1835: A Chapter in the History of the British Commonwealth*; (Toronto: Macmillan, 1962).

49. In one sense, the Quebec School does not see the Conquest of 1760 as the major watershed in French-Canadian history. From the standpoint of social and economic history, the period 1791-1800 is perhaps a significant juncture. Ouellet's work seems to indicate this, as does André Vachon's *Histoire du notariat canadien* (Quebec: PUL, 1962), chapter 3, "Le Prolongement du régime français 1760-1791."

50. Fernand Ouellet, "L'Enseignement primaire: Responsabilité des églises ou de l'état? 1801-1836," *RS* (Apr.-June 1961): 27-42.

51. In an article entitled "Etienne Parent et le mouvement du catholicisme social," Ouellet wrote, "Like most seminary graduates, Etienne Parent was not ready to enter an economic world based on free competition and the underlying bourgeois virtues of a pragmatic education that emphasized initiative, hard work, and the subordination of all things in life to reason." *BRH* (July-Aug.-Sept. 1955): 99.

52. Jean Hamelin and Fernand Ouellet, "La Crise agricole dans le Bas-Canada 1802-1837," *Etudes rurales*, (a journal of L'Ecole pratique des hautes études, Paris), (Oct.-Dec. 1962): 36-59. This article was reprinted without graphs in *CHAR* (1962): 17-33.

53. The systematic study of the seigneurial regime was one of the main goals of the Quebec School. In "Un Problème économique et social," *BRH* (July-Aug.-Sept. 1953): 157-161, Ouellet showed that the system discouraged the establishment of a capitalist economy, particularly because it hampered the buying and selling of real estate. It also discouraged efficient agricultural development, because it did not provide for setting up villages. Marcel Trudel has given a detailed description of the system in *The Seigneurial Regime* (Ottawa: Canadian Historical Association, 1963), the French version of which came out in 1956.

54. A.R.M. Lower, "Two Ways of Life: The Primary Antithesis of Canadian History," *CHAR* (1943): 12.

55. Although one cannot prove any real relationship, some French-Canadian historians may have been instrumental in stimulating the present changes, as indicated by the following observation: "There is a tendency today to view Quebec's potential with greater realism. Maurice Séguin's teaching at the University of Montreal has had an enormous influence, as have the writings of Guy Frégault and Michel Brunet." Vaugeois, *L'Union des deux Canadas*, 218. Historical works generally have a wide reading public, and the layman cares less about their scientific value than the motives and justifications which they bring forward. How true this is can be seen by the reception accorded neo-nationalist works. When Michel Brunet's *Canadians et Canadiens* came out, Jean-Charles Tanguay wrote in *L'Action nationale*: "I cannot recommend this volume too highly to young students who are continuing our constitutional battles and to adults whose attitude has not 'hardened.'" *AN* (May 1955): 840.

56. Jean de la Hire, "Nique à Londres ou à Dieu", *AN* (Sept. 1965): 58-66. This article is a typical example of such confusion.

57. Editorial, "Le Noeud gordien de la 'question canadienne,'" *Le Devoir*, 11 Oct. 1965.

58. Historian Ramsay Cook probably best represented the new awareness of English Canada, as seen in the book written with his Toronto colleagues Saywell and Ricker, *Canada, a Modern Study*, paperback ed., (Toronto: Clarke Irwin, 1964). This is an account of the history of Canada since the Conquest. It seems that the authors give greater emphasis to Brunet's views than do the Laval historians.

59. Again, it must be emphasized that the Montreal School does not subscribe to this view. The severe criticism leveled at the Chicago School by sociologist Philippe Garigue offered ample proof of this. Garigue, *Etudes sur le Canada français* (Montreal: Faculté des Sciences sociales, économiques et politiques, University of Montreal, 1958), 5-16. Moreover, Garigue accepted the "cataclysm" hypothesis.

60. "A l'Heure des espoirs terrestres," *Témoins* (Sept.-Oct. 1965): 12. Both the journals *Témoins* and *Maintenant* were central forces in the revision of the religious values in Catholic and French Quebec during the sixties.

61. Conrad Langlois, "La Religion a fini de bouder les beaux dollars," *La Patrie*; 28 Nov. 1965, 12. Bishop Pâquet's speech is quoted yet again.

62. The initiative did not come from historians, however. Léon Gérin was primarily responsible for the new awareness of educational problems. Guy Rocher, "La Sociologie de l'éducation dans l'oeuvre de Léon Gérin," *RS* (Sept.-Dec. 1963): 291-312. Traditional society was given such an exalted role that in 1949 a French-Canadian medieval scholar exhorted his compatriots to adopt medieval patterns of behavior. Benoît Lacroix, O.P., "Pourquoi le moyen age? Le Moyen Age et le Canada français," *Revue dominicaine* (Apr. 1949): 217-224. Although Quebec in the sixties was in the process of adjusting to the transition so well described by Everett C. Hughes in *French Canada in Transition* (Chicago: University of Chicago Press, 1943), reservations about technological society still continued to exist. Remnants of the past still affect our lives. This is what Fernand Dumont meant when he wrote, "Our rural elites still exalt life on the farm instead of preparing young people for the inevitable move." Fernand Dumont, "Situation de la société canadienne-française," *L'Instruction publique* (Dec. 1962): 285.

Chapter II

1. Among others Jean-Charles Falardeau, "Des Elites traditionnelles aux élites nouvelles," *RS* (Jan.-Aug. 1966): 131-150; Jacques Brazeau, "Les Nouvelles Classes moyennes," *RS* (Jan.-Aug. 1966): 151-163; Hubert Guindon, "Social Unrest, Social Class and Quebec's Bureaucratic Revolution," *Queen's Quarterly* 71, no. 2: 150-162; Léon Dion, *Nationalismes et politique au Québec* (Montreal: HMH, 1975), passim. This group can be fairly easily defined by education (arts and social sciences) and occupation (journalists, poets, *chansonniers* or writers and performers of satirical and topical songs, civil servants, teachers, social workers, union officials, and so on).

2. N.-E. Dionne, *La Nouvelle-France de Cartier à Champlain* (Quebec: C. Darveau, typography, 1891); Marcel Trudel, *Histoire de la Nouvelle-France*, vol. 1, *Les Vaines Tentatives, 1524-1603* (Montreal: Fides, 1963).

3. John Hare, Reginald Hamel, and Paul Wyczynski, *Dictionnaire pratique des auteurs québécois* (Montreal: Fides, 1976).

4. Page references to this work and Trudel's *Vaines Tentatives* will generally be given in the text hereafter.

5. Dionne, 18; see also 11, 15, 18, 78-80, and 93f., in which he severely criticized the "cupidity" and "avarice" of the traders.

6. Jean-François La Rocque de Roberval (ca. 1500-1560) was a member of the French nobility who became a Protestant convert. He was appointed lieutenant-general of New France by Francis I to found a colony. This courtier saw the royal commission as a chance to repair his fortunes. He established a settlement at Cap Rouge made up of felons from the various prisons of the kingdom, but it lasted only a few months. Cartier, who was his subordinate during this expedition, acted as a guide, since this was his third voyage to New France and he was familiar with the St. Lawrence Valley. Cartier had preceded Roberval to America, and met him at Newfoundland, where he refused to follow the latter toward the Quebec region. Cartier returned to France in haste, believing he had a cargo of gold; it turned out to be only quartz and iron pyrites. *DCB*, 1:422ff.

7. "What folly and want of foresight! Why did Roberval not return to his country with this wretched group, who were to be made yet more miserable by starvation and illness? Why fight against odds that strong, hale, and seasoned men might have overcome, when he had only the dregs of society or sailors picked up here and there...people unfit to form the nucleus of a sound colony" (Dionne, 35).

8. Troilus De La Roche de Mesgouez (ca. 1540-1606), a Breton marquis and viceroy of New France, established a settlement of felons on Sable Island in 1598. During the winter of 1602-1603 some members of the island colony mutinied, and the attempted settlement was abandoned.

9. Benjamin Pâquet, *Le Liberalisme*, lectures given at Laval University, 2d ed. (Rome: Imprimerie Polyglotte, 1877), 63f.

10. Ibid., 64-74.

11. Ibid., 74f.

12. Pierre Savard, "Le Journal de l'abbé Benjamin Pâquet étudiant à Rome 1863-1866," *Culture*, 26, no. 1 (Mar. 1965): 64-83. Savard himself applied the description of "liberal" to Pâquet's thought, echoing nineteenth-century commentators.

13. Chauvin was a Dieppe merchant who obtained the trading monopoly for New France in return for an undertaking to colonize it, in accordance with colonial policy of the period. He was a Calvinist who had distinguished himself in the religious wars against the League. *DCB*, 1:209f. The religious affiliation of sixteenth-century traders is a crucial factor in understanding the value judgments of earlier historiography.

14. "If Henri IV had sacrificed less to the Calvinists' demands, Acadia would not have undergone the vicissitudes that destroyed the highest hopes of its founders" (p. 18). "The heretical mentality underlying these settlements" of Brazil and Florida "also caused their failure.... The Calvinist outlook subsequently prevented Port-Royal

from succeeding as well" (p. 88). Incidentally, the Brazil and Florida expeditions are only mentioned in passing, in a note at the end of the book (pp. 272-277). The New France of the clerico-conservative writers was Catholic.

15. The body of nineteenth-century historical writing contains very few references to the British colonial model, among them Garneau (first edition), a few pages in Sulte, and perhaps some minor writers like H.-J.-J.-B. Chouinard, who wrote in 1882, "While all of feudal Europe was fighting on the battlefield...the social and intellectual movement that gave birth to the Reformation and the Renaissance in literature and art brought a breath of freedom to the various peoples." Chouinard then evoked the idea of America as the land of freedom and equality, the land of popular rights. He changed his mind after this "deviation," however, and wrote that aboard the merchant ships "came the missionary...setting out for infidel lands to harvest souls in lieu of those lost in the regrettable foundering of consciences known as the *Reformation*." H.-J.-J.-B. Chouinard, *Paul de Chomedey, Sieur de Maisonneuve, fondateur de Montreal* (Quebec: n.p., 1882), 13f.

16. Dionne, 95; see also 90f., and 280-282.

17. N.-E. Dionne, *Jacques Cartier* (Quebec: Imprimerie Léger Brousseau, 1889), 3. This work was awarded a prize by the lieutenant governor of Quebec. See also N.-E. Dionne, *Samuel Champlain fondateur de Québec et père de la Nouvelle-France....* (Quebec: A. Côté et Cie, 1891), 1:viii. Trudel writes of Champlain's religious outlook that "we must first set aside the dedications that cannot be by Champlain, because of their style (and it is in one of these dedications that the salvation of a soul is placed above the conquest of an empire)." *DCB*, 1: 198.

18. See the preface to the first edition of Trudel's *Louis XVI*: "It is odd that a historian should have to apologize for including footnotes and a bibliography. History in French Canada is still comfortably entrenched in rhetoric courses, and the research historian who attempts to be scientific is very much looked down on. The first type of history is based on source material, and is perhaps, after all, most likely to get at the historical truth. In adopting the scientific method, I am merely following in the brilliant footsteps of that erudite historian, Guy Frégault." Marcel Trudel, *Louis XVI, le Congrès américain et le Canada 1774-1789* (Quebec: Edition du Quartier Latin, 1949), x.

19. See the condemnation of the positivist theories of Seignobos by Canon, later Archbishop, Georges Courchesne, "L'Enseignement de l'histoire au cours moyen et universitaire," *Société historique de Montréal. Semaine d'histoire du Canada...* (Montreal: Société historique de Montréal, 1926), 377-388. Some outlines of methodology suggest St. Augustin's thesis of the two cities or Bossuet's *Discours sur l'histoire universelle* as a basis for interpretation. Others emphasize the Roman

Catholic code of ethics or the supreme importance of revelation in evaluating human behavior, and as a criterion of ultimate truth.

20. In 1963, the Jesuit Jean Leclerc justified providential and moralistic history in relation to interdisciplinary studies and the distinction between pure and applied science. Jean Leclerc, "L'Histoire providentielle, morale ou patriotique est-elle legitime?" *RSCHEC* (1963): 81-87.

21. Marcel Trudel, *L'Influence de Voltaire au Canada* (Montreal: Fides, 1945), 2:256.

22. See, for example, Marcel Trudel, *Le Régime militaire dans le gouvernement des Trois-Rivières, 1760-1764* (Trois-Rivières: Editions du Bien public, 1952), 129-133.

23. Marcel Trudel, *Chiniquy* (Trois-Rivières: Editions du Bien public, 1955).

24. Review by Charles-Marie Boissonnault in *Revue de l'Universite Laval* (June 1955): 900.

25. Boissonnault, 903, 905.

26. *Le Droit*, 27 Apr. 1955, quoted in *Mes Fiches*, no. 326 (October 1957).

27. Lemieux to Arthur Bergeron, curé of Wickham in Drummond county, 15 June 1957. Copy, PAC, MG. 30, vol. 6, series 828, general correspondence, 1900-1963.

28. Albert Tessier, "France nouvelle ou simple colonie commerciale?" *Cahiers des dix*, no. 22, (1957): 44.

29. Tessier, "France nouvelle...", 44.

30. Léon Roy, *Les Terres de la Grande-Anse des Aulnaies et du Port-Joly* (Lévis: n.p., 1951), 15.

31. Trudel, *Champlain*, 9.

32. Tessier, "France nouvelle...", 45.

33. Trudel's approach even drew comment from some of his pupils, as in a review of *Champlain* by Abbé Georges-Etienne Proulx: "With two or three exceptions, the texts given emphasize this less than creditable side of Champlain, and tend to give the impression that their choice was based on somewhat polemical motives." *L'Enseignement secondaire* (Oct. 1958): 47.

34. Marcel Trudel, *L'Esclavage au Canada français. Histoire et conditions de l'esclavage*, (Quebec: PUL, 1960).

35. Review in *Revue dominicaine* (March 1961): 124.

36. Trudel, *L'Esclavage*, 319.

37. Regarding Trudel's statistical argument, see also *L'Esclavage*, 134.

38. Marcel Trudel, "L'Objectivité en histoire," *RHAF*, 3 (Dec. 1951): 315, 319.

39. Trudel, *Les Vaines Tentatives*, ix.

40. Ibid., 79, 85, 106, 114, 168, 244, 249, 267.

41. Lionel Groulx, *La Découverte du Canada* (Montreal: Granger, 1934), 170-173, 196-198, 210-215, 228ff., and 264.

42. Ibid., 235; see also 228f.

43. Ibid., 148.

44. Ibid., 213: "Actually, it was the first explorers, among others, who gradually influenced royal policy toward an evangelizing mission." When Francis I mentioned the evangelizing aim of Cartier's third voyage in the commission of 1540, Groulx gave the king the benefit of the doubt: at least "one can credit him with sincerity whenever piety agreed with policy." Ibid., 232.

45. Cf. ibid., 82, 103, 104, 111.

46. Trudel, *Les Vaines Tentatives*, 88. On his negative comments as to the missionary zeal of colonial undertakings, See also pp. 99, 11f., 121f., 129-131, 154, and 224.

47. Marcel Trudel, *Histoire de la Nouvelle-France*, vol. 2, *Le Comptoir 1604-1627* (Montreal: Fides, 1967), 105-107.

48. Andre Vachon, review, *RS* 3 (Sept.-Dec. 1967): 415.

49. Trudel, *Le Comptoir*, 156, 164.

50. Groulx, *La Découverte du Canada*, 240f, 251ff.

51. Trudel, *Le Comptoir*, 125, 140f., 232f.

52. Even historians suspected of being "liberal" in the nineteenth century considered Cartier the discoverer of Canada. Edmond Lareau wrote in 1888: "The English historians maintain that the result of Cabot's 1496 voyage was the discovery of the American continent north of the Strait of Belle Isle. This claim is questionable, to say the least." Edmond Lareau, *Histoire du droit canadien...* (Montreal: Librairie générale de droit et de jurisprudence, 1888), 1:2. In the subsequent pages, Lareau, like Louis XVI's minister Vergennes, pointed out that Cabot did not formally take possession of the territory, as Cartier had done.

53. This statement is attributed to Amable Berthelot in a manuscript by Maximilien Bibaud. Maximilien Bibaud, "Extraits d'auteurs étrangers honorables pour le canadiens," folio 10, verso, Maximilien Bibaud Papers, Quebec National Library, ms. section. Bibaud wrote, "The first and only volume of transactions of the Quebec Literary and Historical Society appeared in 1820. One of the most remarkable papers was written by A. Berthelot, a former member of the legislature, to refute the English claim of having discovered Canada."

54. For a survey of the voluminous literature devoted to Cabot, see *Review of Historical Publications Relating to Canada*, (Toronto: 1898-1900), 2 (1897):30-41, 3 (1898):32-47, 4 (1899):122-124.

55. Vachon, review, *RS* 3 (Sept.-Dec. 1967): 415.

56. H.P. Biggar, *The Early Trading Companies of New France: A Contribution to the History of Commerce and Discovery in North America* (Toronto: University of Toronto Library, 1901).

Chapter III

1. "The Historian and His Society: A Sociological Inquiry—Perhaps," *Doing History* (Bloomington and London: Indiana University Press, 1972), chapter 3.

2. See my book, *Man and His Past: The Nature and Role of Historiography*, (Montreal: Harvest House, 1982).

3. As illustrated in the collection of writings edited by Robert Allen Skotheim, *The Historian and the Climate of Opinion* (Addison-Wesley, 1969).

4. For more information, see Norman Taylor, "A Study of French Canadians as Industrial Entrepreneurs," Ph.D. thesis, Yale University, 1957. Parts of the study have been published: "French Canadians as Industrial Entrepreneurs," *Journal of Political Economy*, 68, no. 2 (Feb. 1960): 37-52; "The Effects of Industrialization: Its Opportunities and Consequences upon French-Canadian Society," *Journal of Economic History*, 20, no. 4 (Dec. 1960): 638-47.

5. See Conrad Langlois, "Cultural Reasons Given for the French-Canadian Lag in Economic Progress," *Culture*, 21: 152-170.

6. See Harris's review of Cameron Nish, *Les Bourgeois-Gentilhommes de la Nouvelle-France, 1729-1748* in *CHR*, 1, no. 4 (Dec. 1969): 449.

7. This school of thought was led by historians like Marcel Trudel, Jean Hamelin, and Fernand Ouellet, discussed more fully in chapter 1 of the present work. See also my chapter in André Beaulieu, Benoît Bernier, and Jean Hamelin, *Guide d'histoire du Canada* (Quebec: PUL, 1969), 33-52.

8. André Garon, José Igartua, and Jacques Mathieu have summarized the debate in *RS*, 6, no. 3 (Sept.-Dec. 1966): 305-310.

9. See Fernand Ouellet, "M. Michel Brunet et le problème de la conquête," *BRH*, 62, no. 2 (Apr. May-June 1956): 29-101. *ESHQ* gives a more detailed account of his assumptions.

10. The first chapter of the book is devoted to the historiography of the problem. The conclusion "Une Bourgeoisie coloniale: Une Thèse," pp. 173-184, sums up the argument. For a summary of the whole discussion, see Nish, *The French Canadians, 1759-1766: Conquered? Half-Conquered? Liberated?* (Toronto: Copp Clark, 1966). In "Une Question historiographique: Une Bourgeoisie en Nouvelle-France?" Robert Comeau and Paul André Linteau have examined the arguments of both schools of thought. R. Comeau, ed., *Economie québécoise* (Montreal: PUQ, 1969), 311-324.

11. The Canadian Historical Association, *Historical Papers* (1968), 22-23.

12. A discussion report has been published in *RHAF*, 24, no. 1 (June 1970): 79-81.

13. José Igartua, "A Change in Climate: The Conquest and the 'Marchands' of Montreal," Canadian Historical Association, *Historical*

Papers (1974), 125-126. Igartua argues that the traditional nationalist conviction about the Conquest's harmful effect on the French-Canadian merchants is probably well-founded. See also his Ph.D. thesis, "The Merchants and 'Negociants' of Montreal, 1750-1755: A Study in Socio-Economic History," Michigan State University, 1974.

14. *Habitants et marchands de Montréal au XVIIe siècle* (Paris and Montreal: Plon, 1974), 488, n. 7.

15. Such was the argument at the beginning of the discussion. See Michel Brunet, "La Conquête anglaise et la déchéance de la bourgeoisie canadienne, 1760-1793," *La Présence Anglaise*, 49-112.

16. *RHAF*, 10, no. 1 (June 1956): 49-68. The article by Bilodeau is the summary of a Ph.D. thesis presented at the University of Montreal.

17. See n. 9.

18. See Robert Rumilly, *Les Socialistes dominent le réseau gauchiste* (Montreal: Robert Rumilly, 1959). In some ways, the condition of intellectual life at the time could be compared to what happened in the United States during McCarthy's anti-Red-Peril crusade. However, it should be noted that Quebec remained a "priest-ridden" province for more than a century. After the failure of the rebellion of 1837, the clergy took over the national leadership of French Canada. A clergy-owned school system began to expand. Colleges and universities under their control trained the professional and political leaders of French Canada. Apart from a few liberal minds, ultramontanism, the set of values which it implied, and the network of social institutions which it favored, flourished in the province of Quebec. Land settlement, schools, hospitals, and trade unions became more and more controlled by the church. The dominant position of the Catholic church has been seriously jeoparidized only since World War II. Until then, Quebec had a social organization resembling that of Spain, hardly challenged by five decades of industrialization.

19. Defined by a group of intellectuals in Marcel Rioux, et al., *L'Eglise et le Québec* (Montreal: Les Editions du Jour, 1961).

20. These concepts (applied to American historiography) are taken from J. Rogers Hollingsworth's review: "Consensus and Continuity in Recent American Writing," *South Atlantic Quarterly*, 1, no. 6 (Winter 1962): 40-50. The consensus school of the 1950s "described an America with a unified past. As classes, sections, and ideologies have melted into myths, a history characterized by consensus and continuity has emerged." The opposite school of thought, represented by writers like Turner, Beard, and Parrington, "had stressed conflict as a basic theme in the American past by emphasizing section versus section, class versus class, ideology versus ideology, agrarianism versus industrialism." When I refer to traditional or consensus historiography, I mean the kind of history that prevailed during the century-long domination of the clergy over the intellectual life of French Canada.

The historians of that period praised the role of the Catholic church in New France, and the moral conduct of settlers and political leaders as well as the seigneurs. The only strong criticism was directed toward the businessmen of the early colonial period. In sum, there was a sense of consensus and continuity between church-oriented historians, the political, seigneurial, and religious leaders of the early colonial period, and the obedient peasant.

21. *Monumenta Novae Franciae*, vol. 1, *La Première Mission d'Acadie, 1602-1616* (Quebec: PUL, 1967), 276, 719. Professor Campeau is sometimes biased when he studies the value systems and religious beliefs of the Amerindians. Lucien Campeau, *La Première mission des Jésuites en Nouvelle-France (1611-1613) et les commencements du Collège de Québec, 1626-1670* (Montreal: Bellarmin, 1972).

22. "Mgr de Laval et le Conseil souverain, 1659-1684," *RHAF*, 27, no. 3 (Dec. 1973), 323-359.

23. "Ni janséniste, ni gallican, ni ultramontain: François de Laval," *RHAF*, 28, no. 1 (June 1974): 3-26. "Aspects doctrinaux de la dévotion à la sainte famille en Nouvelle-France, *"Eglise et théologie*, 3 (1972): 45-68, is another valuable contribution to history by Pierre Hurtubise.

24. *Le Séminaire de Québec sous l'épiscopat de Mgr de Laval* (Quebec: PUL, 1972).

25. *Le Rigorisme au XVIIIe siècle: Mgr. de Saint Vallier et le sacrement de pénitence* (Gembloux, Belgium: Duculot, 1970). For other essays in the field, see Nive Voisine, "La Production des vingt dernières années en histoire de l'Eglise du Québec," *RS*, 15, no. 1 (Jan.-Apr. 1974): 99-103.

26. Blain, "Les Structures de l'Eglise et la conjoncture coloniale en Nouvelle-France, 1632-1674," *RHAF*, 21, no. 4 (Mar. 1968): 749-756. Jaenen, "The Role of the Church in New France," (Toronto: McGraw-Hill Ryerson Ltd., 1976).

27. *The Huron: Farmers of the North* (New York: Holt, Rinehart, and Winston, 1969).

28. "L'Eau de vie dans la société indienne," *CHAR* (1960). In the recent issues of *Les Cahiers des Dix*, André Vachon has published other essays in the field. Vachon is well acquainted with the findings of cultural anthropology.

29. "The Frenchification and Evangelization of the Amerindians in the Seventeenth-Century New France," *Canadian Catholic Historical Association Report*, English-Language section (1968): 57-71. This essay follows and completes the one written by Vachon in 1960. "Amerindian Views of French Culture in the Seventeenth Century," *CHR*, 55, no. 3 (Sept. 1974): 261-291, is a sound interpretation of intercultural relationships.

30. Cornelius Jaenen, *Friend and Foe—Aspects of French-Amerindian Cultural Contact in the Sixteenth and Seventeenth Centuries* (Toronto; McClelland and Stewart, 1976).

31. Raymond Boyer, *Les Crimes et les châtiments au Canada français du XVIIe au XXe siècle* (Montreal: Le Cercle du livre de France, 1966). For the most part, Boyer deals with New France records. André Lachance, *Le Bourreau au Canada sous le régime français* (Quebec: La Société historique de Québec, 1966). In "Les Causes devant la prévôté de Québec," *Histoire sociale—Social History*, 3 (Apr. 1969): 101-111, Jacques Mathieu tried to avoid value judgments. But, as Louise Dechêne has pointed out, "Studies of criminality are currently in fashion—an interesting area, no doubt, but a dangerous one so long as we do not know what the norms were." *Habitants et marchands*, 414.

32. "French Economic and Social History," *Jounal of Interdisciplinary History*, 4, no. 3 (Winter 1974): 435-457.

33. Robert Mandrou has reviewed the recent production according to these criteria in "L'Historiographie canadienne-française: Bilan et perspectives," *CHR*, 51, no. 1 (Mar. 1970), 5-20.

34. During the last decade, one long-term research project in interdisciplinary history has been launched by a group of specialists in the fields of demography and history at the University of Montreal. Hubert Charbonneau, Jacques Légaré, René Durocher, Gilles Paquet, and Jean-Pierre Wallot, "La Démographie historique au Canada—Un Projet de recherche," *RS*, 8, no. 2 (May-Aug. 1967): 214-217; H. Charbonneau et Yolande Lavoie, "Introduction à la reconstruction de la population du Canada au XVIIIe siècle. Etude critique des sources de la période 1665-1668," *RHAF*, 24, no. 4 (Mar. 1971): 485-511; Charbonneau, Lavoie et Légaré, "Le Recensement nominatif du Canada en 1681," *Histoire sociale—Social History*, 7 (Apr. 1971): 77-98; Charbonneau, Légaré, Lavoie, "The Early Canadian Population: Problems in Automatic Record Linkage," *CHR*, 53, no. 4 (Dec. 1972): 427-442.

35. "Economie et société en Nouvelle-France: L'Historiographie des années 1950-1960," *RHAF*, 28, no. 2 (Sept. 1974): 163-186. Frégault, a major figure of the 1950s, and "a convert to positivist methods, sought to impart them to his students by distributing a handbook on methodology entitled *A Guide to Historical Methods*, edited by the Jesuit Gilbert J. Garraghan, and published by Jean Delanglez. It was based on old German models of the late nineteenth century, which relied almost entirely on heuristic argument and the criticism of sources" (p. 169).

36. The Eccles-Lanctôt-Trudel trio belongs to the tradition of "national" historians. Many of their books are devoted to general history and have been translated for the common reader in one of the two major languages of the Canadian community. Their most important studies published during the last fifteen years are: (1) Eccles: *Canada under Louis XIV, 1663-1701* (Toronto: McClelland and Stewart, 1964); *The Canadian Frontier, 1534-1760* (New York: Holt, Rinehart, and Winston, 1969); *Canadian Society during the French Regime*

(Montreal, Harvest House, 1968); *France in America*, The New American Nation series (New York: Harper and Row, 1972). (2) Lanctot: *Canada and the American Revolution, 1774-1783* (Harvard University Press, 1967); *Montreal under Maisonneuve, 1642-1665*, 3 vols. (Toronto: Clarke Irwin, 1963). (3) Trudel: *Histoire de la Nouvelle-France*, vol. 1, *Les Vaines Tentatives, 1524-1603*, vol. 2, *Le Comptoir, 1604-1627* (see chapter 2 of the present work for a discussion); *The Beginnings of New France, 1524-1663* (Toronto: McClelland and Stewart, 1973); *Introduction to New France* (Toronto: Holt, Rinehart, and Winston, 1968); the last title is mainly devoted to the history of institutions and is more complete than André Vachon's *L'Administration de la Nouvelle-France, 1627-1760* (Quebec: PUL, 1970).

37. See for example Marcel Trudel, *La Population du Canada en 1663* (Montreal: Fides, 1973). His *L'Esclavage au Canada français: Histoire et conditions de l'esclavage* explored a relatively new field (see chapter 1, n. 39, and discussion in chapter 2 of the present work). Eccles's "The Social, Economic, and Political Significance of the Military Establishment in New France," *CHR*, 52, no. 1 (Mar. 1971): 1-22, is a sound revisionist essay. One of the more recent books by Marcel Trudel, *Les Débuts de régime seigneurial au Canada* (Montreal: Fides, 1974), is a very detailed statistical description of land ownership up to 1663.

38. *CHR*, (Mar. 1969): 89.

39. *CHR* (Dec. 1969): 449f.

40. Richard Colebrook Harris, *The Seigneurial System in Early Canada: A Geographical Study* (Madison, Milwaukee; London, and Quebec: The University of Wisconsin Press and PUL, 1966). On this very important book, the reviews by Fernand Ouellet, *Histoire sociale— Social History* 1 (April 1968): 152-159, and Jean Blain, *RS*, 9, no. 3 (Sept.-Dec. 1968): 319-322, should be consulted.

41. Even though Braudel prefaced some of his works, Roland Lamontagne never really applied his mentor's methodology. Titles published by Lamontagne are: *La Galissonnière et le Canada* (Montreal: PUM, 1962); *Chabert de Cogolin et l'expédition de Louisbourg* (Montreal: Editions Leméac, 1964); *La Vie et l'oeuvre de Pierre Bougues* (Montreal: PUM, 1964); *Succès d'intendance de Jean Talon* (Montreal: Editions Leméac, 1964); *Aperçu structural du Canada au XVIIIe siècle* (Montreal: Editions Leméac, 1965); *L'Atlantique jusqu'au temps de Maurepas* (Montreal: PUM, 1965); *Ministère de la marine Amérique et Canada, d'après les documents Maurepas* (Montreal: Editions Leméac, 1966); *Problématique des civilisations* (Montreal: PUM, 1968); *Textiles et documents Maurepas* (Montreal: Editions Leméac, 1970); *Maurepas et Pellerin d'après les sources manuscrites* (Montreal: PUM, 1972).

42. For a good example of the scepticism of senior scholars regarding new methods, see the comment of André Vachon, "La Restauration de la Tour de Babel ou 'La Vie à Québec au milieu de

XVIIe siècle,'" *RHAF*, 24, no. 2 (sept. 1970): 167-250) on the "provocative" essay by Jacques Mathieu, "La Vie à Québec au milieu du XVIIe siècle: Etude de sources," *RHAF*, 23, no. 3 (Dec. 1969): 404-424.

43. Other essays on New France published before 1960 with a "scientific basis" belong to interdisciplinary history; they were not written by historians as such.

44. *CHR*, 42 (1961): 336.

45. For example, Fernand Dumont, *RS*, 1, no. 2 (Apr.-June 1961), 263f. The best review was done by an economist, Pierre Harvey, in *AE* (Oct.-Dec. 1961): 537-548.

46. The word *structure* refers to the economic and social structure of a given society, its forms of economic organization, social strata, etc. Structural changes are usually slow. *Conjoncture* refers to more short-term economic and social trends or circumstances: economic cycles, crisis, growth, inflation, and so forth. Historians study these by means of series of price and wage statistics, many of which they must laboriously reconstruct themselves. In fact, however, such series reflect the same realities as the consumer price index, the unemployment rate, and the like, in our own society.

47. This aspect has been challenged by Peter Nicholas Moogk (see n. 72).

48. See also Micheline D'Allaire, "Conditions matérielles requises pour devenir religieuse au XVIIIe siècle," in *L'Hotel-Dieu de Montréal, 1642-1973* (Montreal: Editions HMH, 1973): 183-208.

49. J.F. Bosher, "French Protestant Families in Canadian Trade, 1740-1760," *Histoire sociale—Social History*, 7, no. 14 (Nov. 1974): 179-201; "Le Ravitaillement de Québec en 1758," *Histoire sociale—Social History*, 5, no. 9 (April 1972): 79-85.

50. At the 1972 meeting of the Canadian Historical Association, Pritchard read a paper entitled, "Maritime Traffic Patterns Between France and New France to 1760"; see also his "Voyage of the *Fier*: An Analysis of a Shipping and Trading Venture to New France, 1724-1728," *Histoire sociale—Social History*, 6, no. 11 (Apr. 1973): 75-97.

51. See his *La Construction navale royale à Québec, 1739-1759* (Quebec: La Société Historique de Québec, 1971). For Mathieu, the low quality, scarcity, and cost of Canadian wood prove that the type of ships built in Quebec at the request of the metropolis were not those which matched Canadian resources. In the history of international trade, Mathieu wrote a suggestive article: "La Balance commerciale en Nouvelle-France—France—Antilles au XVIIIe siècle," *RHAF*, 25, no. 4 (Mar. 1972): 465-497.

52. One can get an idea of Dubé's approach to the subject in "Origine sociale des intendants de la Nouvelle-France," *Histoire sociale—Social History*, 2 (Nov. 1968): 18-33.

53. *Un Marquis du Grand Siècle: Jacques-René de Brisay de Denonville, gouverneur de la Nouvelle-France, 1637-1710* (Montreal: Editions Leméac, 1965).

54. *La Vérendrye et le poste de l'ouest* (Quebec: PUL, 1968); *Nouvelles études sur les La Vérendrye et le poste de l'ouest (Quebec: PUL, 1971).*

55. *Maurepas, ministre de Louis XV, 1715-1749* (Montreal: Editions Leméac, 1967). *La Pensée et l'action coloniales de Maurepas vis à vis du Canada, 1723-1749* (Montreal: Editions Leméac, 1972).

56. For example, the review of Lionel Laberge's *Rouen et le commerce du Canada de 1650 à 1670* (Quebec, 1972), by Jacques Mathieu, *RHAF*, 26, no. 3 (Dec. 1972): 437.

57. *RS*, 12, no. 2 (May-Aug. 1971): 143-183.

58. Ibid., 177.

59. *RHAF*, 27, no. 2 (Sept. 1973): 163-179.

60. A good example of this is Raymond Douville and Jacques-Donat Casanova, *La Vie quotidienne en Nouvelle-France—Le Canada, de Champlain à Montcalm* (Paris: Hachette, 1964).

61. "Les Français hors de France aux XVIe et XVIIIe siècles," *Annales*, E.S.C. (Oct. 1969): 671.

62. "The Social, Economic, and Political Implications of the Establishment in New France," *CHR*, 52, no. 2 (Mar. 1971): 1-22.

63. Jacques Henripin, *La Population canadienne au début du XVIIIe siècle: Nuptialité, fécondité, mortalité infantile* (Paris, 1954).

64. Jean Hamelin, *Économie et société en Nouvelle-France*, 38. Hamelin echoes the assumptions of administrators.

65. *Frontenac, The Courtier Governor,* first published in 1959, is perhaps the best book ever written by Eccles.

66. *Le Monde,* 1 Nov. 1974.

67. "Following the great work of Herald A. Innis, *The Fur Trade in Canada: An Introduction to Canadian Economic History* (Toronto, 1927), the economic history of Canada has regularly been written in terms of the rise (and occasionally, fall) of her exported staple product. What is a staple? It is a product with a large natural resource content. Some part of its fabrication must take place at the spot even if only in the trivial sense of seizing it away from Nature. The staple is a product which does not require elaborate processing involving large quantities of labor or rare skills.... The staple is a product which will bear transport charges and which is in international demand." Richard A. Caves and Richard H. Holton, *The Canadian Economy: Prospects and Retrospects* (Harvard University Press, 1959): 31.

68. Marcel Trudel, *Introduction to New France,* chapter 6.

69. R.-L. Séguin, *La Civilisation traditionnelle de l'habitant,* 538-541.

70. A few pages were devoted to land mobility (287ff). Louise Dechêne studied the parish of Pointe aux Trembles. She concluded that a great geographic stability existed among the peasants. Perhaps the sample was rather too small for the conclusion to be applied to

the whole colony. Marcel Trudel's important book, *Les Débuts du régime seigneurial au Canada,* came to different conclusions through a very detailed collection of data for the whole community. The contradictions between the two writers may be explained by the fact that they worked in different periods: 1627-1663 for Marcel Trudel, and 1642-1731 for Louise Dechêne. Trudel agreed that almost all seigneury owners kept their *censive* during the founding decades.

71. For such statements, see Eccles, *The Canadian Frontier, 1534-1760* (Toronto, 1969), 94.

72. Peter Nicholas Moogk, "The Craftsman in New France," Ph.D. thesis, University of Toronto, 1973; some of the findings have been published: "Apprenticeship Indentures: A Key to Artisan Life in New France," Canadian Historial Association, *Historical Papers* (1971), 65-83; "In the Darkness of a Basement: Craftsmen's Associations in Early French Canada," *CHR*, 57, no. 4 (Dec. 1976): 399-439.

73. Like Hamelin (*Economie et Société*) and Eccles (*The Canadian Frontier*). See Dechêne, *Habitants et Marchands*, 215, n. 136.

74. "Government and private interest in New France," *Canadian Public Administration*, 10 (1967), 244-257.

75. Fernand Ouellet, *Histoire sociale—Social History*, 8, no. 16 (Nov. 1975): 372-382; Hubert Charbonneau, "A Propos de démographie urbaine en Nouvelle-France..." in *RHAF*, 30, no. 2 (Sept. 1976): 263-274.

76. According to the 1681 census, "There are many more young women than young men between twenty and thirty years of age, particularly in the areas where the most coureurs de bois are recruited," that is, the Montreal and Trois-Rivières districts. The figures were as follows: District of Montreal: 66.3 males to 100 females; outside the city limits, the ratio was 46.3 males to 100 females. The difference between sexes was not so high in the Trois-Rivières region— 83.8 males for 100 females, but one can conclude that a large number of young men from the rural area participated in the fur trade. Charbonneau writes: "It follows that only the difference in emigration can explain these figures."

77. Once more exemplified by Jacques Mathieu's recent survey of New France. See Jean Hamelin, et al., *Histoire du Québec* (Toulouse: Privat, 1976), chapters 4, 5, and 6.

78. Fernand Ouellet, "Historiographie canadienne et nationalisme," *Transactions of the Royal Society of Canada*, 4th ser. (Ottawa, 1975), 13:36f.

79. These sources are not, however, without their own limitations. For a critique of the use of inventories after death, for example, see Jean-Pierre Wallot and Gilles Paquet, "Les Inventaires après décès à Montréal au tournant du XIXe siècle: Préliminaires à une analyse," *RHAF*, 30, no. 2 (Sept. 1976): 176-182.

80. Louis Lavallée, Jean Blain, Louis Michel, and others have also

undertaken new research based on notarial documents. See Louis Lavallée, "Les Archives notariales et l'histoire sociale de la Nouvelle-France," *RHAF*, 28, no. 3 (Dec. 1974): 395-403.

81. *RHAF*, 23, no. 2 (Sept. 1969): 185-207.

82. "La Justice seigneuriale en Nouvelle-France: Le Cas de Notre-Dame-des-Anges," *RHAF*, 28, no. 3 (Dec. 1974): 323-346.

83. The *Dictionary of Canadian Biography* edited by the University of Toronto Press is a huge collective effort by professional historians to publish critical biographies. In so doing, historians participate in shaping the collective memory of the nation. The first three volumes deal with New France: vol. 1 (1967) covers the years 1000-1700; vol. 2 (1969), 1700-1740; and vol. 3 (1974), 1740-1770.

Chapter IV

1. See, for example, Claude Fohlen's reservation in *Revue historique* (July-Sept. 1967): 143.

2. *RS* (Jan.-Apr. 1967): 92.

3. This expression is used by epistemologist Adam Schaff, *History and Truth*, (New York: Pergamon Press, 1976).

4. Quoted by Léon Halkin, *Eléments de critique historique* (Liège: Dessain, 1966), 209. Halkin defines the use of this particular device (*le futurible*) in reference to a text by Raymond Aron: "If we wish to ascertain the causal significance of the battle of Marathon, we ask ourselves, 'What would have happened if the Greeks had not won,' and try to determine whether Greece would have developed differently in various significant areas." Halkin, 211.

5. The "would have" or "might have" device occurs, for example, in *ESHQ*, 209, 379. I have done a more systematic survey of *Lower Canada*, noting the following examples: *LC*, 10, 31, 32, 47, 48-49 (several times), 90, 93-94, 113, 117, 134 (twice), 135 (three times), 140, 152, 155, 157, 173, 259, 274, 282, and 327. Ouellet expresses his regret that the rebellion was national in character on pp. 157, 173, 182, and 282 especially. Other instances (e.g., *Bas-Canada*, 272, 289, 305, 332, and 393) do not appear in the English version.

6. "Unfortunately, because of the crisis in its agriculture, Quebec was unable to profit from this favourable situation" (*ESHQ*, 18); in the early days of British rule, "Unfortunately, the shipments of merchandise had been too great for the country's capacity for absorption. The merchants were thus forced to dump their stocks at low prices and often even at a loss" (p. 56); "Unfortunately, the year 1779 was followed by five more years during which crops were more or less paltry" (p. 116); with regard to "fruitful prospects" Ouellet remarks that "unfortunately, the reality was not quite so simple"

(p. 119); "Unfortunately, the Corn Laws did not recognize distinctions between colonial and foreign produce" (p. 137). See also *ESHQ*, 141, 142, 220, 375, 415, and 436, and *Bas-Canada*, 199 (cf. *LC*, 127).

7. Maurice Séguin, *La "Nation canadienne" et l'agriculture 1760-1850* (Trois-Rivières: Boréal Express, 1970). Predecessors with a similar view of "the good seigneur" include Marcel Trudel in *The Seigneurial Régime*, Guy Frégault in *La Civilisation de la Nouvelle-France*, and Brother Marcel Joseph (also known as Georges-E. Baillargeon) in "Les Canadiens veulent conserver le régime seigneurial," *RHAF* (June, Sept., Dec. 1953, and March 1954).

8. These calculations were done on the basis of a late eighteenth-century estimate. See *Rapport des archives du Canada*, 1892, p. 14.

9. Henri Brun, *La Formation des institutions parlementaires québécoises* (Quebec: PUL, 1970), 138.

10. Ibid., 139.

11. The following are examples of Ouellet's typical use of negatives in *Lower Canada*, when discussing the second half of the eighteenth century. New France "had not attracted immigrants" (*LC*, 8); "the advent of the Loyalists does not seem to have aroused any great fear or hostility in the French Canadians (*LC*, 10); "the English-speaking comprised less than 25 percent of the urban population" (*LC*, 17); the Anglo-Protestant business bourgeoisie was not interested in the Catholic clergy, nor was it republican or revolutionary, and did not view society as an ethnic battleground (*LC*, 16-18); nationalism in the sense of "the French-Canadian collectivity" was not yet born (*LC*, 19); the rural population did not question church and seigneurial dues, and did not see the 1791 constitution as a political régime designed to overthrow the old social order (*LC*, 20); the constitutional regime "did not attract a large contingent of illiterate peasants and tradesmen to the assembly" (*LC*, 26). Several other instances occur in chapter 1 and elsewhere.

12. Ryerson made a point of demonstrating the antidemocratic bias of such "Fathers" of Confederation as G.E. Cartier and George Brown. He quoted the comment attributed to Sir John. A. Macdonald about the need to protect minority interests—the rich being always less numerous than the poor. According to Macdonald's biographer Joseph Pope, he "viewed universal suffrage 'as one of the greatest evils that could befall a state.'" In 1861, Macdonald "had argued that 'unless property were protected and made one of the principles upon which representation was based, we might perhaps have a people altogether equal, but we should cease to be a people altogether free.'" S.B. Ryerson, *Unequal Union*, 355, 356; see also 254, 354.

13. Review in *Etudes rurales* (1967): 91-92.

14. Emile Dubois, *Le Feu de la Rivière-du-Chêne: Etude historique sur le mouvement insurrectionel de 1837 au nord de Montréal* (St. Jérome, Imprimerie J.-H.-A. Labelle, 1937), 45. These figures provided by the Patriote camp should be accepted with caution.

15. Jean Hamelin and Yves Roby, *Histoire économique du Québec, 1851-1896* (Montreal: Fides, 1971), xix.

16. S.R. Mealing, "The Concept of Social Class and the Interpretation of Canadian History," *CHR* (Sept. 1965): 211-212.

17. *Revue du Centre d'études du Québec*, no. 1 (Apr. 1967): 48.

18. A. Greer, *CHR* (Sept. 1981).

19. For example: "This capitalist bourgeoisie was not, then, the product of colonial patronage. Its economic strength, although it was linked to the preferential system, was due to its economic activity and not, as some would have it, to favouritism" (*ESHQ*, 417).

20. On his concept of progress, see for exemple *ESHQ*, 201, 207, 386, 440-441.

21. Maurice Crubellier, *Histoire culturelle de la France XIXe—XXe siècle* (Paris: Colin, 1974), 98, 135, 136, 213, 312, 429. This theme was reiterated in *L'Enfance et la jeunesse dans la société française 1800-1950* (Paris: Colin, 1979).

22. Thomas Chapais, *Cours d'histoire du Canada* (Quebec: Garneau, 1921), 2:254.

23. For example, see José Igartua, "A Change in Climate: The Conquest and the 'Marchands' of Montreal," *Historical Papers* (Toronto: The Canadian Historical Association, 1974), 115-134.

24. Gerald Tulchinsky, "Une Entreprise maritime canadienne-française: La Compagnie du Richelieu 1845-54," *RHAF* (March 1973): 559-582. Also, G. Tulchinsky, *The River Barons, Montreal Businessmen and the Growth of Industry and Transportation* (Toronto and Buffalo: University of Toronto Press, 1977). See Ouellet's review in *RS*, 18 (May-Aug. 1977).

25. W.T. Easterbrook and Hugh G.J. Aitken, *Canadian Economic History* (Toronto: Macmillan, 1967), 164.

26. Paul Cornell, Jean Hamelin, Fernand Ouellet, and Marcel Trudel, *Canada: Unity in Diversity* (Montreal: Holt, Rinehart, and Winston of Canada, 1968), 156.

27. Review of *Bas-Canada* in *RS*, 19, no. 3 (Sept.-Dec. 1978): 408.

28. For example, Isidore Lebrun, *Tableau statistique et politique des deux Canadas* (Paris, 1833), chapter 8, for the 1830s. At the end of the 1840s the newspaper *L'Avenir* published figures which perhaps overestimate income derived from tithes, but are nonetheless an indication of the clergy's wealth.

29. Pierre Goubert, *L'Ancien Régime* (Paris, Colin, 1969), 1:121.

30. B. Plongeron, *La Vie quotidienne du clergé français au XVIIIe siècle* (Paris: Hachette, 1974), 23. I have used his 1818 statistics, which he considers reliable.

31. The figures quoted are from ACAM, *Registre de la chancellerie*, 2:80. A copy of this document preserved in the Vatican Archives was supplied by Lucien Lemieux.

32. Quoted by Claude Galarneau, *La France devant l'opinion canadienne* (Quebec: PUL, 1970), 336.

33. Jean Queniart, *Les Hommes, l'Eglise et Dieu dans la France du XVIIIe siècle* (Paris: Hachette, 1978), 300. For a survey of works on the subject, see pp. 297-306. On rural origins for the same period, see F. Boulard, *Essor ou déclin du clergé français* (Paris: Cerf, 1950), chapter 7. For further details on the Quebec situation, see Serge Gagnon and Louise Lebel-Gagnon, "Le Milieu d'origine du clergé québécois 1775-1840: Mythes et réalités," *RHAF* (Dec. 1983): 373-397.

34. Cornell, Hamelin, et al., *Canada: Unity in Diversity*, 177.

35. This was very likely the case for notaries, who numbered one for every 2,655 Lower Canadians in 1791, and one for every 1,976 in 1834. André Vachon, *Histoire du notariat canadien* (Quebec: PUL, 1962), 126.

36. Gilles Paquet and Jean-Pierre Wallot, *Patronage et pouvoir dans le Bas-Canada 1794-1812* (Montreal: PUQ, 1973), 116-122.

37. A. Greer, review in *CHR* (Sept. 1981).

38. "Historiographie canadienne et nationalisme," *Transactions of the Royal Society of Canada*, 4th ser., (Ottawa, 1975), 13:36f.

39. Gérard Filteau, *Histoire des patriotes*, reprint (L'Aurore, 1975). In his account of the rebellion, McArthur stated that the government was aware of the danger of revolt, "and as early as 1836, active preparations were made to resist an insurrection." At St. Eustache, the rebels combatted "a much superior force." Adam Shortt and Arthur Doughty, eds., *Canada and its Provinces*, vol. 3, *British Dominion*, part 1, (1913), 361-363.

40. Fernand Ouellet, *Papineau: Textes choisis* (Quebec: Cahiers de l'Institut d'histoire de l'Université Laval, n.d.), and the pamphlet *Papineau: Un Etre divisé* (Ottawa, Canadian Historical Association, 1961).

41. Blair Neatby to Maurice Careless (17 May 1968). This letter was copied and forwarded to the members of the Canadian Historical Association.

42. Although Ouellet spoke of "violation of the liberty of the press" (*LC*, 82) in his account of the arrest of the editors of the *Mercury* in 1806, he makes no such comment regarding the similar arrest of those connected with the newspaper *Le Canadien* in 1810.

43. N.-E. Dionne, *Pierre Bédard et ses fils* (Quebec: Laflamme et Proulx, 1909), chapters 7, 8, and 9.

44. Henri Brun, *La Formation des institutions parlementaires québécoises 1791-1838* (Quebec: PUL, 1970), passim.

45. Ouellet, in describing Bédard and Papineau, was giving a picture of the middle classes as a whole. These classes were also subject to an "inferiority complex," (*Bas-Canada*, 204), giving rise to "isolationist attitudes" (*LC*, 131). Their schizophrenic view was visible in their refusal to grant the funds to build a St. Lawrence canal system, although the integration of the two province's economies had made it a necessity.

46. In analysing the insurrections, Ouellet made explicit reference to B. Porchnev, *Les Soulèvements populaires en France de 1632 à 1648* (Paris, 1963). Cf. Ouellet, *Eléments d'histoire sociale du Bas-Canada* (Montreal: HMH, 1972), 353, n.

47. Marc Bloch, *Apologie pour l'histoire* (Paris, 1949). Louis Gottschalk, et al, *The Use of Personal Documents in History, Anthropology, and Sociology*, newsletter 53 (New York: Social Science Research Council, 1945).

48. Pierre Vilar, "Histoire sociale et philosophie de l'histoire," *Recherches et débats*, no. 47 (June 1964): 55ff.

49. Anon., *L'Histoire sociale: Sources et méthodes* (Paris: PUF, 1967), 32.

Chapter V

1. See my comparative analysis of Ouellet's and Séguin's theses in *Livres et auteurs québécois* (1970), 190-192.

2. Fernand Ouellet, in a review of Brunet's *Les Canadiens après la conquête...* in *Livres et auteurs québécois* (1969), 171-181.

3. P.A. Sorokin invented the neologism "quantophreny" to designate the abusive use of statistical argument in the human sciences. *Dictionnaire des philosophes* (Seghers, 1962), 259.

4. Fernand Ouellet, "La Mentalité et l'outillage économique de l'habitant canadien-français. A Propos d'un document sur l'encan," *BRH* (1956): 131-139.

5. Trudel gives a similar portrait of the habitant under French rule. Marcel Trudel, *Introduction to New France* (Toronto: Holt, Rinehart, and Winston of Canada, 1968), 218-223.

6. Jean Hamelin, et al, *Histoire du Quebec* (St. Hyacinthe, Quebec: Edisem, 1976), 284ff.

7. Hilda Neatby in *Revue du Centre d'études du Québec*, no. 1 (April 1967): 49.

8. In a lengthy review Pierre Tousignant remarked on this habit of presenting statistics so as to support his line of argument. *RHAF* (Dec. 1980): 417.

9. Review in *RS*, 19, no. 3 (Sept.-Dec. 1978): 410f.

10. Ouellet in a review of Gerald Tulchinsky's *The River Barons*, in *RS*, 18, no. 2 (May-Aug. 1977): 309-311. Ouellet wrote that the book was "methodologically indefensible" and asked, "What, in the final analysis, is the position of the individuals or groups mentioned by G. Tulchinsky in the Montreal business community as a whole?"

11. Ouellet gives the tithe product for 46 parishes in the Montreal region in 1834, 1835, and 1836, referring to *RAPQ* (1943-1944): 243, 386. I have checked this, and there is no reference to tithes. *RAPQ* (1944-1945): 243, gives the figures for 1837 (based on the harvest

of 1836). I assume that the series for the previous years were found in the ACAM *Registres*.

12. I am merely giving the broad outline of Ouellet's argument. Since he took his annual birth and death figures from *JHALC* 1823 (*LC*, 357), he could only refer to the annual totals for the years 1794-1822.

13. Ivanhoe Caron, "La Colonisation de la province de Québec 1821," *Annuaire statistique* (Quebec, 1922), 361-369. See unnumbered table between pp. 366 and 367.

14. The consolidation of the 1825 census which I consulted was published in the *Quebec Almanack* of 1827. The extremely rapid economic and demographic growth of this parish has been discussed by Alexandre Paradis, *Kamouraska, 1674-1948* (Quebec, 1948), 165ff.

15. It should be remembered that the methodology of "serial history" existed before Pierre Chaunu invented the term, as the works of Labrousse show. Chaunu was taken to task by Jean Marczewski, who outlined his own methodology in *Introduction à l'histoire quantitative* (Paris: Droz, 1965). The Chaunu-Marczewski debate was published in the *Cahiers Vilfredo Pareto*, no. 3 (Geneva: Droz, 1964). According to Marczewski, "the serial history of which M. Chaunu speaks is...the first stage of quantitative history" (p. 177). It is empirical in nature, compared to reconstructions based on calculations of national statistics or other mathematical models. Despite such challenges on both sides of the Atlantic, however, serial history has survived. Alongside the classical treatises in historical criticism, it now forms part of the methodological corpus brought together in various textbooks, for example, Jean-Alain Lesourd and Claude Gérard, *Histoire économique*, 2 vols. (Paris: Colin, 1963), and André Nouschi, *Initiation aux sciences historiques* (Nathan, 1978). Early mention is found in Charles Samaran, ed., *L'Histoire des méthodes* (Paris: Gallimard, 1961), 847-965. André Corvisier has made it available to undergraduate students in *Sources et méthodes en histoire sociale* (Paris: S.E.D.E.S., 1980).

16. Richard Chabot, Jean Hamelin, and Fernand Ouellet, "Les Prix agricoles dans les villes et les campagnes du Québec d'avant 1850: Aperçus quantitatifs," *Histoire sociale* (May 1982): 83-127.

17. Fernand Ouellet, "La Mentalité et l'outillage économique de l'habitant canadien-français," *BRH* (1956): 131-139.

18. See, for example, R. Bellemare, *Les Bases de l'histoire d'Yamachiche* (Montreal: Beauchemin, 1901), 143.

19. Joseph Trudelle, *Charlesbourg* (Quebec: F.N. Faveur, 1896), 53.

20. I take the view that Charlesbourg was either the main or only territory contributing to the formation of St. Ambroise. In Appendix F or R (the print is not clear) of *JHALC* 1823, the statistics for births, marriages and burials in St. Ambroise for 1794 were included in the table for Ancienne Lorette. The St. Ambroise table provided annual figures from 1795 on. Charles Trudelle, in *La Paroisse de Charlesbourg*

(Quebec: Coté, 1887), mentioned the subdivision of Charlesbourg frequently (pp. 30, 49, 57, 133-134, 151-157). It seems likely that St. Ambroise was formed from Charlesbourg only, there being no proof to the contrary.

21. Thomas Chapais, *Cours d'histoire du Canada* (Quebec: Garneau, 1921), 2:113-115.

22. In *Notes historiques sur la paroisse de St. Léon* (Trois-Rivières: Editions du Bien public, 1916), 1, Amanda Plourde wrote: "Eighty-five freeholders of the Chacoura division (of Louiseville) presented a petition to Mgr. Hubert, Bishop of Quebec, on December 27, 1796, asking that their township be declared a parish." A chapel was erected in 1798, which was consecrated in 1802 when the registers were begun. The first resident curé arrived in 1805.

23. The population figures for St. Grégoire are from Pierre-Maurice Hébert, *Saint-Grégoire, Ville de Bécancour, comté et diocèse de Nicolet* (N.p., n.d., ca. 1975), 7.

24. Jean Roy, Daniel Robert, and Louise Verreault-Roy, *Les Populations municipales et paroissiales de la Mauricie, 1850-1971*, Research Group on the St. Maurice Region, booklet no. 3 (Trois-Rivières: Université du Québec à Trois-Rivières, 1980), 136. In 1722 the fiefs of Tonnancourt and Godefroi, on which St. Grégoire de Nicolet encroached when created at the beginning of the nineteenth century, were taken care of as "a mission by the curé who may be established in the parish to be erected for Nicolet and Bay St.Antoine, until there is a sufficient number of inhabitants for a parish to be erected thereon." C.-E. Deschamps, *Liste des municipalités dans la province de Québec*, bilingual edition (Lévis, 1886), 778. This illustrates the sort of complicated changes that characterize the general development of Quebec.

25. The following information has been taken from a wide variety of material. Particularly useful in estimating the population of concession roads or *côtes* that went to form parishes were H. Magnan, *Dictionnaire historique et géographique des paroisses, missions et municipalités de la province de Québec* (1925); C.-E. Deschamps, *Liste des municipalités de la province de Québec*; and Serge Courville's master's thesis, "Origine et évolution des campagnes dans le comté des Deux-Montagnes, 1755-1971," University of Montreal, 1973. In addition, numerous parish monographs provided useful details, there being a lack of more systematic regional studies here as elsewhere.

26. Anon., *Ste. Scholastique 1825-1975* (N.p., n.d.) In addition to this monograph, details on subdivision were supplied by officials in the parishes of St. Benoît (letter from Jacqueline Viau to Serge Gagnon, 27 Oct. 1981), in Ste. Scholastique (letter from the curé, Georges Duquet, to Serge Gagnon, 27 Oct. 1981), and St. Hermas (letter from the curé, B. Desjardins, to Serge Gagnon, 4 Nov. 1981).

27. *JHALC*, 45 (1835-1836), appendix BBB.

28. Courville gives 4,343 inhabitants.

29. Courville gives 4,880 inhabitants.

30. This figure is taken from Courville.

31. Courville, 97.

32. Quoted in Albert Faucher, "L'Emigration des canadiens-français au XIXe siècle," *RS*, 3 (Sept.-Dec. 1964): 280.

33. Shortt and Doughty, *Canada and its Provinces*, 4:594.

34. (Claude-Henri Grignon), *L'Eglise historique de St. Eustache* (St. Eustache, 1979), 5.

35. Deschamps, *Liste des municipalités*, 426.

36. Courville, table 3.3: "L'Habitant en 1825 dans le comte des Deux-Montagnes."

37. There were 234 new parishes set up, according to an estimate by Albert Faucher, *Histoire économique et unité canadienne* (Montreal: Fides, 1970), 154f.

38. Serge Gagnon, René Hardy, et al., *L'Eglise et le village* (Leméac, 1979), 143.

39. I am currently engaged in a long-term research project on personnel management in the church from the end of the eighteenth century until the 1830s, this being an aspect of the history of ecclesiastical personnel.

40. Georges Langlois, *Histoire de la population canadienne-française* (Montreal: Albert Lévesque, 1934), 173. Stanley Ryerson (*Unequal Union*, 60), took the figure of 20,000 departures between 1830 and 1837 from Firmin Létourneau, *Histoire de l'agriculture* (1950), 106. The question is whether these people left for good. New light has been shed on this matter by Y. Lavoie, *L'Emigration des canadiens aux Etats-Unis avant 1930* (Montreal: PUM, 1972).

41. Serge Courville, "La Crise agricole du Bas-Canada. Eléments d'une réflexion géographique," *Cahiers de géographie de Québec*, 24, no. 62 (Sept. 1980): 193-224, and (Dec. 1980): 385-428. John McCallum, *Unequal Beginnings: Agriculture and Economic Development in Quebec and Ontario until 1870* (Toronto: University of Toronto Press, 1980), ch. 3. R.M. McInnis, "A Reconsideration of the State of Agriculture in Lower Canada in the First Half of the Nineteenth Century," in Donald H. Akenson, ed., *Canadian Papers in Rural History*, vol. 3 (Ganonoque, Ont.: Longdale Press, 1982), 9-49.

42. In Jean Hamelin, et al., *Histoire du Québec* (Toulouse: Privat, 1976).

43. Normand Séguin, *La Conquête du sol au XIXe Siècle* (Quebec: Boréal Express, 1977).

44. "In the 1831 census, an area declared occupied of between 180 to 250 arpents more often referred to the total area of lots held by the censitaire, wherever they were,...than to the area of a single lot on which he resided." Serge Courville, "Rente déclarée payée sur la censive de 90 arpents au recensement nominatif de 1831: Méthodologie d'une recherche," *Cahiers de géographie du Québec* (April 1983): 53. See also p. 60, n. 6: "This aspect of the census makes it partic-

ularly risky to calculate the average area occupied and cultivated, using as a basic unit the concession road or parish of the time, since there is no indication of the location of secondary lots, which might just as well be in a neighboring *côte* or parish as near the residential lot. One should therefore be very careful in interpreting changes in the average area of land from one census to another." After pointing out that parish subdivisions between censuses increase the margin of error when calculating changes in developed land, Courville stated: "It is often on the basis of such mistaken information that some researchers have concluded that land development fell off in the old, riverside parishes between 1830 and 1840 or 1850, even going so far as to give this as the reason for 'dramatic' exoduses which these same parishes supposedly suffered during this period." This statement challenged the tables in *LC*, 358, 359, 372, and 373.

45. Jacques Boucher, "Les Aspects économiques de la tenure seigneuriale au Canada (1760-1854)," in Philippe Salomon, Georges Frêche, and Jacques Boucher, *Recherches d'histoire économique* (Paris: PUF, 1964), 194-198. Ouellet dismissed Boucher with a typically peremptory judgment, unjustly referring to his effort at comparative history as "rather fruitless" (*ESHQ*, 394).

46. Joseph Bouchette, *A Topographical Description of the Province of Lower Canada....* (London: W. Faden, 1815; St. Lambert, Quebec: Canada East Reprints, 1973).

47. Marc Guillaume, *Eloge du désordre* (Paris: Gallimard, 1978), 45.

48. See Michael Sean Cross, "The Shiners' War: Social Violence in the Ottawa Valley in the 1830s," *CHR*, 1973. This article is well worth reading, and has not received the attention it deserves.

49. See D. G. Creighton, "The Economic Background of the Rebellion of Eighteen Thirty-Seven," *CJEPS* (Apr. 1937): 322-334.

50. Henri Masson, *Joseph Masson dernier seigneur de Terrebonne, 1791-1847* (Montreal: Henri Masson, 1972), 210.

51. This statement is based on accounts cited by Ouellet in "Les Insurrections de 1837-38: Un Phenomène social," *Histoire sociale* (Nov. 1968): 68-77.

52. On the drop in international trade at the time of the rebellion, see *ESHQ*, 674ff. For the international financial and commercial crisis, see *LC*, 278-282. The Shiners' War, which was a violent struggle between the Irish and French Canadians for control of jobs in the Ottawa Valley lumber industry, reached its height in 1835-1837. Some of the brawls took place fairly near the center of social unrest in 1837. Michael Cross, "The Shiners' War."

53. On the Casgrains, see Paul-Henri Hudon, *Rivière-Ouelle, 1672-1972* (Comité du Tricentenaire, 1972), and Elisa-Anne Baby (Mme C.-E. Casgrain), *Mémoires de famille: C.-E. Casgrain*, 2nd ed. (Quebec: n.p., 1891).

54. This account and the many that follow are from the card index

which I am creating for the study on church personnel management mentioned in n. 39 above. I have omitted full references to avoid burdening the text.

55. See, for example, Charles Samaran, et al., *L'Histoire et ses méthodes* (Paris: Gallimard, 1961), 901-908.

56. See Chaunu, chapter 3 regarding declarations of merchandise.

57. T.J.A. Le Goff, "The Agricultural Crisis in Lower Canada, 1802-12: A Review of a Controversy," *CHR* (Mar. 1974): 19.

58. Jean Roy, et al., *Les Populations municipales...de la Mauricie*, 97.

59. Ouellet called historians' attention to village growth (*ESHQ*, 93, 169-170). Between 1810 and 1820, Bouchette mentioned several large villages: St. Thomas de Montmagny with 90 houses and 500 inhabitants; Louiseville with 30 or 40 houses; Nicolet with 50 houses; Laprairie with 100 houses; Boucherville with 90 to 100 houses; St. Ours with 60 houses; St. Denis with 60 houses; St. Hyacinthe with 80 to 90 houses; Sorel with 150 houses; and Ste. Geneviève de Berthier with 90 houses.

60. Originally from Philadelphia, Thomas Maguire resigned from the directorship of the St. Hyacinthe Seminary to represent the Canadian clergy in London and Rome between 1829 and 1830, which was why his treatise was printed in Paris.

61. Although a systematic survey of the correspondence is not complete, it has progressed sufficiently to allow me to put forward this and other hypotheses.

62. McCallum, *Unequal Beginnings*, 27-29.

63. Daniel Robert, "Les Préoccupations pastorales des éveques de Trois-Rivières, 1852-1898," M.A. thesis, Université de Québec à Trois-Rivières, 1982, 172.

64. *Mandements, lettres pastorales et circulaires des évêques de Québec*, (Quebec: H. Tetu and C.O. Gagnon, 1888), 2:488.

65. Le Goff, "The Agricultural Crisis," 19.

66. Fernand Ouellet, "L'Agriculture bas-canadienne vue à travers les dîmes et la rente en nature," *Eléments d'histoire sociale du Bas-Canada* (Montreal: HMH, 1972), 37-88.

67. Figures cited by Germain Lesage, *Histoire de Louiseville 1665-1960* (Louiseville: Presbytère de Louiseville, 1961), 163.

68. Ouellet, *Eléments d'histoire sociale*, 45, n. 8.

69. Nicole Gagnon, review in *RS* (Sept.-Dec. 1978): 411.

70. Jean-Paul Bernard, review in *RHAF* (Sept. 1973): 290.

71. Michael D. Behiels, review in *CHR* (June 1978): 226.

72. Gilles Paquet and Wayne R. Smith mention it in "L'Emigration des canadiens-français vers les Etats-Unis...," *AE* (Sept. 1983): 439, n. 37.

73. "This new measure had so terrified country folk that several persons reportedly hid various members of their families to avoid

the conscription that ignorant people thought this proceeding implied." PAC, MG 24, 1-109, "Journal de François-Hyacinthe Séguin, notaire, Terrebonne, 1831-33," 51f.

74. This calculation is based on the date of the registers being opened, as listed by Richard Chabot, *Le Clergé et la contestation locale au Québec*, (Montreal: Hurtubise HMH, 1975), 35-39.

75. "Professors Wallot and Paquet maintain that demographic pressures did not exist, and that land was not scarce." There was no proven basis for this view, Ouellet said, giving his table of population fluctuations in fifty-three parishes, which also appeared in *Lower Canada*. Fernand Ouellet, "Le Mythe de l'habitant sensible au marché," *RS* (Jan.-Apr. 1976), 126, 127.

76. Claude Fohlen, "Au Canada, un siècle après la Confédération," *Revue historique* (July-Sept. 1967): 143.

Conclusion

1. Cf., Fernand Dumont, *Anthropologie en l'absence de l'homme* (Paris: PUF, 1981).

2. Philippe Ariès, "L'Histoire des mentalités," Jacques Le Goff, et al., *La Nouvelle Histoire* (Paris: Retz, 1978), 402-432. The entire work is indicative of the new emphasis on culture in recent French historiography.

Index